THE
406 TABLE

KAREN R. BARBEE

Serving up meals, memories, and history, one dish at a time!

Knudson Farm, 1980s - Shonkin, MT

Photographs by Karen R. Barbee (unless otherwise noted)

Photograph editing done by Intermountain Business Consulting
and Ayana Shovar

Editing, cover and interior design by Intermountain
Business Consulting

Food styling by Karen R. Barbee, Bunkhouse Barbee Productions

ISBN: 978-1-5323-9644-1

Published by Karen R. Barbee, Bunkhouse Barbee Productions

© 2019 by Karen R. Barbee
First Edition 2019
Second Printing 2020

Extra copies of this book can be ordered by going to:
bunkhousebarbee.com

Printed in USA

DEDICATION

In loving memory, I dedicate this book to my grandmother, Margaret Heintz. Gramma was an amazing woman, whose meals and desserts were always served with a heaping side of family history.

It was at Gramma's 406 Table, that I first learned the art of hospitality. She was a hostess extraordinaire. Her meals and desserts were as memorable as the love she "dished out." The aroma of love, wafting from the walls of her kitchen matched those of her loving arms, always waiting to embrace you. She was generous with her love, meals and storytelling.

In conversations with my family, everyone would always say the same thing about the woman we loved. Each one of us would rejoice in the opportunity to have one more day or meal with her. She was the most amazing person in my life. She was a teacher of love, a follower of Christ and a meal maker of the greatest kind. With the greatest affection and admiration, Gramma, this book is for you. Thank you for everything!

Secondly, I must add, that without my sisters, none of these stories would exist. Thank you for the memories! Without you, there would be no stories to tell and no book to write.

Savannah, my daughter, you inspire me daily to be a better version of myself. The joy of being your Mom is such a blessing! During the years, all the parties and birthdays, celebrating "You," gave me opportunities to exercise my creative muscles. Farm life gave me my roots, but you gave me my wings!

PREFACE

Welcome to *The 406 Table*! The following pages are tidbits of Montana history, short stories of growing up on a farm near the "Birthplace of Montana," and recipes, that through the years have become known as my "Old Faithfuls!"

Our family farm was located northeast of Great Falls, near Shonkin, whose population was a total of two! Knudsonville, our little pretend township in the prairie of our dreams, was named after my step-father's last name of Knudson. Our make-believe town had a blacksmith shop, bunkhouse, church, barn, playhouse, library and of course, the farmhouse.

Knudsonville, consisted of a blended family, with five girls, a menagerie of animals, lots of imagination, a pet deer named Dew Drop, and a crazy dog named Ole'. Farm life in the 1960's had us doing our own dances of the Twist, the Pony, and the Mashed Potato. My sisters and I bonded over music and dancing. Music became our love language and gave us something in common. We cut a rug on the old shag carpet...the color choice, none other than harvest gold! We raced through our Saturday chores, so we could watch Dick Clark and his *American Bandstand Show*. We studied the make-up, hair styles and fashion, while waiting for the "Top Ten" songs of the week. Music filled our summer days, tasty meals were a highlight, and the farm gave us our roots. Our childhood playground on the farm, fueled our imaginations and took the five country girls from crayons to perfume.

A drop leaf Duncan Phyfe was *our* 406 table. It had winged extensions and a center opening for two more leaves. All our school dresses were laid out, cut and sewn on it. Every fabulous birthday and holiday meal was presented on its beautiful walnut surface. Competitive games of Tripoley and Yahtzee were played on the ol' girl. She was a witness to artistic endeavors and stood still for crafty ideas and school projects. Family and Montana history were shared around the curved borders of her wooden edges. Wedding plans, birth announcements, college entrance forms, and life's simple exchanges happened around her. Our 406 Table, if she could speak, would hold volumes of memories, a banquet of words, and a buffet of food delights.

Montana, is referred to as a small town with long streets. The state has something for everyone. For our family, a few vacations, created memories of a lifetime. Between the walls of my beloved Treasure State, you will find two national parks, epic scenery, historic communities, recreational opportunities, and numerous notable characters.

I love the quote that has been credited to, but not confirmed, by President Abraham Lincoln, "My favorite state has not yet been invented. It will be called Montana and it will be perfect."[1] Amen to that! Many historians believe Lincoln was our greatest president. I too, believe he had great insight. On May 26, 1864, he signed into order, that Montana would become a territory. This proclamation gave way to our statehood in 1889.[2]

How far does Montana's reputation span? In 1975, at the age of 16, I was singing with America's Youth in Concert in Europe. While in Rome, Italy, two choir members and I decided to take a taxi. We had high hopes of seeing the famous leather outerwear company, Pappagallo. The taxi driver was conversational and wanted to know about the Americans in his back seat. In broken English, he said he dreamed of seeing the land of the free and the home of the brave. He asked us where in America we were from. New York and Indiana were my taxi companions' answers, while Montana was mine. He got so excited when he heard I was from Montana. He almost crashed the vehicle on the winding road, as he began waving his hands in the air, saying, "bang, bang, shoot 'em up cowboys, John Wayne!" The taxi driver loved spaghetti western movies and was disappointed in the notion that we still did not ride horses to town!

The taxi driver, like so many other people I have met through the years, still believe in an imaginary way, that gunfights ensue daily and dirt roads are lined with covered wagons heading west in search of gold, land, and a new frontier. These day dreamers also hold images of buffalo roaming the prairie, and that cowboys and Indians are still at war. Commonplace images include country dances, trail rides, and campfires. Although these activities do happen, they usually include great food, friendship, and rather tall tales. However, this chance meeting with the taxi driver, illustrated how legendary Montana really is and what a privilege it is to call it home, then and now.

The 406 Table, shares simple stories of the Big Sky Country, highlights of history, and my childhood memories. The book's recipes are food portraits, which pay tribute to them all! I agree with John Steinbeck, "I'm in love with Montana, for other states I have admiration, respect, recognition, even some affection, but with Montana it is love. And it's difficult to analyze love when you're in it."[3]

My first 406 Table

ACKNOWLEDGEMENTS

I would like to thank Tammy of Intermountain Business Consulting for her editorial guidance. Her technical, artistic, and analytical talents have made my book more than I dreamed. I could write endless pages about the amazing talents of my friend, who took my vision and made it more than I could have ever imagined. She, created my website for my former business, "Events I Do." Her computer abilities are outstanding, her investigative spirit is amazing, her work ethic...the best. Tammy is the most talented person I know!!! There is nothing she cannot do and she amazes me daily. How do you thank someone who offered more than you ever asked? She always had my best interests in mind, first and foremost, in design, lay out, and editing. Collaborating with Tammy, elevated my book endeavor beyond my wildest expectations. She has been cheerleader, monitor, accountability partner, and editor. Her professionalism is first rate, no job is too difficult and it's done to perfection! Attention to detail, creativity, and design mastery are just some of the gifts she possess. Thank you for everything! Only you and I know how hard you worked to do this amazing task! I presented Tammy with my vision, ideas, and book concept, known as "a hot mess." Tammy's lay out, editorial endeavors, input and ideas have made my adult 'wish book' something I am so proud of. Thank you so much Tammy!

Jim Lilly, thank you for being the willing partner in taste testing, hauling things here and there, and always saying that "I was onto something," when another idea came to mind. I appreciate your support, encouragement and your ability to live in the chaos of my creations. Also, thank you, Jim, for the additional photography assistance and managing the prop details. I will always be grateful for the 'money shot' you patiently helped to accomplish while in the snow, cold, and wind. Thank you!

Nancy Ruud Cole, Doreen (Dori) Miller, Diane (Tudie) Moore, Savannah Lilly, Janice McKiernan, Sherry Fiddler Velarde, Sandy Fox, Elizabeth Rowan, Nicole Buchenholz, Debbie Miller, Darcy Corbridge, and Willow Jessen you have been my cheerleaders, and I am so grateful for your love, support and belief.

Doreen (Dori) Miller, Diane Worrall, and Lisa (Pitsch) Weber contributed additional photos of Glacier National Park, Fort Benton, Montana, Bannack, Hamilton, and the Bitterroot Valley. Additional 5 Mile Ranch photos were taken by Nancy Ruud Cole and Crystal Nichols. A special thank you to Dori Knudson Miller for the farm pictures, and the metal flower photo. Ayana Shovar and Tammy Goodman were responsible for photo editing. I also wish to thank Susan Blair Anderson for additional editoral assistance. To all of you, I say thank you! Food and entertaining photos were taken by myself as well as many other Montana photo treasures. I am so grateful to my friends who were willing to take extras and be where I could not. You are the best!

I wish to acknowledge my mom for the encouragement and support to accomplish my dreams. When I auditioned for the European singing tour, she graciously sewed clothes for me to wear, believing that I would be accepted. When I decided to start my wedding and events business, she was all in, listening to my ideas and reinforcing with loving encouragement. One day a box arrived with gorgeous cake stands, cake cutting utensils, and tiered dessert caddies. She contributed to my event business by gifting me with those gorgeous standout tablescape serving items and an enthusiastic belief I could be successful in my business endeavors. Thank you so much, Mom, it meant the world to have your support!

I would also like to acknowledge the teaching staff of Highwood Public Schools. As a student, I witnessed their endless hours of work, making learning an exceptional experience. The faculty spent private monies to enhance our education. Marie Haagenson was the first and second grade teacher who created ceramic gifts for her students at Christmas time. Marie was an amazing teacher, who was gifted and caring. She was the foundation of our rock solid education. Ruth Zanto was my 5th and 6th grade teacher and a gem. At Christmastime, Ruth chose a book individually suited for each of her students. One year my gift was penned with the following, "everytime a page is read, something new is learned." Her encouragement of reading, made me a voracious reader. Personalized pencils with our names accompanied the book, making us feel important. Ruth suffered through illness with grace and dignity and my admiration for her is endless. Sharon McGowan was thoughtful and often gave me words of encouragement. Thank you. Mr. Edwin (Ed) Dignin, I owe you so much! Your English classes were tough and for that I am most grateful. I never realized how much you taught me until I wrote this book! Thank you, Mr. Dignin. Doris Rowe and Pat Long were my music teachers. Their passion and love of music gave me musical opportunities to exercise my voice. Thank you so much. Additional faculty and staff of Highwood Public Schools made learning and those teachable moments of my youth, exceptional. Thank you to everyone.

Special thanks goes to Elizabeth Guheen, director of The Charles M. Bair Family Museum and P. J. (Paula) Beezley for Bair Museum photo. Additionally, I would like to thank Patrick Booth of Mystic Creek Studios, for free use of his photo of the Conrad Mansion. Thank you to the following: Brit Clark, Conrad Museum manager, Darlene Gould, Daly Mansion director, Jenna Peete, Moss Mansion director, Corinna Sinclair, Moss Mansion operations manager, Erin Sigl, owner of the Copper King Mansion, Maria Gibbs of the Copper King Mansion, and Chris Nixon, owner of the Lehrkind Mansion, for granting permission to allow the mansions to be included in the book.

Legal counsel was provided by Miller, Korzenik, Sommers, Rayman LLP in New York, New York. A special thank you to David Korzenik, senior partner and Zachary Press, Esq., for helping with the necessary legal advice and taking time to counsel a "small fish!"

For more copies go to:
bunkhousebarbee.com

Tammy Goodman
Intermountain Business Consulting
intermountainbc.com
406.580.1678

Disclaimer: Any recipes that have titles referring to famous people or places are my creations, and not from them, their estate or any affiliation to their celebrity.

INTRODUCTION

My career in the hospitality industry has spanned 32 years, unless you count my 4-H years in the Chuck Wagon, during the Chouteau County Fair. My first 'real' restaurant experience, began after high school graduation, at the Totem Cafe in West Yellowstone, Montana. It is there, that I realized how much tourists envied the locals. The Cattle Company, a renowned Steak House in Billings, Montana taught me the 'ins and outs' of the restaurant business. Through the years, more restaurant opportunities ensued. I managed the historic Pink House Restaurant, in Genoa, Nevada, where the owners had once turned away John Wayne and Jimmy Stewart, as they didn't have a reservation. Also, the famous actors who were filming *The Shootist*, were waitlisted for weeks and found out that actors were not as valuable as the local trade. Locals were considered the "regular" celebrities, no exceptions.

I also found employment with the Tombstone Pizza mogul, Ron Simek. After he and his brother Pep, sold the pizza empire to Kraft, Ron headed west to Nevada.[4] A state with no personal income tax enticed the entrepreneur and encouraged him to develop a new business venture. Ron's roots were in dairy farming, and he was grounded in the notion that land and lots of it, was always a good investment. He purchased the famous Harvey Gross Ranch in Northern Nevada, nestled at the foothills of the Sierras, outside Lake Tahoe.[7] The legendary ranch, once owned by Hugh D. Auchincloss, was frequented by the young Jacqueline Bouvier Kennedy. Jackie had spent numerous summers on the ranch perfecting her equestrian riding skills, as the ranch was once owned by her stepfather, Hugh D Auchincloss.[5]

Ron's new business venture, Little Mondeaux Lodge, was a 20,000 square foot building that could accommodate fine dining, three different wedding locations, and banquet facilities for up to 350 guests.[5] A trap and skeet range, plus sleeping suites, enhanced the 3,600 acre working ranch.[6] During my job interview with Ron, he inquired about my Montana roots and if I knew where Belt was. Belt, Montana was a hop, skip, and a jump from where I went to school in Highwood. Ron stated that, Belt, had the highest sales of any Tomb-

stone Pizza route across the U.S.! The Belt connection, was a bonding coincidence, as was our shared childhoods of growing up on a farm. In its first year of operation, we won and proudly accepted, "Best New Small Business in Nevada" award. During my employment at the Little Mondeaux Lodge, I learned everything there was to know about weddings, events, and celebrations. They were as historic as the property's location. I became a student and studied how the "big guys" spent money and learned the art of staging and wowing clients! The on the job training at the lodge, laid the foundation for what was later to become my own business.

Homesick for Montana, I returned to the Big Sky Country. Here, I was inspired to marinate my creative ideas with my hospitality background, mix in some hard work, and dish out business cards. My business, "Events, I Do" had me busy as an events coordinator. I used creative and imaginative ways to highlight various events, reinforcing my company's tag line, *It's All In The Details*. I always believed in under committing and over producing. I took budgets and stretched them into dreams. My farm girl ingenuity paid off in many ways. Through vision boards, dream events were created, and friendships forged. A particular hotel hosted several of my events. During one event, an employee of the hotel walked into the banquet room. After a few minutes of assessing it, she stated, "I just knew it was your event. I always know your events, they have that something extra!"

As you peruse the pages of *The 406 Table*, it is my hope that you find a little something extra to add to your meals, a bit of history to talk about, and I hope my farm stories will bring a little humor your way. I have added a few event decorating ideas just to "stir things up," also, a ranch wedding, which has Montana inspired details, makes an appearance too. All in all, there is a little something for everyone and a lot about Montana.

CONTENTS

Farm Stories

Country Roads, Take Me Home

I was six years old when Gramma told me about my new life on the farm. I was going to have three new sisters and a life away from her. I studied her face, as she shared of the day's events, listening intently to everything she said. I remember her house dress, with its soft dainty floral pattern, printed on chambray colored cotton. The Peter Pan collar was etched with rickrack trim, and a tired apron wrapped around her waist. This was the picture I held in my mind, as we made our way to our new life.

There was much to prepare, for the two and a half hour trip to Shonkin. Gramma made a wonderful breakfast and continued to describe all that awaited us. She smiled, as I copied her tradition of dunking her toast triangle into her coffee. However, I dipped my piece into Real Gold orange juice!

I drank in every moment with my amazing grandmother. I had so many questions. She filled my mind with answers, while giving a reassuring smile, which expressed everything was going to be alright. She lovingly stroked my hands. Her warm, comforting caress made me feel protected and loved. It was during this embrace that she said my new step-father Skid, was having a birthday party. When we arrived, there would be a dinner, followed by birthday presents and a farm celebration. This is where I would meet my soon-to-be family.

Panic and anxiety set in. A birthday? I had no gift! I was not prepared, as no one had told me. At an early age, I had witnessed Gramma's giving spirit on numerous occasions. She graciously offered lilacs from her yard to brighten someone's day, tasty homemade treats, a caring phone call, or a wrapped gift, to make a loved one feel special. Her acts of generosity and kindness had impressed upon me, that I too, wanted to be a giver. My step-father's birthday was a perfect opportunity to exercise my gift giving skills. I realized I needed Gramma's help to find a gift. Unfortunately, it was Sunday and no stores were open. What was I going to do? Her house was now my only shopping option. Gramma didn't

have guy stuff, as she had been a widow for ten years. Every suggestion, I overruled, and Gramma was tiring of the "let's find a birthday gift" game.

Finally, the overly patient matriarch made two suggestions. To convince me, she had to become the greatest saleswoman of the year. With much hesitation, I chose the only item I felt would be the most acceptable. However, I wasn't completely convinced. Gramma, weary from my endless pursuit, finally won me over and allowed me to believe that it was indeed a good choice. She said that the gift had a masculine edge and it was what every man could use.

Unfortunately, I still needed to find something to wrap it in. Gramma's second offering was her bubble gum pink, floral wrapping paper. Gramma had multiple boxes of special occasion cards, but only one choice of wrapping paper. She had never learned to drive. Therefore, when she liked something, she bought all they had. Evidently, that year it was the pink, floral paper! Despite my hesitancy, she again assured me that the choice was indeed perfect.

Shortly thereafter, my aunt and uncle arrived to pick us up. We were off to see our new home, sisters, and travel the country roads that would take us there. Despite getting lost on the way and needing directions from a local farmer, we made it to Shonkin and found *our* farm.

As we entered our new home, the screen door rattled behind us. The aroma of love drifted from the kitchen and greeted our senses. This was the first of many celebrations that our farmhouse-style 406 Table hosted. It was a delicious feast including a homemade double-layered chocolate cake and vanilla ice cream. The hi-fi stereo was piled high with a multitude of gifts and cards for my step-father. Hastily, I unpacked my suitcase and retrieved *my* gift and cautiously placed it in the pile with the others. All the other gifts had masculine wrap with dark subdued colors, but my bright feminine-wrapped gift stood out glaringly, like a sheep in a herd of cows!! Looking at the ghastly present, wrapped with its bright pink flower print, I felt very uneasy. It was a stark contrast to the the manly wrapped gifts. However, I was still hopeful that my present would be better than the wrapping paper looked!

The array of suitable and appropriate male gifts being unwrapped, were met with delight. Robust approvals made their way around the table. The scrumptious dinner began working its way up my throat, as I realized my gift was the next one that would be opened. Panicking, I mentally began planning my escape route down the country road, back to Gramma's house. I considered hiding, but didn't know where I could go. I needed to get out of there, and fast! I thought perhaps my new bedroom might work. Unfortunately, the moment arrived before I could even finish formulating my getaway plan and the bubble gum colored gift was opened. Sickness washed over me as my step-father Skid, pulled out the black and white....skunk figurine salt and pepper shakers, that Gramma had sold me on! There I sat, red faced and embarrassed over my stinkin' gift! The farmhouse grew quiet while shame and humiliation ran over me, like a tire on road kill. I bolted from the table and bounded into the bedroom, that was

soon to be mine. Embarrassment and disappointment fell down my face, along with the tears I was sadly wiping away. With a quiet gentleness, Skid entered the bedroom. He sat next to me and warmly thanked me for the gift. He reassured me, saying he loved the present and felt it was perfect. The man, I would later learn, was one of few words. Yet, in that moment, he had expressed all the right things. Our hearts connected during that intimate moment, as did our father-daughter relationship. His gracious, tender manner helped to restore my confidence and provided me some much needed comfort.

No one ever mentioned my stinkin' gift again. However, those shakers stood watch over the family's activities for years, while they sat perched on the back of the farmhouse stove. Recently, I saw a similar pair of shakers in an antique shop. Their price tag was quite spendy! Fortunately, there is no dollar value you can place on special

Road To The Farm

moments of the heart...the first father-daughter bonding moment over my skinkin' gift! Priceless!

Harvesting New Memories

Farming is an amazing endeavor. It requires fortitude, dedication, optimism, and a desire to believe in a gamble against Mother Nature. The struggle of whether or not Mother Nature was going to be a friend or enemy was only one obstacle that farmers had to contend with. Riding the highs and lows of grain prices and knowing when to sell was another. For small farm operators, there was a constant fear of losing it all to the big operators. The odds a farmer had, in order to win against wind, grasshoppers, drought or hail, were riskier than an amateur playing craps in Vegas. Thick luscious crops, were a farmer's hope and dream, along with getting the grain in the storage bins before hail or strong winds got ahold of it. A "bumper crop" were wondrous words, not often heard. However, farming should be renamed, "risky business." So often, Mother Nature did her thing and ruined the hopes of a bountiful crop to fill one's bank account.

Grain fields turning from luscious green to a rich golden hue have a beauty that evokes a feeling of patriotism. The "amber waves of grain" depiction in the song, America the Beautiful, had a special meaning for farm kids. In music class, I remember feeling the pride of singing about the glorious beauty that grew in our backyard. The hearty grain stalks, stood like sentries guarding our farm. They waved, as we rode our bikes on the back roads, while going nowhere in particular. The rustle of the drying stalks made a song all their own. Their melody was a deep and rich whistle. When the wind blew through them, they sang the harmony of soft sanding sounds and lovely notes of dried leaves being crushed on a late fall day.

Growing up in the country provided regular opportunities for our imaginations to run wild. We explored the Wild West, built an imaginary town, and participated in the most wonderful parades that our minds could imagine. There were benefits to having vivid imaginations, as we were taken to places beyond the borders of the grain fields, which surrounded us.

Summer's harvest created even more playtime fun. The exciting activity of the combine's engine humming, the filling of Skid's Coleman cooler with iced tea or lemonade, signaled life was about to change. Harvest was all about getting the cut grain into the storage silos before Mother Nature could wreak havoc and ruin the crop, or the volatile price of grain became unfavorable. Skid would chew on cut samples of wheat to see if the moisture content was correct, for harvest to begin. Samples were then placed in used coffee cans and driven to the elevator to verify the moisture level which Skid's discerning taste test already knew.

Once the taste test and elevator confirmed the "go ahead" to start harvesting, our farm life revolved around the cutting of grain. Grain mermaids suddenly appeared, as my sisters and I floated through the deep sea of cut grain in the back of the truck. As we rode on the mounds of grain or swam beneath them, our imaginations had more opportunities to make-believe we were somewhere else. The cool kernels of the grain played between our toes. We swam laps from one end of the truck bed to the other, scooping up the handfuls of gold, like miners at Sutter's Creek. However, our gold rush came with a few stink bugs, grasshoppers, and beetles. As grain miners, we sifted and cleaned the kernels, making our own pan of gold and chewing the precious nuggets into gum. There was an artful way of performing our wheat-gum technique. After popping a small handful of kernels into our mouth, a firm crunching action would occur from biting through their hard outer shells. This was followed by an increase in saliva and spitting out the chaff, until the soft and sticky "chew" was exposed. Our jaws tired quickly, as much chewing was needed until the final product emerged....a homemade sticky-style gum. Wrigley's was no match for a farm kid!

As we rode through the grain fields, another idea floated to the surface of our imaginations. There above the grain dunes in the back of the wheat truck, we built a dreamy parade float, complete with a royal queen and two enthusiastic princesses. Tudie drove our magical float, Dori held court as our beauty queen, while my sister and I were her loyal princesses. There in the endless grain fields, we learned everything necessary about a proper

parade wave. We mastered the *wrist, wrist, wash the window* action, that all members of royalty perform. To the scores of our fictitious onlookers, we smiled, waved, and proudly nodded our heads in their direction. Although confetti was never thrown out of the grain truck, an assortment of dead bugs were! The bugs served as our imaginary candy that our parade onlookers were anxiously anticipating. We were grain royalty and proud of it!

Yellowstone National Park

What's a vacation? Where is Yellowstone? What is Old Faithful? Those were the questions my parents had to answer, once they announced harvest was over and we were going on vacation. I was six years old when I saw Yellowstone National Park for the first time. The year was 1965. A bumper crop of that year's harvest of wheat and barley, had our spirits as high as the hot August heat. With an ample bank account, our family loaded up the Chevy Impala, hit the long dirt road and traveled to Yellowstone.

As we journeyed, my parents painted vivid images of the park, describing what we would soon see. Nature's canvas would hold visions of boiling, steaming hot pots, giant bears, vast wildlife, and the Old Faithful Geyser and Inn. While sitting in the front seat between my parents, I had the unfortunate experience of overhearing their conversation about the ghost of Old Faithful Inn and whether or not the sightings were true. The story of the headless bride haunting the halls of the historic hotel had me fearing she would make an appearance while we were there! Apparently, the new bride had died in room number 127. The evil groom, had violently murdered his bride during their honeymoon stay and stashed her head in the crow's nest of an upper balcony. Over the years, numerous apparitions had been seen of her in a white gown, carrying her severed head under one arm, while roaming the hallways at the inn.[8] Good grief! I wished I hadn't heard that story! Now there was even more to pay attention to and look out for. I wanted to keep an eye out for bears. But the ghost? Not so much!

The beauty of Yellowstone National Park, made it feel like a mythical place. Every year tourists have come from around the world to take a glimpse of the renowned water fountain, known as Old Faithful Geyser. The hot water wonder erupts 15 times a day, every 94 minutes, expelling 3,700-8,400 gallons of water per eruption, and rises approximately 130 feet in the air.[9]

The white billow of steam, which dances its way to the clouds, never disappoints the waiting crowd. Her continuous precision leaves a sense of awe in one's spirit and we were all speechless that summer over the fountain's beauty. Only a natural wonder was capable of doing that!

A short distance away, the Old Faithful Inn was equally breathtaking. The massive wooden structure is an architectural feat. Some of the inn's decor, consists of twisted lodgepole balconies, intricately hand forged lanterns, an enormous clock, and a four sided stone fireplace, which are all crafted works of art. The wooded fortress, was built between 1903-1904, with lumber harvested from surrounding forests.[10]

On its east wing, the Porte Cochere, is created with beautifully cut log columns, a massive awning, light streaming lanterns, a red front door and a gigantic lock. Its deep, wooden sitting chairs, provide the perfect opportunity to drink in the surrounding majestic views. Evergreen laden boughs, remind visitors of nature's provision of lumber for the resplendent lodge.[10]

Subsequently, Old Faithful Inn is the largest log hotel in the world.[11] A majority of the construction to build Old Faithful Inn, was performed in weather conditions so severe, that crews had to be rotated, to endure the intolerable cold, desolation, and primitive work conditions.[10] The result? Magnificence!

Our family's top priority was to see 'Yogi Bear and his band of brothers," however, avoiding the ghost-bride was mine! As we moseyed along the narrow two-lane highway in our cramped, hot car and gazing at nature's handiwork, we smelled something a little strange. Initially, we randomly accused each other of being the responsible party for the foul odor. Finally, our parents explained that the sulfur in the hot pots caused the fetid, rotten egg smell. Well, that cleared up a lot of the "who done it" finger pointing!

The roads were narrow and winding, causing traffic to move slowly through the park. In addition, tourists frequently stopped to take pictures, halting the flow. As traffic continuously slowed and stopped, our hopes of seeing Yogi or one of his buddies, diminished. Our patience as back seat observers, was also evaporating. However, there are certain advantages to slow meanderings, as you get a much clearer vision of what your surroundings are. Suddenly, what appeared to be a boulder or big dark moving clump, was headed our way! Realizing it was a bear, we quickly remembered that a lodge employee told us that a bear's favorite candy was lemon drops. With unimaginable excitement, my sisters and I promptly threw handfuls of lemony candies out the open window. We couldn't believe our eyes! Fear gripped us as the bear reared up on its hind feet and scared the remaining lemon drops right out of our hands! In sheer panic, we raced to roll the windows up, as the bear sauntered over to us for more sweets. As we swiftly drove away from the bear, silence ensued for miles. Everyone realized that the lemon drops were the bear's dessert, but we could have easily been his main course!

This was the first of many adventurous trips I have taken to the famous park. For me, Yellowstone is an emotional experience. Her beauty, natural wonders, wildlife, and geysers are enchanting. Old Faithful Inn and the famous geyser are also breathtaking. The scenery of Yellowstone Park is something one must see for themselves!

In 1970, the park placed a ban on feeding the bears and animal proof containers were installed throughout the park to keep garbage in and the bears out.[12] Although I am all grown up now, I feel like I have been feeding my own hungry bears for years! I have numerous *tried and true* recipes that are frequently requested, and favorites of my family and friends. I call these my "Old Faithfuls." Just like our trip to Yellowstone, my recipes will create memories of their own. They are so delectable, I guarantee that they will disappear as fast as we did, while escaping the hungry bear!

Donna

Long summer hours, found my sisters and I making playtime our top priority. We created entertaining projects from our imaginary prairie community of Knudsonville. Our fictitious store clientele, were thrifty, hardworking individuals, and the best people around. The fruit of our labor, was selling goods to these prairie folk, who came to town to fill their empty pantries. As *store owners*, we couldn't wait to share the newest bolts of fabric with the farm wives who daydreamed of a pretty new Sunday dress. We fashioned big ideas out of our fanciful inventory of basic cotton, sent from a big city mill. Our store provided more than pantry staples, it was a playground of big business, dressmaking supplies, and also bore an invisible sign which read, "Friends, you are welcome here."

In the basement Donna, our oldest sister, was working on sewing projects while we sold our canned goods to imaginary shoppers. The whining rhythm of the sewing machine sounded so much different than Gramma's. I watched in awe, as the new electric version hummed its way tirelessly, down pieces of fabric. The old treadle machine that Gramma used, was foot operated and slow, however, Donna's had a need for speed. Our game of store was interrupted by the small glow of light, shining from the foot feed and down onto the fabric, as if it were lighting the way. Curiosity got the best of me and I took a leave of absence from my store duties. I inquisitively walked over to Donna and asked her what she was making. "Oh something," she vaguely replied. She was going to school in the fall and was preparing a suitable wardrobe for her college entrance, but the dress she was sewing, was too small to have fit her petite figure. It was also way too big to fit any of our baby dolls. Realizing that I was not making headway with an answer from Donna, I went back to playing in our store.

Our summer was coming to a close and soon Donna would be moving away from the farm and heading to college in Bozeman. One afternoon, she told my sister and I, that she had something special for us. Once again, our 406 table hosted another memorable family moment. There, on its aged wooden surface, lay two large white boxes. We stood at the table, stiff as soldiers and afraid to move. Donna softly nodded her head and said, "Go ahead, open them." We were confused. Did she mean us? With trepidation and a slight bit of reluctance, we removed the lids off of our mysterious

boxes. Layers of bright red tissue paper revealed the most beautiful dress I had ever seen! My dress was created from a small checked linen fabric which was woven with dark Dijon and chocolate/black colored checks, complete with a sailor tie. The special gift, became the ensemble for my first day of school. I loved the dress so much, I wore it until it was in tatters. I was only willing to retire the pinafore, when I had outgrown it. The dress was such an incredible gift, as was Donna, my new sister.

When Donna came home from college that Christmas, we eagerly awaited stories of her school days. As an artist, she was wonderfully gifted, as a sister, sweet and loving. Donna was also thoughtful and beautiful. Her soft flaxen blond hair and shining blue eyes were inherited from her father, as were her many artistic talents. Although watercolor was the medium that Donna was most familiar, clay and charcoal became new avenues for her artful ways. On the afternoon of Christmas Eve, my sisters and I were sitting in the living room, when Donna brought out a thin package. The last gift to be placed under the tree. Donna situated it next to the large heavy box, with a gift tag that said "Dad." We were very curious about the packages that she brought. She said we could try to guess about the thin one addressed to Mom. My enthusiasm had me hollering, "Pictures!" and Donna replied, "Of who?" I thought quickly and answered "Us!" She was taken quite by surprise, with my correct answer and disappointed that our guessing game had ended so quickly.

On Christmas morning, Skid opened his totem pole-like sculpture. The unique object bore a sphere, crescent moon and star, resting on a square platform. The totem structure was created with white fired clay. It appeared Skid was just introduced to modern art! Mom opened her gift last. She shed happy tears, as she sat in awe over the amazing gift of love. Donna had sketched charcoal portrait drawings of my sister and I. The pictures, just like the dresses she had made, were heartfelt gifts of acceptance. Thereafter, the stunning portraits hung on our dining room wall. My picture, and the artist which created it, are both beloved treasures of my heart. Although, I no longer have the favorite dress of my childhood, I do have the portrait and the memory of Donna, who was so generous and loving.

Donna's artistic talents were abundant. She created masterpieces, whether it was from the kitchen stove, her electric sewing machine, or simply her hands. I have been told that watercolor painting is a very challenging medium. Many artists leave watercolor and choose to paint with oil or acrylic, instead. It was just like Donna, to choose the hardest medium and make it look like the easiest!

In March 1985, *The Western Heritage Art Show* in Great Falls, Montana, selected Donna's work titled, *No Fields To Plow*, as best in show. Interestingly, water color was the category of which she won! The winning painting, depicted two old worn antique tractors as its main subject. Through Donna's artistry, the revival of their spirit told a tale, as they sat side by side, weary from years of exhausting work. The "good ol' boy" tractors in the painting, retired from their years of farm life, are seen resting by tall, slender prairie grasses. Donna's mastery of paint brush to paper, made the aged implements celebrities. Her award was one which was distinguished and highly coveted. The judges recognized what we already knew, Donna was an award winning artist!

Several years after receiving her award, Donna was called to her Heavenly home. I imagine she is there, collaborating with Charlie Russell, another notable Montana artist. From Heaven, the two artists now create magnificent heavenly paintings. When a sunrise or sunset is particularly beautiful, I imagine Donna and Charlie sitting side by side, sharing stories about Montana, and sending a little more color our way.

Shonkin Style

Grain fields escorted the dirt carpeted road to Shonkin, Montana, and marked the changing seasons. Each year, the wheat and barley fields of intense green, turned to harvest gold, then to winter's brilliant white. Mature, fragrant, wild rose bushes of soft orchid and vivid yellow, delivered the sweetest fragrance. Random, lonely hollyhock stalks, still stood tall, where once a farm house had been. Thus, I have lovingly referred to hollyhocks as "the prairie woman's rose." These remnants were reflections that the little community of Shonkin, population two, had once been more robust in its census numbers. In June 1880, the town had 170

citizens. Statistics from 1882, indicated there were 97 buildings, 968 cultivated acres, 41 miles of fence, 15 miles of irrigation, and 197 dairy cows. In addition, there were 24 families, 19 bachelors, and 15 school students. The once bustling community was never rebuilt after Owen (Ownie) Connolly had set a fire torching the once prosperous prairie town.[13]

While driving down the dirt road to Shonkin's only store, dotted clusters of pink prairie roses next to an abandoned home, were a frequent summer scene. The wild rose bushes, sent a pleasant aroma that the hollyhocks were unable to accomplish. The prairie grasses, slender and beautiful, had an innocent, rich smell, much like a spring rain. All of these scents, lovely and memorable, were no match for the sweet, heady scent of the purple lilacs standing alone on the rural, grassy floor. There were no street lights or signs in the small, isolated town. The wild roses, lilacs, and hollyhocks, were Nature's welcome signs and the only visible evidence that you were entering the once bustling prairie community.

Shonkin was the capital of *our* farm life. The Post Office/General Store had several shelves of donated books for "checking out," milk and bread in case you "ran out" and a few "get by goods." The ol' girl had a false front exterior, with a single gas pump, whose metal numbers flipped and dropped with a thunderous clunk. Narrow, uneven hardwood planks, were worn and tired from the many steps life had dealt them. The old wooden floor, with its squeaky song, was background music for the front door clang and window pane clatter. Cheerful, red geraniums were wintered in the picture window, offering a lovely contrast to the stark white of winter. Aged driftwood arms held the crimson floral blooms. They intertwined, like a perfect pair of elegant ballroom dancers.

The store's bookkeeping practices were simple. A recipe box was kept under the worn wooden counter. A pencil notated the date of one's purchase and the total amount, with no signature required. Monthly statements were 'settled-up' when you picked up your mail. All transactions were handled with the honor system. No one questioned the recipe box or its proprietors. A modest candy case rested on top of the checkout counter. It was small with two shelves, encased in glass. Its entire inventory was a total of about 10 treats. The selection of candy bars was limited, to make room for other gems. The valuable gems, were Yogo sapphires from Utica and Montana sapphires from across the Treasure State. We chewed on fancy thoughts of how one of those sapphires in the candy case, would make a stunning ring for us to wear. We began digging into the idea that rockhounding would be fun, but the thought of unearthing a beautiful Montana sapphire, would be even better!

The store owners were also part-time sapphire scavengers. The post office/general store closed at two on Saturday's, so the couple could go explore the mountains for glittering gems. When there was a find, it was carefully cut, polished and placed in small protective foam boxes. There, nestled in the candy case, was the evidence of their weekend endeavors. No candy bar could have tasted as marvelous as the Montana sapphires looked! The store's inventory of precious gems, not under lock or key, spoke volumes about our community. Trust was abundant.

During an election year, the post office/general store served as a voting precinct. A long banquet table held the ballots, pens, and other pertinent information. Starched white sheets were hung up by wires, to create two individual voting booths. The old wooden stove provided needed warmth, but it was no match for the political hot air that ensued around election time! Games of Pitch and Cribbage were frequently played, tempering political conversations.

The proprietors witnessed generations of farm families growing up and making their way into the world. Their little store provided a convenient place for local conversation. Pacing men, would shoot the breeze, while waiting for the mail. Farm wives would catch up with one another and share about each other's families. Often, a treasured recipe or two would emerge, in these conversational exchanges.

Daily trips to retrieve the mail were adventurous ones. By noon, the mail was sorted and placed into the intended mail boxes. Each box had its own winning combination. Ours was, one complete rotation to the left, all the way back to the right and back again to the left. The small hard, ridged nob, was cranky through years of use, but always accommodated our anxious little hands.

It was thrilling to open the little bronze paneled window box and see what life had delivered us!

On occasion, our mail carrier from Great Falls, Montana, delivered more than mail. Cold winters, drifted roads, and winter sickness, often gave our mail carrier a part-time job. He would carefully search the aisles for needed sundries in the big stores of Great Falls and deliver them along with a road report. Thankful, were the handful of secluded farm wives who benefited from his gracious purchase of big town necessities. Calling in an order and paying for a long distance phone call was a small price to pay, for a needed bottle of cough syrup or another essential item that was not a staple in our humble little store. The mail carrier's services made him a celebrity and a candidate for weatherman due to his knowledge of the road conditions. His ability to deliver a big city grocery item was more important than Santa!

As my sisters and I grew up, we started anticipating the placement of our catalog notice from Spiegel and Aldens in our country mailbox. We couldn't wait! Once the card had been retrieved from the box, informing us the catalog was on its way, we were on high alert! When the treasured catalogs arrived, playtime halted and our imaginations were redirected to the fashion world. The wonderful images within the pages, brought a little bit of big city life to the country. Sears, Penny's, and Montgomery Wards were nice to look at, but Alden's and Spiegel were a bit more, "highfalutin!" Endless hours were spent daydreaming about the inspiring items found in the coveted pages of the *Wish Book*. My sisters and I took turns carefully flipping and examining page after page while discussing one another's wish list.

In 1975, I received my last letter from the old post office with a postmark from New Jersey. The envelope contained my letter of acceptance to tour with America's Youth In Concert. My cassette recording and audition tape were the last mailings I sent from the country post office. The nationwide audition chose 250 choir and 175 orchestra students from across U.S. high schools to perform concerts throughout Europe. We recorded an album in New York and gave our last concert in the breathtaking St. Patrick's Cathedral. In old Box 43, my parents received letters and postcards from Italy, Switzerland, Austria, France, and England describing my many travels and experiences.

A former music teacher at Highwood Public Schools, Doris Rowe, made my audition tape possible and was instrumental in making my music dream materialize. She and her family were dear friends of ours and they lived in the Shonkin mountains. Doris was also a ranch wife and downright wonderful person. There are no words to thank her for making the impossible, possible!

Ole', Driver Dog Extraordinaire

The pedigreed wire fox terrier, with his coarse, curly fur coat of white and smatterings of caramel colored spots, had legs like springs. He was hyperactive with a need for speed. He chased his tail like a spinning top, making constant circles all around us. Ole' was not one for hugs and loving attention, he was alpha dog and proud of it! He also had brute strength, with noxious gas to match! To top it off, his rancid breath was atrocious. Ole's sour stomach was as legendary as his obnoxious behavior. His eating style was a whole other story! He never wasted an ounce of time and would easily swallow a huge serving dish of food, in one efficient gulp.

The dog felt he was king of the farm and was everywhere a vehicle happened to be. His pogo-stick-like legs were a nuisance, as the dog could aptly jump into any vehicle before the door was even completely opened. He would aggressively, run down the road with his stunted little legs, as we pulled into the lane leading to the farm. He provided his own directions to drivers, as he ran alongside any vehicle driving up to our yard. The mutt felt that being everyone's traffic escort was his full-time job, while guarding the farm was simply a hobby. However, the farm dog's real passion was driving. My sisters will attest to Ole's uncanny ability to understand all the correct driving procedures and what to do behind the wheel.

The four-legged irritant was impatient with all the female drivers, as he watched them frequently pop a clutch or grind a gear. Skid's policy was that all his daughters would know how to drive a stick shift, no exceptions. The frustrated dog would swing his head in the direction that the gear shift should be moved. If it was done wrong, he would drool, nip, growl, and release a little brewing frustration from his backside! The dog would crank his head aggressively to the left or right, attempting to signal the driver which way to turn the steering wheel. When the engine revved up, ready to shift into a new gear, Ole' had already craned his head, impatiently directing the driver on what to do next. We all knew that Ole' wished he could have had the ability to drive. However, the dog was never wrong with his instructions. Frustrated? Yes!

Ole's motto was always, "Let's go!" Where? Anywhere! He was a travelling, adventurous guy and ready at a moment's notice. Everyone had to master the skill of getting into a vehicle and quickly close the door, or the dog would be in like a flash. I remember pretending to walk past a vehicle while Ole' was distracted, then racing to get into it before he could manage his hostage takeover. In the event the beast managed to hijack his way into the truck cab, we knew we were doomed. Once Ole' got into a vehicle he wouldn't leave. Space in the truck cab was limited and Ole' managed to occupy most of it.

One late summer night during the horse races in Fort Benton, Ole' was involved in holding another victim hostage. Under Montana's big sky and darkness of night, Ole,' the *farm cop,* heard faint sounds of a vehicle motor. He was keenly aware of the rumbling sounds of a stalled engine and with his imaginary badge in tow, the beast went to investigate the situation. There, he discovered the grumbling sounds of a truck parked on the county road.

The following, is an account of a phone call my mom received the next morning, regarding Ole' and his evening investigation: "Are you missing something?" was the caller's inquiry. Mom was surprised by the question and quickly took a mental inventory. The exhausted neighbor began describing the events of his evening. "I pulled over by your place late last night and got out of my truck, to check my tires." Checking the tires, was a term loosely used by men, to empty their bladders. The neighbor, it seemed, had spent the day at the race track, complete with libations. He said that when he got back in the cab, he was unaware the dog had snuck in to hitch a ride!

The neighbor was not expecting any uninvited passengers. To make matters worse, in the 1960s, alien abductions and U.F.O. sightings were the subject of many newspaper articles and television programs. There was an unsettling feeling across the country, that creatures from the unknown were watching or living among us. People were often seen looking to the sky for clues and information. Was it a star or starship? There was great fear of being abducted by aliens and taken to places unknown. Travelers felt uneasy, especially during complete darkness, worried if a possible alien encounter could steal them away from the life they knew.

Upon entering the truck cab, our neighbor stated he heard and felt moist, heavy breathing from some being, waiting there for him. He was unaware that our "alien" dog had decided to go for a joy ride and slipped slyly into the inviting truck cab. The man said he sat in the dark, terrorized by the mysterious travelling companion. The frazzled farmer decided he needed to quickly create an exit plan. Nervous and shaking, he flooded the engine with his efforts to get the truck started. There in the darkness of night, the creature growled, nipped and drooled, while the terrified neighbor had difficulty executing his driving skills. He explained that Ole' was irritated every time the man ground a gear. The hostile takeover, had made our neighbor so overwrought, he wasn't even capable of the simple task of shifting gears!

It is likely, the alcohol probably didn't help either!

However, the awkward twosome eventually made their way to the farmer's home. When they arrived, Ole' went ballistic! Each time the man reached for the door handle to make his exit, Ole' came unglued. Afraid of what would happen, our neighbor scrapped the idea of exiting his truck and the two spent an uncomfortable night in the vehicle. When morning's light came, the furious farmer's wife discovered the duo in the truck, worse for the wear. At the end of the phone call, the exhausted farmer pleaded with Mom to come get the dog as soon as possible, as he couldn't take another moment with the animal. Our sentiments exactly!

Chokecherries, The Gift That Kept On Giving

My sisters and I, have childhood memories involving various buckets, old ice cream containers, or anything with a handle, that we could use to collect chokecherries found along a hillside in the Shonkin mountains. Chokecherry syrup and jelly were the staples in our winter pantry. The jars also made their way into gifts at Christmas or as a thank you, for a kindness shown. The aroma of the ruby berries simmering on the stove is a fragrance I've never forgotten.

It was birthday time for Skid, which created a welcome diversion from the many conversations about the gas thief, who was driving into our backyard and stealing gas, from the big tanks behind the shop. The idea of someone coming to our remote location and filling up on fuel, was not a pleasant thought. Aliens and gas thief conversations were joyfully sidelined, while we discussed birthday gift options for Skid.

While in Great Falls, getting equipment parts, groceries, and other necessities, we found a present for Skid. Finding the ideal gift for the patriarch was challenging, as the Pet Rock we got him last year bombed! We were rather excited with the discovery and purchase of our clever wine making kit! This kit included two plastic square vats/jugs, caps, tubing, directions, suggestions, and an opportunity of a lifetime.

Skid was welding metal yard statues, tables and figurines, for extra farm income and gifts. We were entertaining the idea that homemade wine, could also be sold next to the variety of his welded art objects at the local arts and crafts fairs. Pairing the homemade wines and welded art, was a business collaboration we thought could help fill the pocketbook, during lean times.

After careful study, purchasing yeast, and other miscellaneous ingredients, the wine making adventure was about to begin. A recipe card was used to document the start date, the times which the valves had last been turned, and any other pertinent information. So, we began the daily ritual of watching the little crimson berries turn to wine, discussing their progress, and how soon the harvest of chokecherry wine would occur. As the vessels brewed the wine, an aroma of excitement and optimism began filling the prairie air. There was enthusiastic hope of the new hobby turning into a business opportunity. In the event hail, grasshoppers or low grain prices ruined harvest, there was now an income back-up plan. We had done it! We found a gift that was memorable and a potential money maker.

Excitement brewed, as did the wine. The last stages of fermentation were nearing and uncorking the vessels of plastic, piqued our anticipation. However, one late evening, we were suddenly jarred awake. Everyone jumped up out of their beds and ran to see what was going on. What was that shooting noise, we all wondered? Was it a hostage take-over by aliens or had the gas thief broken into our farmhouse? The sound of rapid fire was shooting everywhere around us. Suddenly, we heard Skid say, "I'll get my gun!" This was not good!

We continued to hear more gun fire and popping noises. Someone eventually found a light switch. When the light uncovered the darkness and revealed our kitchen, we froze in our tracks. There in the kitchen we all stood, with our mouths wide open, as we watched the fermented explosion, drip and ooze from the ceiling, the cabinets, and onto the floor. The claret red goo, slimy, and foul smelling, made us nauseous and cover our noses. The odor was overwhelming, rotten to its dripping core. That summer night, we heard Skid saying, "Maybe there was too much yeast. Maybe next time, plums ...yes plums!"

"NO!" we shouted in unison, as the lights were turned off and the mess was abandoned until morning.

Unfortunately, there was no new career for the farmer. His wine business dream, came and went. One thing was for certain, if any aliens were looming about, or the notorious gas thief heard the commotion that night, they would have certainly hit the road or the sky! The stench was awful, but the memory, like the cleaning, lived on for days! The wine making kit was always remembered as the gift that kept on giving. That night however, was remembered as, "The night the lights went on in Shonkin!"

Utica, Blue For A Day

Mom loved growing up near Moccasin, Montana. My grandparents had sold their ranch in Rudyard, in 1944 and settled on new dreams in Central Montana. My mom had eight older brothers. She was the only girl and the youngest of the Heintz children. Sunday family dinners, complete with sister-in-laws, future weddings, and little nieces and nephews to adore, made the farmhouse joyful for the only daughter. Mom often shared stories of Gramma's towering cakes that were so high, that the nearby Judith Mountains, looked miniature by comparison. Gramma also enjoyed serving fluffy, buttery pancake breakfasts piled high, with fried eggs in between. During the depression, the inexpensive breakfast was frequently served as dinner.

I remembered the smile Mom sported, while describing how she and Puddles, her four-legged childhood dog, roamed Macaroni Hill. The odd name bestowed upon the hill, always made me wonder if it was a childhood creation or the real thing. The cheerful, blue wildflowers, dotting the meadow and roadside edges, permeated my mind, as she described their beauty. Mom's vivid description made me wonder if the color of the blue wildflowers was as beautiful as the Big Sky I loved so much.

During a conversation around the breakfast bar one morning, Mom started reminiscing about the wonderful church picnics she loved to go to as a young girl. The annual event was held in Utica, Montana, not far from the Heintz farm and ranch outside of Moccasin. The historic area near Sap-

phire Village, was the summer picnic spot. It also was the location for the painting *A Quiet Day in Utica*, created by the famous western artist, Charlie Russell. His many artwork pieces depicted the small mining area of Utica, Sapphire Village and Central Montana. Mom stated that Utica still had buildings that were "scene stealers" in Charlie's paintings.[14]

She also told us about the rare gems that were mined, where Charlie had once called home. Mom said the cornflower blue, of the rare Yogo, had the same hue as the delicate wildflowers of her youth. Her words painted a powerful picture. She said that although the Yogo mine had closed, rumor had it, that a lucky camper would occasionally spot a blue bauble shining in the soil. Soon, we were pondering the idea, that a camping adventure to Utica and Sapphire Village, just might lead us to a Yogo!

Chatter, cooking, and packing ensued. "Our Blue Adventure," was happenin' and boy were we

excited! As we turned onto the back roads leading us to Utica, Mom once again saw the familiar flowers from her childhood, with lush green crop fields and mountains as their backdrop. Puddles, though long gone, sent his memory to run alongside our camper, guiding the way and I soon realized that Macaroni Hill was real after all. Perhaps Mom's stories of a Yogo being randomly discovered would also be true for us!

Several hours passed, as we prepared our campsite and evening meal. Hot dogs, bbq'd potato chips, potato salad, and cookies were laid out. As a treat, shrimp salad made the night before, helped turn the meal into a real banquet! Mom's delicious dinner had her future miners dining in rather high-style. Mom's announcement of "Dig in family!" had us all laughing. We knew the *dig-in* reference had more than one meaning. While we were finding the riches at the bottom of our plates, we all hoped to find the same in our buckets of dirt the next day!

Eventually, the night air and long journey had us sleeping restfully under the stars, in our home-made camper. Early the next morning, coughing, fatigue, sickness, headache, and gasping for air, woke Dori up. A gas leak from the camper's stove sent an asphyxiating grip through the small camper. The small slightly cracked window next to Dori's pillow, gave her enough oxygen to wake from a deep sleep. The difficult task of waking everyone up and trying to help each person to fresh air, was not an easy one for Dori. At only 10 years old, she had the ominous responsibility of helping our gas saturated bodies, get outside the camper. Vomiting, choking, and debilitating headaches, were hitting us like a wrecking ball to an old brick building. Fortunately, the mountain air assisted Dori, and God helped too!

Somehow, we managed to make it to the local hospital in Lewistown, where we were treated and released into Gramma's care. A few days later, we were homeward bound. As we headed down Highway 87, past the Hobson turn off, heading home, we all looked in the direction of Utica thinking of what might have been. Our dashed dreams of sapphires and exploring the sites that Charlie had painted, were never to be. Yet, we were most grateful we were on top of the ground and not underneath it, which was indeed a miracle!

Dew Drop

Our journey to find a blue treasure was disheartening and the trip home was subdued and quiet. As we settled back into our daily farm routine and chores, we made peace with the reality that no lovely azure baubles would be placed on our fingers. Nevertheless, we were always on the hunt for fun, playtime, and new adventures.

Our party line rang with some interesting information, which took our little minds on a detour from the camping disaster and onto a new journey. Mom answered the phone and we heard the words, "Really." "Hmm." "Well let me see." and "Sure, we can be there this afternoon." We were exceedingly curious about the telephone conversation and we gathered around mom, like flies to a picnic.

As we traveled to the neighbor's farm, we daydreamed of what may be awaiting us. Would this surprise be as fantastic as our imaginations were creating, or were we being childish in our excitement? At the end of the road waiting for her new family, was a Bambi look-alike. An unfortunate accident with a train, took the life of the deer's mother and her twin. The doe-eyed beauty, whom we named Dew Drop, became our newest family member. She was a delightful and loving little creature.

Dew Drop would nuzzle her face into your lap, as her way of hinting that she wanted attention and some gentle strokes around her face. When you complied with the petting, she fluttered her ears with approval. Her kisses were the loving licks she gave our hands and our faces. There was a grateful look in her beautiful eyes and a playfulness about her spirit that we all enjoyed.

We all loved Dew Drop, and wanted to share our excitement of our new family member with everyone around. We considered sending birth announcements, but chose to announce her arrival on our party line. There were always numerous eavesdroppers on the phone line and we knew the news would travel faster than we could write!

Gramma taught us the song, *You Are My Sunshine*, making it a childhood musical memory. Although we frequently played the radio for Dew Drop, we decided our new farm baby should have

her own sweet song. We sang the sunshine song to her, but when the 'dear' part came, we referred to it as 'deer' and sang the word at the top of our lungs! Even Ole' would stop barking to listen to our chorus. We delighted in our cleverness, laughing and singing at the same time, amusing ourselves while entertaining our special pet. Every time we greeted Dew Drop with her morning bottle, we sang, "You'll never know 'DEER' how much I love you, please don't take my sunshine away!"

The adoption of sweet Dew Drop that summer, taught us so many things. We all enjoyed mothering the little orphan found near the railroad tracks. Each of us embraced her as though she was another member of our family. We had many typical pets through the years, but Dew Drop was unique and special. After all, she was the one we "deerly loved!"

Bunkhouse Play

Ah, the bunkhouse! Many a farm and ranch had one and we were no exception. The small dwelling gave my big imagination many creative

opportunities, that provided abundant youthful memories. Countless hours of endless play, fashioned my sisters and I into formidable ranch owners. *The Big Valley*, a television program about the Barkley's, a ranching family, was a mere copycat for what my mind's eye envisioned. The Barkley's spread couldn't hold a candle to the bustle of activities and adventures happening in *our* playground. Hours were spent moving the cowhide, sweeping, redecorating, organizing the makeshift game table, rearranging the same pictures and calendar. As ranch proprietors, we decided things needed a little spiffin' up. Once the time consuming work was completed, we always discovered that everything in its original location, was indeed perfect. The whole place was just a little cleaner and tidier for the imaginary cowboys, coming in from the range.

One item that we never moved, was the old kitchen stove. We polished and cleaned her up and she prepared the best meals in our fantasy world. We pretended to create comfort food and fabulous desserts, on the old worn out and unemployed stove. Our neglected workhorse had seen better days. Her burners were intact, but her spirit was tired. Her spring loaded handle could have been a gym exercise as it was a workout to crank. Yet, after the bunkhouse range was painstakingly cleaned, her white enameled surface glistened like a fresh blanket of snow.

The unassuming bunkhouse provided a platform for my imagination, to transform popular television westerns into pretend playtime. Television programming had many ranch inspired series, but they couldn't hold a candle to my imaginary and epic cinematic works. In the playground of my mind, my sisters and I were accomplished independent women, yet strong and caring, much like Audra and Mrs. Barkley. They had The Big Valley, but we had Knudsonville. The drama of our playtime didn't include gunfights or shoot outs, but was merely an opportunity for the riders coming in from the range, to enjoy a well-presented "spread" of delicious food. We were hands-on owners, showing our appreciation for those imaginary hard working cowboys, who rode the range and protected our stock.

Bunkhouse play filled our many summer hours with hard work, amusement, and happy memories. I truly believe that all the fictitious meals made in the bunkhouse of my youth, have contributed to the creative meals and desserts that I make daily, for my real "hands."

A Circus Of Events

Once again our party line rang, delivering exciting news. Donna, now a newlywed, called and invited us to the Big Top. The circus was coming to Great Falls. Donna had just moved to Carter, which was only 30 miles north of Great Falls. She said we would spend the night in her newly decorated guest room. Leaving from Carter, instead of the farm, would make it easier for us to go to the circus. We were thrilled, as she gave us the rundown on the agenda, and when to arrive in Carter.

We reached Donna's home with wide eyes and big dreams. None of us kids had ever been to a circus before! It was an exciting opportunity to see the Big Top and spend time with our oldest sister. Donna greeted us with chilled lemonade, complete with fresh mint from her garden. She made bolo-

gna sandwiches and navy bean soup. After her husband Gary arrived from the field, freshened up, and had a quick bite to eat, we proceeded to Great Falls.

The smell of circus food permeated the evening air, as we neared The Big Top tent. The ambient lighting was dim, however, our enthusiasm could have lit up the tent all by itself! Warm buttery popcorn, roasted peanuts, pink cotton candy on funnel sticks, and assorted toys, met our inquisitive eyes.

The array of circus toys was dizzying. Where did one little kid start? Pennants, inked up and printed to commemorate our big top experience were for sale, as were clown dolls and large boxes of candy. Rounding the corner, the greenhorn farm girls were met with the most wonderful vision... fur monkey trapeze artist dolls! Quick, someone get the smelling salts! What was a kid to do? Our humble post office/general store did not have delightful clown dolls, or the fantastic flipping fur monkey toy!

Our excitement took over and so did Gary. The overpriced toys were being thrust into our little faces by an aggressive circus employee, attempting to entice the first-time circus goers into purchasing them. The circus barker figured he could convince the starry-eyed farm girls into buying all his loot. However, he met his match when Donna and Gary stepped in and stopped his hustling sales pitch! They conservatively bought only one fur monkey toy and one circus pennant.

We soon found excellent seats inside the Big Top and settled in with our sugary treats and drinks, as well as the one fur monkey, to be shared three ways. Our attentive eyes were eagerly anticipating the greatest show on earth. Soon, the acts began. We were mesmerized by the circus, while passing the new little fur toy back and forth.

During intermission, Gary leaned in and told us he was going to go and get another toy monkey for *cheap* once the circus was over. He explained that employees of the circus, discount food and toys when the show ends, so that they don't have to move all the things from one town to another. Was it possible that another toy could come back to the farm with us? Did Donna's husband really have the inside scoop regarding the comings and goings of the circus world?

While the circus show continued, we marveled over all the thrilling sights of the Big Top. When the show ended, Donna sat with us while Gary strode through the thick crowd in search of another fur monkey. After a while, Donna said it was safe to get up and work our way through the thinning crowd. While walking toward the exit, we saw Gary, "the grinning gambler," with another fur monkey trapeze doll! We couldn't believe our eyes, and we realized he really did know how the circus world worked after all!

Riding home in the back seat, sat the three weary circus goers, filled with exciting memories of bright Big Top lights, shining in their eyes and one extra *bargain* monkey toy to share. The joy of our adventure was heightened by Gary's wheelin' and dealin' ways!

The Greatest Show On The Prairie

Our circus adventure and fun time with Donna, inspired a big idea. Tudie, two years younger than Donna, had an imagination beyond belief. Whenever she came up with a plan, I knew our play time was going to be epic! Dori was always Tudie's creative partner in crime, their playtime adventures made me a benefactor of the inspired schemes, which emerged from her vivacious imagination. The endless talk of our circus adventure, had Tudie dreaming up new playtime fun. This time, the farm was going to be turned into a Big Top, *farm-style*.

Big Top conversations were under way and the farm was energized with circus talk. There was much ado about everything! The execution of the circus extravaganza taking place on our farm, involved many hours of prep work. Tudie, was the self-appointed ring leader and mistress of ceremonies. She called a prep meeting on the harvest gold shag rug. It was determined the barn, the corral, and surrounding areas, all needed cleaning. No canvas Big Top would be erected, as our prairie circus had more of a rustic air about it.

Tudie and Dori practiced their horse riding tricks, while also fighting off horse flies, and Ole' constantly hovering under foot. I remember them doing their acrobatic practices: handstands, back flips, and hanging off the saddle, while riding endless circles inside the corral. The novice riders, with

their amateur horse riding skills, soon looked more professional. It was incredible how they transformed into skillful circus artists. Their perfected horse riding skills were amazing and certainly circus worthy! Tudie's silver baton flew through the air, and she caught it with the greatest of ease. However, Ole' was ever present, in case she didn't. The baton skills acquired from being a member of the majorettes, came in handy as she became the mistress of ceremonies. Her baton twirling talents were also going to be showcased during the circus extravaganza.

Careful consideration of all things farm; from inspirational props, to animals, was fair game in our circus. There was an air of ingenuity and anticipation looming over the homestead. A spiral notebook, left over from playing library and store, was used to script the *big show*. It was shaping up to be a premiere event, putting Shonkin on the circus map!

Act assignments were given to each of us. Tudie was Ring Mistress, and her lovely assistant was Dori the Great. While our youngest sister was Sacagawea, an Indian princess who once

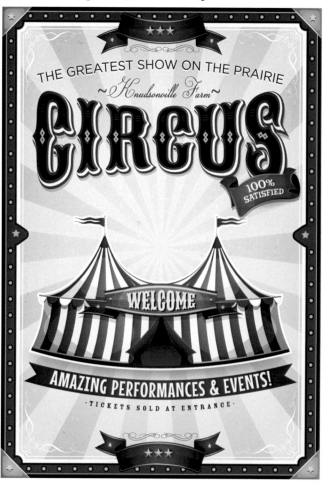

travelled through Montana near our farm. As for me, I was the unthinkable… Frances the Fat Lady!

There are no small acts in any show, and in this case, the bigger the better! Pillows had to be stuffed and tied around my small frame, to give the illusion of plumpness. An old wig was powdered and silver framed, round granny glasses, topped off my costume. I carried my shame-based sign, "Frances The Fat Lady" to announce who I was. Tipper, the grey striped kitty, was a circus act as well. Her costume consisted of a baby bonnet, and a collar with bells to add the finishing touch. Our youngest sister's Indian princess dress, and brown paper headband with feather, made her look like a young Sacagawea. She pulled a rusty little red wagon with metal fencing on it. The fencing bundle was tightly wound and covered with a white sheet, fashioning it as a Conestoga wagon. Tudie and Dori were fitted perfectly in classic, colorful tumbling and acrobatic attire, consisting of cut-off shorts, tank tops and sleeveless blouses tied at the waist. Their beautiful tans were a natural accessory.

Still, there was one more act which needed to be added to the cast of characters…..Ole'. We all knew that he'd show up anyway, so we devised a role for the dastardly dog. Snickers turned into robust laughter, as we considered the many possibilities for the mutt. He had a certain amount of predictability: barking, nipping and stinking up the joint. So, creating a circus act for him was a challenge. Costume creations, befitting the dog's personality and his wild behavior, had us stumped. One evening while preparing the farm's Big Top area, we heard the dinner bell and strode to the house. We went through the fence and securely closed the gate. Suddenly, Ole' started jumping up and down. His spring-like legs, helped him bounce up and down like a Mexican jumping bean. There it was! The revelation of an act, Ole' could be the star of. It was thrilling to think we could dress him up and get the better of the ornery creature.

A vest, fashioned from his dog house rug, would be tied around the beast. The rug's southwestern design, with its stripes of turquoise, red, gold, and green were perfect for his outfit. An old Mexican sombrero topped off his getup. Dressing the mongrel was an arduous undertaking, as holding the dog still, was a difficult struggle, exacerbated by his noxious gas. It took all of us to tether the beast for his costume fitting, transforming him from "driver dog" to "Mexican jumping bean." We decided after the challenging task of a dress rehearsal, putting his costume on could wait until right before the show.

The day had finally arrived to unveil *The Greatest Show On The Prairie*. Hay bales were placed outside the barn for seating. Many of our neighbors came, looking forward to the entertainment. The attendees all carried Awake orange juice cans, cleaned and full of coins, to purchase goodies from our concession stand. Mom contributed with her own delicious fair food. She made rice krispies bars, chocolate chip and oatmeal cookies, cinnamon rolls, ham sandwiches on her homemade bread, complete with potato chips and pitchers of cold lemonade. Our concession stand sales were as hot as the summer heat. We sold out in a flash!

The guests made their way to our imaginary Big Top. Enthusiasm came too, as they were the best audience ever! A portable radio provided background music, giving our guests something to listen to, other than Ole' barking, growling and cutting loose a string of gaseous sounds! Soon, our Big Top would reveal its circus acts under the Big Sky.

Tudie graciously thanked our guests for coming and announced the parade of circus acts that would start the show. Sacagawea began the procession, rounding the burn barrels and making an imaginary path towards the "circus tent." I was next, followed by Dori then Tudie. Tipper ran through the hay bale seats, jingling all the way! Someone was supposed to escort the dog for his rotation in the circus acts. Although no one was certain what happened, all of a sudden, our circus on the prairie, was interrupted by the Mexican jumping bean. Ole' began running through our guests, while chewing and pulling at his costume. As he was gnawing at his ensemble, his sombrero flew haphazardly in the air, snapping from side to side behind him. As Ole' twisted and tugged, trying to pull off his vest of many colors, his berserk moves made him appear like a Go-Go dancer on American Bandstand. We were used to him chasing his tail, but this was a whole new dance move! Everyone stood there speechless. He was determined to aggressively tug at his costume, tearing at the fringe with bear teeth, while attempting to strip it off. He was full-on "matador vs. bull" mode. The bullfight was on and he had no intention of losing! One of the amused guests said, "How did they get him to do that?" I shook my head, and replied, "For the love of Pete, he's nuts!" Finally, Ole' made his circus exit, but not without first leaving a foul smelling trail, letting us know what he thought of the whole thing!

Our guests were busy discussing the show and giving us a profusion of complements. The Big Top was a success, even Ole's "act" was a hit! The hot summer sun, absence of shade, and my mounds of pillows and clothes, had me thirstier than the dry desert. After taking several large swigs of lemonade, I headed to the house. Upon arriving, I discovered the mysteriously missing platter of rice krispies bars, laying on the kitchen counter. Carefully, I carried the treats in one hand, while juggling my fat pillows in the other. As I made my way back to the Big Top, the unthinkable happened. The Mexican jumping bean, saw the sweet platter of treats and decided they were his reward for a job well done! The beast lunged right into me. The collison sent the treats flying through the air, like they were a trapeze act. Our gracious guests picked the straw off the rice krispies bars and still paid top dollar for them. All in all, *The Greatest Show on the Prairie*, was a hit. As for Ole', he stole the show! Our circus memories? Outstanding!

Tipi Time

The shelterbelt possessed rows of trees with furrows racing down the dirt, slowly curving around like a river bend. Every late spring or early summer, Skid took the John Deere and plowed through the shelterbelt that protected the farm from harsh winter winds. Straddling the soft, wavy mounds of freshly plowed dirt, undulating from high to low, was like playing jump rope. Each step, felt like we were maneuvering around an obstacle course. Lifting our little feet up and over the freshly plowed furrows of dirt, felt as if we were frolicking in flour.

An evening jaunt for ice cream from the Tastee Freeze in Fort Benton, provided us an opportunity to learn a little Montana history. Not far from the ice cream shop, were the remains of a historic

Army fort and a keelboat, used in the movie about Lewis and Clark. I remember collecting random arrowheads and finding Indian beads in the dirt around the old wall of the historic fort. These were reflections of a life when Indians roamed the prairie and the cavalry came west to settle the frontier.

We were told that Indians lived in tipis and used tanned animal hides, to cover the outer shell of the dwelling. The fortress was easy to assemble and take down, whenever they made camp at different places. The native's nomadic ways, typically had them wintering in one area and summering in another.

We then learned the story of a young woman, who was part of the famous expedition of Lewis and Clark. Sacagawea was a Shoshone Indian princess, who traveled with the notable explorers. They credited her as an invaluable asset, while they journeyed through the Louisiana Purchase. Her knowledge of terrain, weather, Indian tribes, and food sources, made her a priceless companion.[15] She was a legend, and we assumed that she was also beautiful, after all, she was a princess. She had dark braided hair and a dress made of tanned hides, heavily adorned with colorful beads. She also wore soft moccasins, as she scouted for berries to make pemmican for the expedition crew.[16]

The tales of lodging and tipi encampment were soon going to create another playtime adventure on the farm! Sacagawea was a fascinating subject and the idea of a tipi was even more exciting. Descriptions of the historical journey of Lewis and Clark, and their Indian guide Sacagawea, made the dusty, hot evening drive home go a little faster. Our minds were consumed with the pride of the expedition, their discovery of finding our great state, and the realization, that those travelers walked where we did!

The accounts of Lewis and Clark inspired us and we decided our little frontier town of Knudsonville was going to have a new building for summertime play. We explored all remnants around the farm. Leftover scrap pieces of wood, nails, string, cardboard boxes, and miscellaneous scrap piles, had us pondering numerous ideas. We soon ruled out building a fort for our township, as the construction skills needed were a bit too difficult. However, a tipi had a little "je ne sais quoi." This task put us on a mission

to find the perfect location for our native dwelling.

As with any real estate endeavor, location, location, location, factors into the proper site for a new building or structure. Protection from howling winds and Ole's disruptive and destructive behavior, had us considering several camp locations for careful placement. While we traversed the farm we passed the shelterbelt, and realized it was a perfect place for our tipi replica. We felt Sacagawea would have loved the location also!

The shelterbelt was a barricade from Mother Nature and her wrath. Storms and age wore a few tree limbs down, right to the ground. The broken branches were tired and weary from protecting our farm from harsh winter storms. We dug up the broken branches from under the dried grass next to the dirt furrows. The pieces of wood were given one final duty; to frame our tipi. Careful design was under way, as we stripped off the small excess branches and dried leaves. We made certain the branches measured equal lengths, to properly form the tipi structure. Building the skeleton of our dwelling was time consuming, but exhilarating. Everything was

starting to take shape, in our "chore of discovery!" Even Ole' seemed to nod with approval! We stood in amazement as we lined up our branches, leaning them all in towards the center, to make a proper tipi top. The wide circle of limbs was indeed looking like a real Native American fortress! It was an exercise in patience, as we had to navigate around the dirt furrows and Ole', who was always in the way! We then realized that our tipi needed a way to keep the top tied together. Just as we were deciding how to accomplish the task, all the limbs suddenly fell to the earth, from which they came. Ugh! We took a much needed lunch break and chewed on ideas of how to tie our new playtime home together.

Shop rags, twine and wire didn't seem to be suitable items for the shelterbelt creation. We realized securing the frame of our tipi was paramount to its sturdiness, but how? We perused Skid's work benches and the bunkhouse too. Frustration was setting in, like the storm clouds overhead. Elmer's glue was suggested, while shoelaces from our sneakers was a distant thought. After several hours of shrugged shoulders and disapproved ideas, we took one more tour of Knudsonville, determined to find the perfect resource to tie our lodging together.

Somehow our investigation of the garage was overlooked. We quickly entered, hoping it held our solution. There it was! What a sight to behold! Hanging from the shelf, was a discarded chamois car cloth. The golden leather/suede square was indeed perfect. It had frontier written all over it. We pretended it was a tanned hide, a gift from one of Sacagawea's Indian friends. The cloth was cut into strips and tied, to rebuild the tipi top. The top was much sturdier this time and we stood in amazement and pride as we looked at our tipi. We felt we were kindred spirits to Lewis and Clark, their expedition, and to Sacagawea.

A few extra strips of the chamois cloth were cut fine and thin. My sisters wove them into their pigtails and their braids to look like a native Indian. This was exciting stuff! We ate Slim Jim's and beef jerky, pretending it was the pemmican Sacagawea had taught us how to make. We also added instruments to the tipi experience. Our pow wow music was made from oatmeal containers for drums, and paper plates filled with navy beans, then stapled together, to create tambourines. We drilled

Sacagawea statue in Three Forks, MT

soda pop tops with an awl, threaded wire through the hole, and hung it on the outer edge of the plates, so they looked like real tambourines. We colored Native American figures on the musical instruments. We used chicken feathers, gathered from the chicken coop, to adorn the instruments and our hair. The harmonica was the last instrument to be included in our musical repertoire.

We stuffed one of Skid's red bandana handkerchiefs with extra jerky, snacks, and little baggies of Lucky Charms cereal. We thought that the "magically" delicious cereal would bring us a little luck, to keep our tipi standing. While we were in the kitchen gathering our treats, we also grabbed macaroni and cheerios. We thought these additions would make great beads for our necklaces and bracelets. The leftovers would be used as bartering items for any future expeditions we might undertake.

Tudie grabbed her baton for the pow wow dancing. An empty Milk Duds box, with its flaps opened wide, was blown into, to make a deep bugle call to our pow wow festivities. We loved our tipi, and thought it was a magnificent addition to our frontier prairie town. No tanned hide covered our fortress, as we knew Ole' would have revamped his circus act and tore it off the tipi shell, just like he had done with the rug off his back! All in all, our little "expedition" was a summertime, playtime hit.

Although challenging to build, the tipi was a

tribute to Sacagawea. We recognized her importance as a guide to Lewis and Clark and their expedition. The tipi gave us a sense of pride, as we felt we connected to the spirit of the Indian princess, who once walked where we had. We pretended that she was our friend and that she taught us her culture. We dreamed of including her into our own sisterhood. Sitting inside the tipi, that hot summer day, we rejoiced in our accomplishment. With Slim Jim's in hand, we raised them to the heavens and said, "To Sacagawea!" Our declaration was a heartfelt invitation for the princess to join our circle of sisterly love.

The shelterbelt provided more than just a location for our "chore of discovery" tipi. It was also shade for our summer activities, as the rows of caragana, poplar, and Russian olive trees shaded us from the hot summer sun. Yet, the tipi creation wasn't the only fun time amusement in the shelterbelt, that summer.

A coffee can was filled with treasures from each of us and buried next to the tipi. In it, we placed our school pictures, to commemorate the year of the time capsule. Jacks, playing cards, coins, a few dollars, treasured rocks, and notes from each of us were also put into the can. The carefully placed objects were special belongings, that we temporarily gave away. The plan was to dig up our buried treasure and retrieve our personal donations the following year. Unfortunately, the buried treasure was never recovered. For many years, we carefully unearthed the burial site, but our coffee can was never found. The consensus of opinions concluded, that Skid had probably plowed over and dug up our childhood treasure. Although, the time capsule is long gone, the memory of it lives on in each of us.

Sonny and Cher

One year our party line blew up with the news that Sonny and Cher were going to come to the State Fair. Unlike many of the other fair performers, we were familiar with their music. We listened to them on the radio and watched them on *American Bandstand*. They were edgy, controversial, show stoppers. Sonny's Roman inspired bowl haircut, made him look as if he didn't have the money to afford a proper haircut. Cher on the other hand, had tresses, made for tossin'! Her blunt bangs and spit-curled sides were stylin'. The singing duo would sway back and forth, as did her bangs, while they sang their songs and keeping the beat. The singing duo wowed us, as they looked adoringly into each other's faces and smiled, while performing their hit. Seeing Sonny and Cher on television was captivating, exhilarating, and inspiring.

We were never short on playtime ideas, but managing playtime activities that all the ages of the farm girls were able to participate in was challenging. Our ages were 5, 6, 9, 16 and 18, so having opportunities for all of us to engage in, was sometimes a stretch for anyone's imagination! Music usually filled in the age gap, setting the stage for bonding and lots of it.

Sonny and Cher's musical performance inspired another opportunity for creativity and music to entertain our imaginations and make a summer day memory. "Live from the Shonkin Prairie, Sonny and Cher!" was Tudie's announcement, and our cue, for Dori and I to come out of the bathroom and into the living room. Tudie announced that the miracle, of the pretend Sonny and Cher, was made possible because their imaginary tour bus had "supposedly" hit the ditch.

With nervous hands, holding a hairbrush and a comb for pretend microphones, Sonny and Cher, farm style appeared. There Dori and I performed the classic, *I Got You Babe*. My short hair with bangs, needing a trim, were combed forward. Dori slept on large rollers, straightening her dark curls. We borrowed clothes from closets that weren't ours and liberally festooned our necks with Mom's jewelry.

We made our prairie debut in the living room, rocking left and right, occasionally holding hands in front of the black and white television, that first introduced us to the "real" Sonny and Cher. It is reported that not much singing took place, as the singing duo was laughing so hard, choking up and forgetting their memorized words. The performance however pitiful, distracted us from looming chores and how hot the summer day was.

There was pure joy in our translation of being Sonny and Cher. We learned a lot: how to make something from nothing, laugh at ourselves and enjoy dancing and singing. Something else happened that day, the blended circle of sisters were bonded in a

way that blood did not provide them. We were a sister act, who for one day, were stars on the prairie.

Sonny and Cher did eventually come to Great Falls, Montana, and were headlining the evening entertainment at the state fair. We were overcome with excitement at getting to see them perform live and laughed over the thought that they might not be as good as we were! How could they be, we thought, causing more giggles. Making the announcement more intriguing, was the scandalous news regarding Cher's gown. Someone on the party line, stated it was a Bob Mackie gold lamé original, and was supposedly worn without any under garments. That news had us speechless!

Pantie lines or no pantie lines, we headed to the show to see for ourselves, if in fact Cher was a "good girl." We always took binoculars to the State Fair, since sometimes we had nose bleed seats. The field glasses were passed down the line, letting everyone get a glimpse at Cher, while hunting to see if she was undie-wear free! The dress was gorgeous, as was Cher. She and Sonny had an image makeover and became very elegant performers. Unfortunately, our seats were too far away to get a clear view, to confirm whether undies were present or not.

In the end, Pantie Gate didn't matter, as seeing them perform was the best night ever! Under the stars, the prairie sisters were backup singers for Sonny and Cher, singing at the top of our lungs. Rumor had it, that there was some serious competition in the grandstands, for the famous husband and wife singing act!

Skid

Skid was an artist, farmer, musician and whistler extraordinaire. Tractor seats were welded into bar stools, driftwood fashioned into a table lamp, curled iron pieces were formed and welded into a coffee table and TV stand. All our bedroom furniture was made by the artistic hands of Skid. There wasn't anything that he couldn't do, including making the best angel food cake, mom ever tasted.

During Christmas, the hi-fi stereo played non-stop, dropping vinyl 33 LPs of Perry Como, Andy

to him, as the combine was full, or that Ole' had let out a string of nasties in the hot cab of the combine and Skid was trying to clear the air of the foul smell!

Describing him as an artist, was an understatement. Every winter the basement became a woodworking shop for Skid's carpentry skills. One Christmas, he made a cradle for his youngest daughter's baby doll. The handcrafted bassinet was removable and could be carried without the frame. He painstakingly painted delicate, light pink piping trim all along the edges. Dori's custom wood stove, with its painted wood burners and temperature knobs, was also a gift from her Dad. It found a new home in the playhouse that he built for us.

The playhouse design was a mini version of our farmhouse. The quaint miniature, was nestled between the house, barn and garage. It replaced our playtime in the bunkhouse, as we preferred our little feminine getaway, over the masculine charm of the bunkhouse. The new building, painted white, with charming pink window trim, had feminine decor. It had windows that cranked outwardly, as a thoughtful installation, making it easy for our little hands to maneuver. The playhouse door was a copycat of the one on the famous sitcom *Green Acres*. During the opening credits Mrs. Douglas the farm wife, was seen poking her head out the top half of the Dutch/barn door. We did the same with our door, greeting one another cheerfully, while singing the Green Acres theme song.

Before we learned the art of driving a real stick shift, we mastered the many rounds around the farm buildings in the "putt-putt." The homemade car was fitted with the motor from the grain auger and only ran when harvest wasn't under way. A *Popular Mechanics* magazine was Skid's inspiration for our childhood wheels. It was the best little car and one Ole', thankfully wanted no part of! The "putt-putt" could navigate hard turns, a gravel driveway, and handle five farm girls. It was the best "Wheels of our life!" Skid's vision and creation was thrilling to drive around. It was an original, just like the creator.

My stepfather's demeanor was quiet, as his mind was doing all the creative talking, filling his soul with new artistic masterpieces to make. He was one of the *original* repurpose, reuse,

Williams, Dean Martin, and Nat King Cole. The classics were holiday traditions, as was the accompanying background of Skid's melodic whistle. I remember trying to prolong my chores so I could eavesdrop a little longer to hear the magical, musical sound. The farmhouse was a concert hall for Skid's musical gift, so beautiful and pure, that meadowlarks were jealous. Now that is saying something!

Patience should have been the farmer's middle name, with having five girls and no sons. He suffered through driving lessons and fender benders. Mechanical geniuses we were not. When he needed help in the shop, his patience was tested, and I mean tested! We, on the other hand, never understood his many hand signals, while making rounds in the fields during harvest. I remember Dori and I constantly wondering what to do next! There were many possible meanings behind his gestures: one more round before a load could be picked up, drive the truck over and recycle craftsmen. He built a wishing well, followed by enormous metal flowers. The petals were retired duck feet, from the plow on the tractor. Large rings were welded perfectly in place, to hold flower pots under the carved metal leaves. He also welded rusted horseshoes into legs for a metal cowboy statue, giving new life to old things. Nuts, bolts, screws, and wire became figurines, that represented farm life, the 60's, or anything else his imagination could come up with.

He pursued other artistic mediums as he made wine glasses from pop bottles, for his ceremonial pour of chokecherry wine. The neck of the bottle was cut off and glued to the bottom, making a stem for the wine glass. Unfortunately, the ceremonial pour never took place, due to the fermented explosion! Soda cans were cut and curved into photo frames. One year, extra-large soup cans became curly-q Easter baskets. Today, when my sisters and I see metal creations in stores or craft fairs, we know he would have already thought of it first. Truly, there wasn't anything he couldn't create with his remarkable workmanship.

Skid maintained a positive outlook, always jovial and kind. He suffered through a birthday Pet Rock gift one year and a birthday card that said "Happy Anniversary!" He never let us believe that the items were inappropriate, just remarking, "Well I'll be." When crops were ruined, he would say, "What next?" not dwelling on the disappointment. Instead he would head to the shop, to deal with the devastation, artistically.

There were two times I cried in his presence, the first was over my stinkin'

birthday gift for him and the other was the loss of the cheerleader figurine he crafted for me. Skid did not have time to make duplicates, so I allowed the figurine to go to the arts and crafts fair as a prototype for orders. Sadly, the cheerleader was accidentally sold, without my knowledge. When we arrived home and unpacked, I discovered my gift was gone. I could not hold back the tears, as I hurriedly raced to my bedroom. He graciously offered to make another, but I would not have it. I longed for the original gift, no replacement would suffice.

As the farm stories close, I find it only appropriate to acknowledge the best man I ever knew. His career was farming, but art was his passion. The farmhouse was filled with memorable moments. Our 406 Table was a workhorse for meals, games, and family exchanges, but it was no match for the childhood Skid provided and the family he included us in. Thank you Skid, for everything.

Beverages

Harvest Cooler, **Lemonade Style**

There is not a summer memory that did not include Skid's Coleman cooler filled with lemonade, sitting in the cab of the combine. The cooler was replenished during afternoon harvest breaks, with more of the lemony thirst quencher.

6 lemons juiced, seeds
    removed
¾ cup of granulated sugar
¼ cup of powdered sugar
3¼ cups boiling water
3 cups cold water

In a saucepan, boil 3¼ cups water with granulated sugar, approximately 5 minutes. Making a syrup. Remove from heat and stir in powdered sugar.

In a large gallon pitcher, mix freshly squeezed lemon juice, 3 cups cold water, and prepared sugar syrup. Stir well. Refrigerate.

Makes 6 servings

Highfalutin Party Punch

This recipe came to me while I was managing the Little Mondeaux Lodge. A prominent political family requested that this recipe be served for their granddaughter's 'highfalutin' lavish wedding. The contract stated that I was to purchase all the ingredients, show no one the recipe and make the family's "secret" punch recipe myself. About that secret recipe? I kept it secret alright, but I've been making it for years. I have served this for my own family's "highfalutin" events. After 30 years, I think it's okay to let the secret out!

12 oz club soda
1 liter ginger ale
1 can frozen white grape juice, thawed, prepared according to directions
5 cups of ice cubes

In a large punch bowl combine all ingredients, including ice cubes. If preferred, ladle punch and ice into pitchers and serve.

 Inside Scoop: Food coloring can be added to the punch to coordinate with a theme of a party. For an ice ring, I use a Bundt or angel food pan, fill ½ way up with water, place flowers or flower petals in container and freeze for 8 hours. Remove and fill until full with water and freeze for an additional 24 hours. Ice cube trays can be frozen with flowers, petals and greenery. Use the same method when making an ice ring. If you are serving the punch outdoors, freeze ice cube trays or ice ring for several days to make sure it is well frozen.

Makes 12 servings for a larger glass, or 16 small glass servings.

Strawberry Lemonade

Place ½ cup of strawberries, stems removed and puree in a blender. Add into lemonade and serve.

Last Chance Gulp Lemonade

This is a cheater lemonade that tastes like fresh!

Helena, Montana is the capital city of the Treasure State. Four desperate miners, in search of gold, came to Helena, and discovered a gold deposit of epic proportions. In a last ditch effort, the miners found the "motherlode" in a stream in Helena. It was the second largest gold deposit to be unearthed in Montana. It was their last attempt in striking it rich, thus the name, "Last Chance Gulch." In over four years' time, beginning in July 14, 1864, over $19 million dollars in gold was mined, in Last Chance Gulch. Helena became famous for the amount of millionaires living there in 1888. There were more millionaires per capita than any other city in the world.[17] This Last Chance Gulp, has some bragging rights too. It is refreshing and easier than making a recipe from scratch, yet it tastes like homemade. Your guests will quench their thirst, right down to the last gulp!

1 can frozen pink lemonade or regular lemonade
   concentrate
3½ cups water
⅛ cup of powdered sugar

In a microwaveable safe container, take one cup of the above water, place in microwave for 1 minute. Remove and stir in the powdered sugar. This makes a simple syrup. Add the syrup to the thawed, lemonade concentrate, then add the remaining 2½ cups water. Stir well. Place in refrigerator to chill. Stir before serving. This lemonade has pucker power!!! If you like a less sour taste, increase water by adding another ½ can of water.

Inside Scoop: When making the lemonade for a larger group, I freeze several trays of the prepared lemonade, in ice cube trays or ice ring. I have used a Bundt pan to make an ice ring as well. Make lemonade ahead of time and fill ice cube trays with the lemonade. Add frozen cubes when serving. These will replace regular ice cubes and will not water down the flavor. Also, for added visual interest, add sliced strawberries, fresh rose petals, or single flowers.

I sometimes offer guests Torani Huckleberry Syrup, or other syrup flavors to enhance the lemonade, making a "Lemonade Stand/Bar." You can always use pureed strawberries to change the flavors, refer to Harvest Cooler, Lemonade Style, on page 26 for the recipe.

Makes 6 servings.

The Flathead Float

"A fine sheet of water," were words used to describe Flathead Lake. The exquisite Montana lake is home to hundreds of birds and multitudes of wildlife. Wild Horse Island is the largest island on the lake and home to more than 75 species of birds, deer, bighorn sheep, coyotes, and bears. The water is perfect for sailing, cruising, and kayaking. Flathead Lake is the largest natural freshwater lake west of the Mississippi, in the lower 48 states. The lake includes 200 square miles of water and 185 miles of shoreline.[18] The Flathead Valley is the perfect growing climate for its famous Huckleberries.[19] If you are unable to float on the Flathead, you can at least toast, to the beautiful lake, while drinking a Flathead Float!

Note: Before making these huckleberry infused beverages, I place the large drinking glasses in the freezer. This helps frost the glasses, making their presentation a little more special.

Huckleberry ice cream or vanilla ice cream
Flathead Lake Huckleberry Gourmet soda or ginger ale
Huckleberry syrup
Glacier Whipped Cream (page 155) or aerosol whipped cream
Tall drinking glass or mug
Straws

For large gatherings or simple parties, I prepare in advance, 2 scoops of ice cream per glass and place in a covered container and freeze. This step helps with faster assembly and keeps the ice cream from getting soft too quickly. If you pre-froze the glasses or mugs, remove them from the freezer and place 2 scoops of ice cream in each one. Pour the soda over ice cream, then place a dollop of whipped cream in each glass, followed by a drizzle of huckleberry syrup. Serve with long spoons and straws.

Inside Scoop: During the summer season in Montana, Wilcoxson's and Meadow Gold Dairy companies feature huckleberry ice cream. Huckleberry soda hits the shelves in the summertime as well. I order Torani huckleberry syrup online, if I do not have homemade syrup on hand.

Hot Chocolate, Cocoa Bar

Within the following hot chocolate recipes, there are a variety of hot drinks that were served to cold kids, while doing winter birthday parties or skating parties at our local ice rink. Many of Montana's winter activities called for a hot mug/cup to warm you up. The variety of spices and flavors are nice options. I have added shaved ice to "cooled" white chocolate/hot chocolate and called them, "A Frozen Snowman." I decorated the labels of individual water bottles and called them a "Melted Snowman," while a large clear beverage dispenser became a vessel for a larger version of the 'melted snowman'. I would place shaved ice in the dispenser and let it float on the top, making it seem as though the snow was melting. Candy canes were used as stir sticks. I often found various flavors in other colors online. Mint and chocolate nonpareils were used to further heighten the flavor. Glass coffee jars were repurposed with scrapbook paper and ribbon, to hold decorative straws. I used sugar in the bottoms of the jars to weigh down and elevate the straws. Neutral serving pieces were revamped with ribbon, bows, and matching papers. I also used gift card tags as labels or recycled Christmas cards, to create labels to identify the variety of beverage flavors. Party favors were jars/clear plastic cups with white cotton candy, decorated with labels, saying the contents was "snowman stuffing."

Pony Express,
Malted Flavor Hot Chocolate

Pony Express riders on horseback delivered saddlebags of mail known as a "mochila" from Missouri to California. Changing horses and riders occurred every 100 miles on the Pony Express Trail. A monthly salary of $100.00 was earned by the risk taking riders, whose weight could be no more than 125 lbs. The most famous rider was Buffalo Bill, who later became the proprietor of The Wild West Show. The Pony Express had a short run, starting on April 3, 1860, and ending October 24th, 1861. The invention of the telegraph delivered information much faster, with the news and other notes inside an envelope in a rider's saddlebag.[20] The most famous delivery was President Abraham Lincoln's inaugural address. The legendary speech of Lincoln was the fastest delivery of the Pony Express, taking 7 days and 17 hours.[21] This creamy hot chocolate would have aptly warmed an express rider. I am certain he would have also delivered a few "notes" of compliments!

1½ cups heavy cream
1½ cups milk
4 oz. box of white chocolate
½ - ¾ cup malted milk powder (used for shakes)
1 teaspoon vanilla
1 teaspoon almond extract

Heat cream and milk in saucepan. Once steaming, but not scalded, add white chocolate. Melt and stir until creamy. Add the malted milk powder, stir well. Next, add vanilla and almond extract. Heat until well mixed. Pour hot chocolate into cups or mugs.

Makes 2 servings.

Inside Scoop: This is rich and sweet! Should you like to drink a frozen snowman, refrigerate the hot chocolate, when it is cooled, add a cup of ice and place in blender, mixing well.

Vigilante Hot Chocolate, Hot Chocolate Spiced Up

I suggest you become a vigilante, and keep a close eye on your cup or mug of this spicy, hot chocolate! The delicious flavors, infused in this hot beverage are almost criminal. Montana history is steeped with self-appointed vigilantes, protecting citizens and communities. Posses of men rode tirelessly, fighting the good fight and making outlaws accountable for their devious ways. Catching a criminal in "the act," often found the guilty one hanging from a rope in the center of town. Locals found themselves taking the law into their own hands and doing what they thought was the right thing. In the small community of Roundup, Montana, a hangman's noose is still on display, right off the main street. A painted mural illustrates the outlaw's horse standing alone, after the hanging took place. Virginia City, Montana, has a famous cemetery called Boot Hill, where many outlaws are buried.[22] Evidence that a vigilante's sharp shootin' ways were indeed effective. Vigilantes aren't the only ones who were packin' some heat. The rich flavors of this hot chocolate, do as well. The surprising heat, is reminiscent of burning campfire embers, warming your spirit. This is perfect for any outdoor Montana adventures!

1 cup milk
2 tablespoons cocoa powder
¼ teaspoon ground cinnamon
⅛ teaspoon ground nutmeg
¼ teaspoon ground Ancho Chili Pepper powder (not regular chili powder)
2 tablespoons honey
Whipped cream and chocolate syrup, optional

In a small bowl, mix dry ingredients. In a microwaveable bowl/mug heat 1 cup milk, for 2 minutes. Remove and add dry ingredients, whisk to make smooth the mixture. Add honey, stir until well mixed. If desired, pour into a mug and add marshmallows, whipped cream or drizzled chocolate syrup, as topping options.

This is an individual serving size.

Inside Scoop: This is full of "heat." It is spicy and will certainly warm you up! It's great for a break during outdoor winter activities. I usually make this in a 2 cup glass measuring cup, as it makes it easy to pour into a cup or mug.

The Grand Union Hotel

The historic Grand Union Hotel, located in the Birthplace of Montana, otherwise known as Fort Benton, Montana, served one guest a little more than hospitality.[23] A cowboy, who had rented a room in the Grand Union Hotel, decided he would ride his horse to his room. The manager told the cowboy that it was not going to happen and that the horse was not welcome. The two men exchanged gunfire, the cowboy received 44 slugs in his body and paid for a room he never slept in.[24] The beautiful Grand Union Hotel opened its doors in 1882, and was reported to be the finest hotel between Chicago and Seattle. The hotel sits off the banks of the Missouri, where Lewis and Clark and their Corps of Discovery traveled.[25] The steamboat era of the upper Missouri, made Fort Benton a bustling community for the vessels to dock, while trading furs and gold. The historic hotel opened seven years before Montana was proclaimed a state and is considered the oldest hotel in Montana.[26] The beautifully restored hotel, is nestled along the river walk and is listed in the National Register of Historic Places. Wonderful dining, beautiful rooms, and picturesque views are waiting for you at this historic hotel!

The Grand Union Hotel
1 Grand Union Square
Fort Benton, Montana 59442
(406) 622-1882
(888) 838-1882

Photo courtesy of Debbie Hamilton

A Grand Union Hot Chocolate

A union of wonderful flavors!

3 cups half and half or light cream
1 cup white chocolate chips or semi-sweet
   chocolate chips
1 teaspoon vanilla
1 teaspoon almond extract

Heat half and half or light cream with white or semi-sweet chocolate chips and simmer. Add vanilla and almond extract. Decorate with whipped cream and/or drizzled chocolate syrup.

This makes 2 large mug portions.

 Inside Scoop: When my daughter was little I made this as a white version, by using white chocolate chips, then adding a little red food coloring to make it pink. As a little girl, it was her favorite color and having pink hot chocolate to drink was a colorful treat! For a fun decoration, make small snowflakes, by melting candy discs into snowflake designs and place in the hot chocolate (see page 33 for snowflake example).

Breakfasts, & Jellies

Berries A Special Treat

Berries Montana's Treasure

Montana has a reputation for its slopes, streams, vistas, and its berries. Chokecherries and huckleberries are gems that rival the rare Yogo Sapphire. All are highly coveted and produce a mouthwatering response. The simmer of berries on a farmhouse stove, signals that the kitchen cupboard will soon have a summer memory and canned perfection for future treats. Both berries make their way into delectable crisps, muffins, pancakes, pies, and beverages. Creative cooks are imagining new ways to utilize the berries and competitions are popping up all across the Treasure State.

Huckleberry Jelly

10 cups Huckleberry juice
8 cups sugar
2 boxes of pectin

In a large stock pot, place berries and follow directions in pectin package. Prepare canning jars and lids according to instructions.

Chokecherries

"Chokecherry Capital!" Those were the words painted on the side of a downtown brick building in Lewistown, Montana. Every September, the Central Montana community of Lewistown, celebrates the "little" berries, in a "big" way. Music, arts and crafts, food and fun, line the downtown streets. The "berry" fun celebration includes a culinary cooking contest using the claret red berry. A pancake breakfast is a highlight of the celebration, as chokecherry syrup is on the menu.[27] Lewistown rolls out the "berry" red carpet, and everyone will find something to see, enjoy, and taste. Take a chance on this event and see how Central Montana celebrates the wild berries of Montana.

lewistownchokecherry.com ✍ lewchamb@midrivers.com

Chokecherry Syrup

3 ½ cups juice
4 ½ cups sugar
1 package pectin
Chokecherries

Add 1 cup water for every 4 cups of clean and washed chokecherries, place in a suitably sized stock pot and simmer on medium heat, until fruit is tender, and skins split. Stirring frequently. Remove from heat and cool. Place a large bowl on a kitchen countertop, use a pillowcase or cheesecloth and place cooked berries in it. Strain or squeeze juice from the berries. My mom always hung the pillowcases from cabinet doors, letting gravity assist with the straining process.

Follow directions on pectin package for jam and jelly preparation, and canning process.

Spice Up Your Mornin',

Biscuits and Gravy

Cold Montana winter mornings called for a little heat. Nothing like a hot breakfast to help take the chill off! Many brunches and breakfasts included my Spice Up Your Mornin' biscuits and gravy. Sometimes this meal made its way down the dinner lane. Why not? Cold nights need a little spice too!

1 can Pillsbury Grands biscuits
16 oz. package of Jimmy Dean regular/
    original sausage
1½ teaspoon onion powder
1¼ teaspoon garlic powder
1 teaspoon chili powder
⅛ teaspoon cayenne powder, optional
¼ teaspoon sugar
1 tablespoon flour
8 complete grinds of black pepper
2 cups heavy cream
⅛ cup milk
Non-stick cooking spray

Preheat oven to 350 degrees.

Spray a cookie sheet with non-stick spray. In a small mixng bowl, combine all seasonings (except flour and sugar) and set aside.

In a large skillet, spray with non-stick spray. Open sausage package and break into pieces, placing into skillet. Sprinkle the seasoning mixture on top of the sausage. Over medium heat, cook sausage, stirring regularly until thoroughly cooked. Drain excess grease.

Sprinkle the flour over the cooked sausage, stir. Add heavy cream, mixing well, then stir in sugar. Place biscuits on prepared cookie sheet and bake according to directions. Continue stirring sausage on low heat, add milk, stirring again. If you like a thin gravy add more milk.

Pour sausage gravy into a separate bowl. Place biscuits in a serving container. I place a cloth napkin over the biscuits to keep them warm.

Serve immediately.

Cinnabar Cinnamon Rolls with Bacon

"The Roosevelt Special" was a six-car operation and a precursor to the motorcade rolling into the Gardiner Basin. The "Elysian Car" was a 70-foot-long railroad car, referred to as the "Rolling White House" for President Theodore Roosevelt's comfort, as he inspected Yellowstone National Park. During his 16 day visit, the car was unhitched and parked along the tracks in Cinnabar, Montana. The location was a perfect landing for Roosevelt to enjoy the beautiful outdoors, wildlife and scenery. Cinnabar was close in location to Gardiner, Montana, which was the first major entrance to Yellowstone. [28] During his stay, the historic arch was being completed and was dedicated to the president, naming it the "The Roosevelt Arch." President Roosevelt placed the last cornerstone on the arch in 1903, covering a time capsule that included a Bible, his photo, local newspapers, and other items pertinent to the date. The grand Roosevelt Arch, in Gardiner Montana, has an interesting welcome sign that reads, "For the Benefit and Enjoyment of The People." [29]

The easy preparation of these sweet and savory cinnamon rolls is definitely for the benefit and enjoyment of the people! Your guests will be amazed at the creation and you will be delighted with how easy they are to make. Give them a try!

17.5 oz. can Pillsbury Cinnamon Cinnabon rolls
12 oz package microwaveable bacon, Hormel Black Label

Preheat oven to 350 degrees.

Prepare microwaveable bacon according to directions. Place cooked bacon on paper towel, to remove excess grease. Open the can of cinnamon rolls and carefully unroll each. Place 3 cooked bacon strips in a line, down the dough and reroll, into a cinnamon roll shape. Place rolls in a baking dish, sprayed with non-stick spray and bake according to directions on the cinnamon roll package. Spread icing on rolls and serve.

The Roosevelt Arch

Motherlode Breakfast Casserole, and Burritos

This breakfast casserole will have you hitting pay dirt, as you "dish up" this flavorful breakfast entrée. A "motherlode" of riches will pan out, whether you serve it as a casserole or into breakfast burritos.

Either way, you have struck it rich!

1 lb Jimmy Dean original sausage
1 medium onion diced
6 large eggs
4 cups frozen hash browns, thawed
2 cups shredded cheddar cheese
½ cup cottage cheese
1¼ cups Monterey jack cheese
½ teaspoon onion powder
½ teaspoon Hamburger Grill Mates
    McCormick seasonings
½ teaspoon dried basil
½ teaspoon dried thyme leaves
2-4 tablespoons butter
Salt & pepper to taste
1 package flour tortillas

Heat oven to 350 degrees.

In a large non-stick frying pan, fry sausage, breaking it into small pieces. Drain the grease, and place in a bowl to cool. Melt butter and fry hash browns, diced onion, salt and pepper to taste. When hash browns are golden, place them in a 13 x 9 greased baking dish. In a large mixing bowl, whisk eggs, add cottage cheese, cheddar and Monterey jack cheese, all herbs, and onion powder. If sausage is cool enough to not cook egg mixture, then place sausage on top of hash browns, otherwise wait until room temperature. Pour egg mixture over the sausage, cover and refrigerate.

Place breakfast casserole, on center rack of oven and bake for 35-40 minutes. Serve immediately.

Inside Scoop: I often turn this baked casserole into burritos. I bake the normal amount of time. Ten minutes before the timer goes off, heat flour tortillas on a griddle or frying pan, wrap in foil to keep warm. Remove casserole from oven and slice into servings for the tortillas. Serve with any of the following: sour cream, guacamole, sliced avocado, salsa, or chopped onions. For a breakfast brunch, I place all these sides out on a buffet table for guests to build their own burrito. The casserole, not made into burritos, is wonderful served with toasted English muffins.

Upside-Down Dinners

Through the years, I made my own family upside-down dinners (breakfast for dinner). Our topsy turvy tradition, was sausage patties, French toast, and orange juice. Often times, I dusted off the good china, matching stemware, silverware, and cloth napkins, for the upside-down dinner. My daughter, Savannah, helped set the table and she called it a feast. Round slices of sausage were made into rectangular shapes. Our delicate tea cups were filled with fresh fruit, sometimes homemade hot chocolate, depending on the time of year. Warm syrup was a must! I made homemade flavored butter rounds, when possible. The melon scoop took the flavored butter to new heights. When Savannah learned to write, she made fancy place cards. When glitter glue was introduced to her little hands, guess where it ended up...on everything! I loved every messy minute. Her enthusiasm made cleaning up, worth it. Perhaps you will bring out your good dishes and make an upside-down dinner, a new tradition for your family.

French Toast

6 eggs
1 teaspoon cinnamon
½ teaspoon nutmeg
2 teaspoons vanilla
3 teaspoons almond extract
2 tablespoons butter, softened
⅓ cup vegetable oil
Half of a ⅓ cup of heavy cream
(milk is okay, however, I prefer heavy cream)
Loaf of French bread

Preheat oven to 350 degrees.

Slice 14 pieces of French bread, set aside. Whisk together or mix with a fork, in a casserole or baking dish, eggs, cinnamon, nutmeg, vanilla, and almond extract. Set aside.

In a large skillet, spray with non-stick spray, melt butter and oil on medium heat. Dredge the slices of bread in the egg mixture and fry both sides, until golden brown. Place on a paper towel-lined plate.

Once all the French toast has been made, place the slices on a sprayed cookie sheet and put in the oven. Immediately, turn oven off. Take sausage and shape into rectangular slices, fry until done. Heat syrup in microwave for a few seconds, to warm, and serve.

Inside Scoop: Sausage can be prepared first and put in oven to keep warm. Fresh fruit can be purchased or prepared in advance and served in a large bowl or individual cups or saucers.

Ranch Hands Benedict,

A Traitor On The Original

6 oz. filet, grilled, then cover with foil and let rest
3 eggs, scrambled and cooked until done
1 English muffin, toasted
3 large egg yolks
1 tablespoon water
¼ teaspoon salt
3 tablespoons lemon juice
1 stick butter, cut into chunks, melted
¼ teaspoon sugar

Prepare the Hollandaise as follows: In a saucepan, spray with non-stick spray. Turn stove on to medium-low heat, add egg yolks, whisk until fluffy/frothy, add water and salt, keep whisking. Watch your heat, so it does not scorch mixture or scramble the eggs. Add lemon juice, whisk well, then add sugar. Continue whisking and slowly add melted butter until the mixture thickens and is glossy.

Slice the tenderloin. Place the two pieces of toasted English muffin on a plate, top with scrambled eggs, place steak strips on top of eggs, spoon hollandaise on top and serve immediately.

Slap Jack Stack, Pumpkin Pancakes

These pancakes have a hint of fall. I often make them in smaller sizes, stacking them high. With homemade pennants on the skewers, they look like a parade of breakfast delights. This pancake batter is a camping staple. Yes, I put it in used ketchup bottles and other containers that can be squeezed and easy to pour.

2½ tablespoons pumpkin spice flavoring
¼ teaspoon cinnamon
2 cups Aunt Jemima Buttermilk Pancake mix
1½ cups cold water

Thanks to Wendi Wetzel of Montana Rustic Accents, in Columbus, Montana for giving me permission to take pictures of her glamping setup.

Heat a skillet or griddle, sprayed with non-stick spray, over medium-low heat. Combine all ingredients until smooth, if the batter is too thick, thin with an additional tablespoon or two of water. Use a ¼ cup measuring cup and scoop batter onto skillet or griddle. When bubbles appear, check the sides to see if the pancakes are golden brown and flip. Makes 6 pancakes or 12 smaller ones.

The Whole Kit and Caboodle,

Breakfast Muffins

These delicious muffins were made one winter morning from items that I had on hand. I had forgotten a neighbor's birthday. The weather and roads were terrible, so I created these delicious muffins using my cupboard's whole, "kit and caboodle." Anytime there was a special event at my neighbor's home, they aways requested these muffins. They are delicious anytime of the day!

1 teaspoon salt

3 teaspoons baking powder

⅓ cup sugar

2 cups all-purpose flour or whole wheat flour

⅓ cup, plus 1 tablespoon brown sugar

1 teaspoon cinnamon

1 teaspoon vanilla

½ of a ⅓ of a cup of honey

1 egg

¾ cup of buttermilk

½ cup of vegetable oil

1½ tablespoon yogurt

½ teaspoon of lemon juice

½ cup peach bits (I buy a small can of peaches, place 4-5 slices in a bowl and cut into small bits with kitchen shears)

Preheat oven to 350 degrees. Place cupcake liners in muffin tins, approximately 12.

In a small bowl, combine the following: salt, baking powder, sugar, flour, and cinnamon. In a large bowl place flour, then mix in the small bowl of dry ingredients. Add egg and oil, mix well. Next, add buttermilk, mix well. Add honey, vanilla and then lemon juice, mix well. Add yogurt mixing well, then stir in peach bits until well combined. Scoop batter into muffin tins and bake for 15 minutes. Turn oven to 375 degrees, bake for 3 - 4 more minutes. Check with a toothpick to make sure batter is cooked in the center, making sure they are baked completely.

Inside Scoop: These muffins are flavorful, but not particularly sweet. Serve with one of my assorted butters, the combination is delicious.

High Stylin' Brunch

I hosted an engagement brunch for a client at my home. The intimate affair for immediate family only, served many purposes: celebrating the engaged couple, and meeting their families, who had decorating visions for the wedding. It was also an opportunity for everyone to see my rental inventory. It was challenging to set a time which everyone involved could get together, so the bride's mother and I, decided this was a simple way to move thru the long list of to-do's! While I executed the delicious celebration meal, the out of town guests were treated to a lovely brunch and the bride's family had a stress free day. The elegant atmosphere set the stage for wedding visions and ideas. The scrumptious brunch was created from many of the items that are recipes in the breakfast section. Elegant serving pieces elevated standard breakfast items. *See photos below for staging ideas.*

Appetizers

Outlaw Party Dip

This chip dip should be outlawed, as you can't get enough of the rich, creamy garlic flavor! My mom made this during the holiday season, serving it with turkey sandwiches. I have kept up the tradition, oh so good!

Ingredients for roasted garlic version:

8 oz. cream cheese, softened
½ cup heavy cream
1 clove garlic, roasted, peeled
½ tablespoon onion powder
½ tablespoon garlic powder
Breath mints!!

Ingredients for quick dip version:

8 oz. cream cheese, softened
½ cup heavy cream
1 tablespoon onion powder
1 tablespoon garlic powder
(more garlic powder can be added, add at teaspoon intervals, until desired taste)

In a mixing bowl, whip cream cheese. When smooth, add heavy cream and mix well. Sprinkle in garlic and onion powder, mix well. Additional garlic powder may be added to desired taste. If you are making this recipe with roasted garlic, peel the clove sections and mash with a fork, then add to the dip, mixing well. Refrigerate until well chilled before serving.

Inside Scoop: The dip needs a sufficient and sturdy chip (I recommend Lays ruffle potato chips). Once the dip has been well chilled, you might want to thin it with a little extra heavy cream, to your desired consistency.

Note: To roast garlic, cut off tips, place in a pie tin with a cup of water, cover with foil, bake for 45 minutes at 350 degrees.

Charcuterie Board

(shahr-koo-tuh-ree)

Charcuterie boards are a French inspired platter, combine fruits, breads, meats, and cheeses. Assorted nuts and French baguette slices, pair well with cured meats, cheeses, spinach dip, pickles, and miniature mustards. Olives and boiled eggs are also nice additions. Small ramekins work wonderfully as serving containers for pickles and olives. Stacking meats and cheeses of varying colors, will add visual interest. Artisan crackers, garlic bagel chips, French baguette slices, and wheat thins are crowd favorites. Grapes, berries, and dried fruits add dramatic color, while prosciutto, salami, and ham contribute to the savory side of the palette. Cheddar, parmesan, and Monterey Jack wedges create depth, while burrata and alouette serve as soft and spreadable cheese spreads. Serving portions are typically 3-4 slices of meat and 1-2 ounces of cheese, per person.

Inside Scoop: When serving the assorted charcuterie items, a wooden cutting board is a preferred serving vessel. However, for large parties or weddings I have used large ceramic tiles from home improvement stores. A long dressing mirror or mirror tiles, add a glamorous flair, when clear plastic bowls and plates are filled with the finger foods and LED candles are interspersed. The clear serving containers, show off the food and the unusual tile or mirror background. Typical charcuterie boards do not use containers for the food items, but I avoid cross contamination and place items in clear containers.

Sweet and Sour Sauce

This recipe is as re-creation of a popular dipping sauce served in the now closed Wong's, a popular Billings, Montana Chinese restaurant. I can tell you that my guests say they would choose this sauce over a typical sweet and sour sauce anytime.

3 tablespoons KC Masterpiece Original BBQ sauce, *if you like a less spicy sauce reduce to 1½ tablespoons of BBQ sauce.*
½ cup apple jelly
½ cup grape jelly
¼ teaspoon garlic powder
½ teaspoon onion powder
Pinch of salt
Cornstarch

In medium size saucepan, place all ingredients, and cook on medium heat. Whisk continuously until the sauce is clear. If you like a thicker sauce, use a 1/3 measuring cup, put 2 tablespoons of cornstarch in and add enough water to measure about a quarter of the way up the measuring cup. This will be thick and paste like. Stir, and add to the sauce and whisk until it thickens. Serve with coconut shrimp, egg rolls, wontons, and deep-fried veggies.

Huckleberry Fruit Dip

8 oz. package of cream cheese, room temperature
7 oz. jar of marshmallow cream
1 teaspoon vanilla
3 tablespoons huckleberry jelly
Sliced apples or assorted fruits

In a medium size mixing bowl, use an electric mixer and beat cream cheese and marshmallow cream until smooth. Add vanilla and jelly, mix until well blended. Refrigerate until ready to serve. I usually serve this with sliced apples. Should you not have huckleberry jelly, serve the dip without it, as it is still delicious.

Inside Scoop: For parties, I slice assorted fruits and stack on bamboo skewers, with the fruit dip on the side. I have also sliced a pineapple in half. Slice one section into chunks and the other half becomes a platform for the fruit skewers to stand in. For a tipi inspired birthday party, I made fruit skewers with a strawberry cut in half to look like an arrow tip. From scrapbook papers I made paper feather cut-outs and glued them on the end. The skewers then appeared as an arrow, to coordinate with the party theme.

Cowboy Caviar

15.25 oz can of kernel corn, drained
14.5 oz can of black beans, drained and rinsed
14.5 oz can of petite diced tomatoes, drain or
     strain tomatoes from juice
½ cup diced red onion
1 teaspoon minced garlic
1 clove garlic chopped fine
½ cup chopped cilantro
½ tablespoon lime juice
½ teaspoon McCormick Hamburger Seasoning
½ teaspoon onion powder
¼ teaspoon chili powder
½ teaspoon cumin
½ teaspoon salt
¼ teaspoon garlic powder
½ cup diced red onion
2 avocados diced (1 reserve one diced avocado,
   to place on top of salsa, right before serving)

In a large bowl, mix all the ingredients, cover and refrigerate.

Inside Scoop: My guests love this salsa! I add the avocado right before serving, keeping it nice and green, and fresh. This is also great on a salad with my Farmhouse Ranch Dressing (page 107). Grilled chicken, topped on a salad with the cowboy caviar is delicious. When I do a taco bar or seafood enchiladas, this is always served on the side.

Shrimp Cocktail Sauce

1 teaspoon lemon juice
3 tablespoons horseradish sauce
½ cup chili sauce (prefer Heinz)
½ cup ketchup
1 tablespoon dried parsley
1 tablespoon finely diced cilantro, optional
½ teaspoon ground black pepper
½ teaspoon salt
½ teaspoon Alpine Touch (a Montana spice, found in
   local stores)
⅛ teaspoon onion powder
Serve with approximately 2 pounds of chilled shrimp

Mix all ingredients together in a medium size bowl until well blended, transfer into serving dish, cover and refrigerate for at least 2 hours. The sauce is best when allowed to rest overnight, letting the flavors marinate.

As an additional recipe, I take an 8 oz brick of cream cheese, spread it on the bottom of a serving dish, layer the cocktail sauce over the cream cheese, and cover it with shredded fresh crab meat. I serve assorted crackers on the side. Always refrigerate these shrimp appetizers until serving.

Inside Scoop: During Christmas I use a tree shaped Styrofoam cone, which I adhere to a platter by using a piece of heavy tape or florist gum, rolled onto the bottom of the cone, sticking it to the platter. Once secured, I use green leaf lettuce and fasten with toothpicks, attaching the lettuce onto the cone, making it look like a Christmas Tree. With cellophane trimmed toothpicks I attach individual shrimp, creating shrimp swirls on the cone, to look like ornaments. Next, I cut an end off of a lemon. Using a paring knife I cut tiny sections out to look like a star and attach to the top of the shrimp tree with a toothpick. I slice 3 - 4 lemons into wedges and place them at the bottom of the tree, like stacked presents. The presentation always gets "oohs and ahhs!"

"High Time" Salsa

It is high time you make this salsa! Serve it with chips, on grilled meats, or fish tacos! When serving grilled or baked salmon, I always have this as a topping choice. The flavors are wonderful. I make a package of chicken tenderloins, marinated in my teriyaki marinade. I grill the teriyaki chicken and top it off with the High Time Salsa. Your guests will love it!

2 avocados, diced
¼ cup fresh chopped cilantro
2 small cloves garlic, peeled and
    finely diced

½ teaspoon onion powder
2 tablespoons lime juice
2 tablespoons honey

1 large mango diced (you can get frozen mango pieces, thaw and cut into
    diced pieces)
½ teaspoon McCormick Grill Mates hamburger seasoning

Mix all ingredients well and refrigerate, until serving

Inside scoop: Sometimes, I grill a small can of pineapple rings and cut into pieces, then mix these into the salsa, especially if it will be served with a marinated teriyaki meat. Often, I grill the rings until golden, place the rings on the grilled meat and top off with the salsa. The presentation is delicious!

Pitch-A-Fit, Atichoke Appetizer

This artichoke appetizer is the best way to start a meal. As the artichoke is cooking and the amazing aroma, is filling your kitchen, your family or friends will be pitching a fit and wondering when they are going to get to dig-in. This is an appetizer must!

2 large artichokes
1 packet zesty Italian salad dressing

1 teaspoon onion powder
3 grinds of fresh ground pepper
Vegetable oil

Place a large stock pot with water ¾ of the way full, on stove and heat until boiling. Cut the top off and the tip points of the artichoke leaves. Then slice a ¼ to ½ inch off the stem and cut an "x" slit on the bottom of the stem. In a coffee cup, pour the packet of Italian salad dressing in, add vegetable oil, a ¼ of the way up the cup. Fill remaining cup with water and stir well, mixing all ingredients. Dredge the cup into the heated water pot, until the cup is empty, add onion powder and pepper grinds. Once the water and spices are at a rolling boil, add artichokes. Cover pot with a lid and turn down heat, to medium. Cook for approximately 45-55 minutes. Check tenderness and readiness of artichokes by using tongs and pull a leaf off. If the artichokes are oversized, more cooking time is necessary. Take tongs and squeeze the artichokes when removing them from the stock pot, draining any excess water. Place in serving container or slice in half and place on a platter. Serve with drawn butter or mayonnaise.

Home on The Range,

Tenderloin Bruschetta

10 oz. package of buffalo mozzarella, sliced thin
Small bundle of fresh basil, stems removed
1 baguette of bread
3 tablespoons melted butter mixed with 1½ teaspoons of garlic powder
6 oz. container of pesto
4 oz. teriyaki pork tenderloin or beef tenderloin

Grill tenderloin according to directions. When finished, cover with foil, to let meat rest and to keep it warm. Slice only after 15-20 minutes of resting.

Preheat oven to 375 degrees.

Slice baguette bread at an angle, place on cookie sheet, then brush or spread garlic butter, lightly on baguette slices. Toast in oven for 5 minutes or until lightly browned. Remove tray of baguette slices, spread a layer of pesto (about ½ to 1 tablespoon) on top of each slice.

Cut tenderloin in thin slices and place a piece on top of pesto, followed by a fresh basil leaf, then mozzarella slice. Place prepared tenderloin baguette slices in oven and bake for 10-15 minutes. Serve immediately.

FARMERS

Petticoat & Bonnet,

Bruschetta

Petticoats and bonnets were foundations of a woman's wardrobe, in the 1800s. Petticoats were considered an undergarment, filling out the width of a woman's skirt. A petticoat was a wardrobe must. Fabric layers of a skirt fanned out and often the lace-ruffled edge of the petticoat, peeked thru. [30] *A bonnet was worn as a fashion statement, but also a practical way of protecting a woman's face from the elements. The large brim of the bonnet diffused the wind and hot sun.* [31] *The "petticoat" crab mixture of this appetizer, peeks through the avocado bonnet. Adorn this appetizer with dill sprigs, to add the finishing touch, much like flower sprays on a lady's bonnet from the 1800s!*

¼ cup mayo
2 tablespoons Dijon mustard
3 tablespoons fresh squeezed lemon juice
1 tablespoon horseradish
1 teaspoon dill
1½ teaspoon Tabasco hot sauce
3 cups crabmeat flaked, imitation can be substituted
2 ripe avocados, peeled and diced
½ teaspoon kosher salt
⅛ teaspoon ground pepper
3 tablespoons butter, melted
Garlic powder
8 slices sourdough bread, toasted

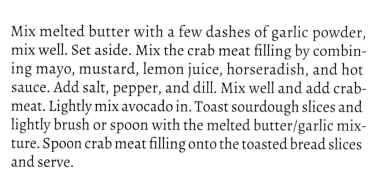

Mix melted butter with a few dashes of garlic powder, mix well. Set aside. Mix the crab meat filling by combining mayo, mustard, lemon juice, horseradish, and hot sauce. Add salt, pepper, and dill. Mix well and add crabmeat. Lightly mix avocado in. Toast sourdough slices and lightly brush or spoon with the melted butter/garlic mixture. Spoon crab meat filling onto the toasted bread slices and serve.

Fresh dill can be added to top, for presentation. I usually serve with a field green salad and side of assorted fresh fruit.

Salmon Suckers

8 oz. cream cheese

6.5 oz. Alouette Garlic & Herbs, soft spreadable cheese spread

4 oz. smoked salmon

½ teaspoon dried parsley

½ teaspoon onion powder

½ teaspoon garlic powder

12 grinds of fresh ground black pepper

Parsley or cilantro leaves

Slices of pimento, radish, or tomato, cut into tiny squares

Lollipop sticks

Ritz crackers

In a medium size mixing bowl, beat cream cheese with an electric mixer on medium speed, then add the Alouette, mixing well. Flake the smoked salmon, add to the mixture and mix well. Add onion powder, garlic powder, pepper, and parsley, mix well. Cover and refrigerate for 4 hours.

Use small spoon, or cookie dough scoop and shape the salmon dip into balls, place each on a Ritz cracker (for easy individual servings) and then on serving tray. When all the dip is formed into balls, place a lollipop stick in center, lay parsley sprigs on top where the stick is inserted. Next, add a pimento, radish or tomato square in the center, making it look like a bowtie configuration. Refrigerate until ready to serve.

Serve with assorted crackers, bagel chips and Ritz crackers

Inside Scoop: Serve the dip with toasted bagels for breakfast or lunch. It is a delicious pairing.

Breads and Butters

Lodgepole Twists

The twisted balcony and handrails of the Old Faithful Inn are the inspiration for these puff pastry works of art. The lodge is a visually creative structure, as are these delicious lodgepole twists. Your guests will keep coming back for more! Serve with salads, pastas or as an appetizer.

1 cup grated parmesan cheese (I like the fancy parmesan best, it is graded finer, otherwise, I suggest grate it fresh)

2 teaspoons thyme leaves

2 teaspoons basil

1 tablespoon garlic powder

1 tablespoon minced garlic

⅛ teaspoon ground black pepper

2 eggs

17.3 oz. package frozen puff pastry sheets, brought to room temperature

Preheat oven to 400 degrees.

In a small bowl, mix cheese, herbs, garlic, and pepper together. Pour mixture onto a large platter or cookie sheet, spreading out, set aside. Whisk eggs in a large baking dish. Spray another cookie sheet with non-stick spray. Using a fork, dip a sheet of thawed pastry dough into egg, covering well. Repeat this by flipping the pastry dough, covering the other side in egg. Dredge both sides of pastry dough into cheese/herb mixture. Place puff pastry on cutting board and cut into strips about 1 inch in width (I use kitchen shears). Twist strips and place on cookie sheet about an inch apart. Continue with remaining dough. Bake for 12-15 minutes, or until they are a golden color.

These puff pastry delights are wonderful, if you are a garlic lover, sprinkle a little extra garlic on each one, right before baking. The dipping sauce options enhance the flavor!

Serve with drawn heated garlic butter, marinara, sriracha sauce, or my Farmhouse Ranch Dressing (page 107).

Old Faithful Inn

Donna's Vegetable Bread

Avocado toast is all the rage! Restaurants serve it with lots of twists, making it savory and ornamental in its presentation. Avocado puree' is one option with sliced figs on the side. Sliced avocado with sprinkled bacon and sliced hard boiled egg, is my daughter Savannah's favorite. Donna's farmhouse vegetable bread, toasted, is the perfect accompaniment for the avocado/egg topping!

½ cup oil
2 eggs
13 oz. can evaporated milk
2 large peeled and sliced carrots
1 stalk of celery, diced fine, no leaves
1 cup fresh parsley leaves, stems removed
1-inch wedge of cabbage, sliced and chopped
3 tablespoons honey
1 teaspoon salt
1½ cups warm water
2 tablespoons yeast (almost 3 packets of yeast)
9-9½ cups whole wheat flour (or you can make a
   flour blend by using 5 cups whole wheat and 4½
   cups regular flour mixed together)
3 bread pans

Preheat oven to 350 degrees.

In a medium saucepan, heat until warm: oil, milk, eggs, celery, parsley, cabbage and honey. Stir, mixing well. Once the ingredients are warm, remove from heat. In a small bowl, mix salt and flour. Set aside. Dissolve yeast in ½ cup of warm water. Let stand for approximately 5 minutes, for yeast to bloom. Using a standing mixer, pour saucepan liquid into mixer bowl and add dissolved yeast, mix well. Then slowly add flour/salt. Using a kneading hook attachment, beat for 10 minutes.

Remove dough and place on a floured surface. Knead by hand, for a few minutes, turning dough over, several times. The dough will have a slight elastic texture. Portion the dough into 3 even loaves. Place in bread pans that have been sprayed with a non-stick spray. Cover each bread loaf with a tea towel or cotton dish towel.

When dough has risen twice its size (usually takes 2-2½ hours for the dough to double, depending on room temperature), bake for 45 minutes. Let bread cool in pans. Remove and place in airtight containers until ready to serve.

City Slickers Sausage Bread

The flavors of this bread are amazing! Your home will smell like a famous artisan bakery! This bread is a family favorite and always shows up when my daughter makes a trip home. When I created this recipe, there was a blizzard outside and I whipped up a meal with items I had on hand. This fabulous bread is the result of making do with what you have.

2 garlic cloves
8 oz. bag of shredded mozzarella cheese
1 bag of Rhodes frozen dinner rolls (36 count)
1 tablespoon onion powder
1 tablespoon dried thyme
1 tablespoon dried basil
1 tablespoon dried rosemary
19 oz. package of Johnsonville HOT Italian sausage

Preheat oven to 350 degrees.

STEP 1

Cut the top off of garlic cloves, place in a small pie tin or heat resistant dish. Add just enough water to cover about a ¼ of the way up the garlic clove. Cover with aluminum foil and bake for 40 minutes in oven. Remove and let cool. Peel outer layers of garlic clove and slide baked garlic out of each clove and dice. Set aside.

STEP 2

In a 9x13 baking pan, spray with non-stick spray and evenly place 24 frozen dinner rolls. Lightly spray the top of rolls and cover completely with plastic wrap to make airtight. Let rolls rise, at room temperature.

STEP 3

Use a sharp knife tip to remove sausage casing, cut into small pieces and place in large frying pan. Sauté sausage and drain grease. Use a paper towel to dab excess grease from pan. Next, add all spices to sausage. Stir until mixed well, then add roasted garlic pieces, stirring again. Refrigerate and reheat sausage mixture when rolls have risen or make right before turning rolls out onto pan.

STEP 4

Use a large cookie sheet or pizza pan, cover with aluminum foil and spray lightly with non-stick spray. Flip risen dough balls onto the pan and spread it out, until it creates a unified layer. Be careful to not create holes in the dough. Spread the meat mixture in the center of the dough and sprinkle mozzarella cheese on top of meat. Fold one side of dough over and carefully tuck under, forming a roll or log configuration and curve ends under as well, making a loose "C" shape. Bake for 18 minutes or longer, until golden brown. Using a stick of butter, rub a little on top of hot bread and serve. This is excellent served with a side salad, pasta, or soup.

Country Fair Cornbread

1 cup cornmeal
1 cup flour
¼ cup sugar
3 teaspoons baking powder
¼ cup butter, melted
1 teaspoon baking soda
⅔ cup plain yogurt
¼ cup creamed corn
¼ cup frozen corn, thawed
1 cup buttermilk
2 eggs
½ teaspoon salt
4 oz. diced green chilies, optional

Preheat oven to 375 degrees. Spray a 9-inch pie plate or 9-inch casserole dish.

In a medium size bowl mix cornmeal, flour, sugar, baking powder, baking soda, and salt. Fluff with a fork, to mix well. In a large mixing bowl, combine, yogurt, creamed corn, buttermilk, butter, and eggs. Add dry ingredients, stirring well to combine. Next, add thawed corn and chilies. Pour batter in pan or dish and bake for 25-30 minutes until lightly golden color. Individual servings from a muffin tin are also nice. Make sure to spray well, with non-stick spray or use double layer of cupcake liners. Pour batter into muffin tins..

Inside Scoop: I make a breakfast sandwich with the leftover cornbread. I fry sausage in squares, and place on toasted cornbread, with fried egg on top. Preheat oven to 350 degrees. Cut squares of cornbread, slice in half and bake for 5 minutes. Turn up heat in oven to broil and bake an additional 2 minutes. Remove from oven, place sausage on toasted cornbread followed by a fried egg.

Best Banana Bread Ever!

My mom and gramma made this bread all the time! It is simply the best banana bread ever!

1¼ cup sugar
2 eggs
½ cup butter softened
1½ cup mashed bananas (3 or 4 bananas, ripe works best)
½ cup buttermilk
1 teaspoon vanilla
2½ cups all-purpose flour
1 teaspoon baking soda
1 teaspoon salt
½ cup chopped walnuts

Preheat oven to 350 degrees. Place oven rack on second rung from bottom.

Grease 2 bread loaf pans, 8½ x 4½ x 2½, set aside.

In a large bowl mix sugar and butter. Add eggs, mix again. Add, bananas, buttermilk, and vanilla, beat well. In small bowl mix flour, baking soda, and salt, then add to the wet ingredients, mix well. Next, add nuts. Mix well and spoon or pour batter into the loaf pans, measuring equally.

Bake for 45-55 minutes. Use a knife to test. If knife removes smoothly without wet or soft dough, remove bread from oven. Let cool for 10 minutes. Run knife around outside edges of bread, turn upside down on a plate, then place upright on a wire rack to cool completely.

Inside Scoop: This bread is wonderful for a brunch or a dessert. I often gift wrap the loaves in large cellophane bags, tied with pretty ribbon and attach the recipe. It is a wonderful hostess or perfect holiday gift!

Pumpkin Patch Muffins

1½ cups all-purpose flour,
   sifted, not necessary, but makes them
   a little lighter
½ cup sugar
2 teaspoons baking powder
½ teaspoon cinnamon
¼ teaspoon nutmeg
½ teaspoon salt
1 cup milk
1 egg
¾ cup canned pumpkin pie filling
¼ cup butter melted
1⅓ cup of semi-sweet chocolate chips

Preheat oven to 375 degrees. Line muffin tin with liner, set aside.

In a large bowl, combine flour, sugar, baking powder, cinnamon, nutmeg, and salt. Fluff with a fork. In a separate bowl combine milk, pumpkin, butter, egg, and add into the flour mixture. Mix well, do not over mix. Stir in 1 cup of semi-sweet chocolate chips and stir well. Fill liners ¾ of the way full, and sprinkle remaining chocolate chips on top. Bake for 15 minutes and turn oven up to 400 degrees and bake for an additional 3-5 minutes. Check at 3-minute mark, to not over brown.

 Inside Scoop: ¼ cup of chopped nuts can be sprinkled on top with chocolate chips.

Butter Me Up!

Maple Butter

½ cup butter, softened to room temperature
2 tablespoons maple syrup

Beat on high speed until fluffy, place in a ramekin and serve.

Honey Butter

½ cup butter, softened to room temperature
¼ cup honey

Beat on high speed until fluffy, place in a ramekin and serve.

Raspberry, Chokecherry, or Huckleberry Butter

½ cup butter, softened to room temperature
3 tablespoons jelly or jam of your choice

Beat on high speed until fluffy, place in a ramekin and serve.

Inside Scoop: When doubling this recipe, place flavored butter in a Ziploc bag, cut corner tip and pipe into ramekins. Use a small melon scoop if desired.

Bunkhoouse Bread

1 loaf sourdough bread
12-16 oz. bag shredded Monterey Jack cheese
2 tablespoons minced garlic
½ cup finely chopped green onion, optional
1 teaspoon onion powder
1 teaspoon thyme flakes
1 teaspoon rosemary springs, crushed
1 teaspoon basil
1 teaspoon parsley
¾ cup melted butter
⅛ cup grated parmesan

Preheat oven to 350 degrees.

Cut bread lengthwise and widthwise several times (making a grid pattern), being careful to not cut completely through the bread. Place bread on a foil lined cookie sheet. Open up the grid pattern on the bread and sprinkle Monterey Jack cheese inside the slits. Combine melted butter, herbs, minced garlic, and onion powder. Spoon this mixture into slits. Then sprinkle parmesan cheese into slits. Wrap bread in foil and place on baking sheet and bake for 15 minutes. Uncover bread and sprinkle the green onion on top (optional) and bake for 10 more minutes. Serve immediately. Serve with marinara or my Farmhouse Ranch Dressing (page 107).

Sandwiches

Sac-a-way Sandwich

Sacajawea Park, Livingston, MT

These sandwiches pay tribute to Sacagawea, the Native American princess, who accompanied the Lewis and Clark Expedition. "At the age of 12, Sacagawea was captured by an enemy tribe and sold to a French-Canadian fur trapper named Toussaint Charbonneau,"[32] who later married her. The husband and wife accompanied the famous Lewis and Clark Expedition and their Corps of Discovery.[32]

Sacagawea was an integral part of the expedition, which began in 1804. As a guide, she had an understanding of the territory that Lewis and Clark were exploring. She also possessed a vast knowledge of wilderness survival and knew edible plants that could provide sustenance, while the adventurers were travelling. Sacagawea had excellent language interpretation skills, making communication possible for Lewis and Clark. As the only woman in the entourage, her presence helped the discoverers to appear as a "peaceful" group, making them non-threatening. [32] It is reported that Clark told Charbonneau on August 20, 1806 that, "Your woman, who accompanied you that long and fatiguing route to the Pacific Ocean and back, deserved a greater reward for her attention and services on that route than we had in our power to give her."[33]

In 1805, Sacagawea gave birth to her son Jean Baptiste, later nicknamed "Pompey," "Pom," and "Pomp," by Captain Clark. The birth of Lil' Pomp was extremely difficult for the young Sacagawea. Some sources state that a tincture of rattlesnake venom was given to her, to assist through the difficult delivery.[34] Three years later, Sacagawea delivered a daughter and sadly passed away a few months later. Clark had developed a bond with Sacagawea's son and after her death, he took custody of Pomp and his sister Lisette. [32]

Across the northwest, there are many monuments dedicated to the Shoshone Indian princess. Three Forks, Montana has a statue of Sacagawea and her son (see page 20). [35] In Livingston, Montana, a park has been named after the young woman.[36] In 2000, a US minted dollar coin was issued, featuring a likeness of the famous guide. [32]

Pack a "Sac" Lunch, is made with this delicious chicken croissant sandwich recipe. You will discover a blend of flavors that are so memorable, they will be on your must make list! Picnics and luncheons will be historic with these delicious sandwiches. Take a "Sac" with you as you explore scenic backroads of Montana, perhaps even following in the famous footsteps of Sacagawea!

Inside Scoop: I have made these delicious sandwiches for an Easter luncheon with a festive place setting used for the presentation. I served the sandwiches, wrapped in parchment paper, with a beautiful bow. I also presented each guest with their own personalized basket of food treasures which contained carryout containers of salads and deviled eggs. My guests had enough food in each bakset for another meal. There was little clean up, as the baskets were taken home.

"Sac" Lunch

This luncheon was so fun to create and execute! That Easter we had 10 inches of snow. However, my beautiful spring and Easter luncheon baskets were much appreciated by my guests. Once again, oohs and ahhs were heard around the table! Food can be fun!

1 cup mayonnaise
1¼ tablespoon Dijon mustard
½ tablespoon regular yellow mustard
½ tablespoon onion powder
⅛ teaspoon garlic powder
1 teaspoon lemon juice
1 teaspoon thyme leaves
2 teaspoons sugar
4 grinds black pepper
⅛ teaspoon salt
3 bouillon cubes
½ cup chopped pecans, chopped very fine
3 chicken breasts
Green or red leaf lettuce
6 croissants

In a large stock pot, filled ¾ of the way with water, add bouillon, ½ teaspoon each of salt, onion, and garlic powder. Cook on medium heat. When water comes to a rolling boil, prepare chicken by using a tenderizing spike punch or poke holes in chicken with fork tines. Place in the hot seasoned water and cook covered for 10-15 minutes, on medium heat. Remove one chicken breast from liquid and check to see if the breast is completely cooked, (no pink inside). When breasts are completely cooked through, remove from heat and allow to cool.

While chicken is cooking, mix all spices together, along with mayonnaise, and mustards. Cover and refrigerate for an hour or two. Chop pecans and cover until ready to mix. Cut green leaf lettuce for all the sandwiches, bag and refrigerate. Next, slice croissants and put in airtight container.

Pull chicken from liquid and place in a bowl, cover and refrigerate, for 1 to 1½ hours. Then, cut into small pieces. In a medium size bowl, combine chicken pieces, mayo sauce and mix well. Then add pecan pieces, mixing well. Spread with a spoon, onto one side of croissant. Place green leaf lettuce on top of chicken mixture. Put sandwiches on a tray and cover with plastic wrap. Refrigerate for several hours, until ready to serve.

Inside Scoop: Sometimes I add cooked bacon. I either dice it and add it into the mixture or simply place two strips of it in each sandwich, right before serving.

71

Lil' Pomp Bites

These delicious little sandwich bites, are a tribute to Pompey, the son of Sacagawea, who was the guide for the Lewis and Clark Expedition. Pompey or Lil' Pomp was born during their expedition travels. He was Sacagawea's first-born child, and Clark became very fond of the baby boy, giving him the nickname, Lil' Pomp. [32]

Native American Indians carried their babies in cradleboards, made from a stick frame, laced together with strips of tanned hides. A carrying sack was made from hides, also sewn together by leather strips, securing the edges for safe travel for their babies. [37] *This Lil' Pomp Bite is a puff pastry cradleboard for the hot dog bite.*

Pompey's Pillar, named after the baby son of Sacagawea, is only 25 miles from my home in Billings. The famous landmark is the only historical evidence of the Lewis and Clark Expedition. Resting on the famous sandstone butte, is the curved signature of Captain Clark, dated July 25, 1806. Native Americans referred to the pillar as "The place where the mountain lion lies." [38] *I can attest to the Indians reference of the mountain lion. While traveling home one night, I saw one of those big cats running alongside the highway, keeping time with my car's tires. It was mammoth in size!*

The boardwalk at Pompey's Pillar, leads to the famous engraving of Clark's signature. You will also pass by a replica of Clark's canoe, enjoy breathtaking views of the Yellowstone River and see the same vistas that Clark and his entourage saw. There is a visitor center where pertinent information regarding the signature engraved over 200 years ago into the butte, can be found. [39]

17.3 oz. box of frozen puff pastry sheets, brought to room temperature
16 oz. package of hot dogs (which has 12 hot dogs)
1 egg white, used to seal edges of puff pastry

For further information
visit: pompeyspillar.org
(406)969-5380

Preheat oven to 375 degrees.

Once the frozen puff pastry sheets have thawed to room temperature, cut the sheets where they have been folded. Take each pastry sheet and cut in half. Place each cut piece on cookie sheet (sprayed with non-stick spray) in a grid pattern. Remove hot dogs from package. Dry each with a paper towel to remove any moisture. Cut the hot dogs in half. Place a cut hot dog, with the round edge towards the top. Center the cut hot dog on pastry dough and fold over. Use the egg white to glue/seal the edges. With the tines of a dinner fork, press around all edges to make stitches marks similar to that of an Indian cradleboard. Fold the top opening down, into a half moon shape, so you can see the papoose (hot dog) peering out.

Bake 'Lil Pomp Bites for 15 minutes. When timer goes off, turn oven to broil and leave cookie sheet in oven. Bake on broil temperature for 3 minutes. Serve immediately with condiments of your choice.

We Found the Beef, Steer Montana

"Where's the Beef?," was an advertising slogan that caused a lot of buzz in 1984. The famous television commercial for Wendy's Hamburger chain, had an elderly woman trying to find the hamburger patty. It suggested that competitive hamburger chains were providing small burger portions. According to the commercial, Wendy's had found the beef and was serving it all day long. The ad campaign was a hit. Clara, the aging woman who shouted, "Where's the beef?" was an even bigger hit.[40]

Well Clara, we found the beef and it is in, The O'Fallon Museum in Baker, Montana. The museum is home to the world's largest steer named Steer Montana. The famous steer lived 15 years and 4 months. His weight was 3,980 pounds and he grew to a staggering 5'9" tall, was 10'4" long, and had a girth of 9' 2'!!! Rumors surrounding the steer's size and how he became a record setter, stated it was a result of the "mash" made from the hearty grains grown on the Montana prairie. The beef pride belonged to a local rancher named Jack Guth. He and Steer Montana, toured stock shows and many circuses.[41] The steer's reputation made headlines equal to his size.

I wonder what drivers thought as they were meandering down highways and rural roads coming upon Jack and his "Beef Beast?" What a sight that must have been! I am certain that the story of the "Big Beef" had listeners thinking it was another tall tale. In case you have been wondering "Where's the beef?" well now you know. Steer your way to Baker and see for yourself, the beef pride of Montana.

Steer Montana Sliders are an easy to make sandwich, that pay tribute to the famous Montana steer!

O'Fallon Museum   Baker, Montana 59313
723 South Main   (406)778-3265

museum@falloncounty.net

Steer Montana Sliders

1 package of Pillsbury crescent rolls
1 package au jus gravy mix
½ lb deli roast beef, sliced thin
8 pieces of Gruyere cheese (swiss or provolone are good
   choices also)
Fresh basil leaves

Preheat oven to 350 degrees.

On a cookie sheet, spray lightly with non-stick spray. Roll out individual crescent triangles, place beef slices, basil leaves, and cheese, evenly on all the triangles. Roll each one from large end to narrow end. Bake for 11-13 minutes, until golden brown. Prepare au jus according to directions and serve in ramekins. Sliders are also delicious with my Horsey Ranch Sauce.

Horsey Ranch Sauce

1½ cups of my homemade Ranch Dressing (page 107)
2 tablespoons raw horseradish

Mix together ranch and horseradish. Serve with Steer Montana Sliders.

Pizza Sandwiches

This recipe is for a large group. It is easy to reduce and make smaller portions. I often make this for party appetizers. Kids absolutely love them, and they are great for a movie night!

1 loaf of French bread
10 oz. can tomato paste
6 oz. bag fancy parmesan cheese
6 oz. bag of pepperoni slices
16 oz. bag of shredded mozzarella
Onion powder
Garlic powder
Italian seasoning

Preheat oven to 375 degrees.

Slice 14-16 slices of French bread and place on a cookie sheet. Put in heated oven for 3 minutes. Remove from oven and flip bread slices over and bake for 3 more minutes. Remove cookie sheet from oven and spoon a light layer of tomato paste on all slices. Next, sprinkle onion powder, then garlic powder, followed by a light sprinkling of Italian seasoning. Place shredded parmesan, evenly on all slices, followed by 3-4 pepperoni slices (depending how large the bread slice is). Sprinkle mozzarella on top of pepperoni. Bake for 7 minutes. Turn the oven to broil and continue to bake for 2 more minutes, until golden brown. Serve immediately

The Stack Sandwich

In Black Eagle, Montana stood a masonry structure known as "The Stack." The amazing structure was approximately 506 feet tall, including a brick chimney. The inside dimensions were 75 ft at its bottom, which then tapers to 60 at the stack's top. The iconic symbol was completed in 1908 as a smelter for the Anaconda Copper Mining Company.[42] The Stack once employed over 1,000 miners and helped grow the community of Black Eagle.[43] The landmark was a visual icon for the Great Falls, Montana area and its residents. Sadly, the stack was demolished on September 18, 1982, forever changing the landscape. [42] For eleven years the masonry building was the largest in the world, setting a record for the small Montana community.[44]

5 lb. package of chicken breast filets (marinated overnight in teriyaki marinade, see recipe page 91)
1 loaf of French bread, slice 2 pieces for each filet
Cooked bacon, 2 slices per sandwich
Butter or mayonnaise
Provolone slices, 1 slice per chicken tender
Green leaf lettuce
Sliced tomatoes
Sliced avocados

Grill chicken, approximately 3-4 minutes per side. Use a meat thermometer for accuracy, as cooking time will vary according to breast thickness. Set a timer for a minute or two before chicken will be done and place cheese on top to melt. Continue grilling, by resetting timer for the additional grilling time. While chicken is finishing grilling, toast breads, then spread butter or mayonnaise on both sides. Stack chicken and preferred topping choices. Use a toothpick so your "stack" doesn't topple over.

Photo courtesy of Wikimedia Commons[45]

Soups, Sides, & Beans

Bridger Bowl Chowder

Snow often piles high in Montana. In the Rocky Mountain region of the western half of the Treasure State, annual snowfall stacks up to 300 inches or 25 feet.[46] Bridger Bowl, is one of 16 Montana Ski Resorts that offer hip-deep powder and exceptional Rocky Mountain Views.[47]

Bridger Bowl Chowder takes the edge off a cold winter's day. The rich and creamy texture is the base for the hearty soup. This is an ever-popular meal choice for my family and the recipe is one of my "Old Faithful's." I am constantly asked for this recipe, your guests will ask too!

6 oz. box of Uncle Ben's Original Long Grain & Wild Rice, fast cook recipe
½ cup all-purpose flour
½ cup chopped onion
3 tablespoons minced garlic (I buy it in a jar in the vegetable aisle)
¼ cup butter
4 cubes chicken bouillon
2 cups of chicken broth
1½ cups peeled and cubed potatoes (about 2 medium size potatoes)
1 cup peeled and chopped carrots
½ teaspoon thyme leaves
½ teaspoon nutmeg
⅛ teaspoon pepper
1 tablespoon onion powder
1 teaspoon chopped rosemary sprigs
15.25 oz. can of whole kernel corn, including liquid
2 cups half and half
3 cups cooked and cubed meat (ham, turkey, or chicken)
Grated parmesan cheese to sprinkle on top, optional

Prepare rice according to the directions on the box, cover and set aside.

In a large stock pot, spray with non-stick spray. To make the chowder, melt butter in stock pot, then add onions and cook until crisp-tender. Stir in flour and whisk for a minute, stirring constantly. Add half and half, all herbs and spices, meat, rice and corn. Next, add minced garlic, stir and cover. Heat on low.

Fill a medium size pot ¾ full with water. Heat until boiling and turn heat to medium-high, then add carrots and potatoes. Cook until tender. Check at 8 minute mark to see if potatoes are fork tender. Continue checking at 4 minute intervals until potatoes are tender. Remove from heat and drain water. Next, add the vegetables to chowder, mix well and serve immediately. Serve with County Fair Cornbread. Offer guests grated parmesan as a garnish.

Note: Often, I cook a 19-ounce packet of Johnsonville Hot Italian Sausage. Remove the casing and tear into pieces and fry in a large frying pan until well cooked. Drain off all grease and pat with a paper towel to remove additional grease.

Inside Scoop: I have turned a muffin tin over, sprayed with non-stick spray and placed individual Pillsbury Biscuits on separate muffin mound. Push the biscuit down the sides so that it will become a bowl. Bake according to directions, Turn upside and ladle chowder in each bowl, place on a platter and serve with an optional side of parmesan.

How The West Was Won, Quick 'Chicken Coop' Soup

32 oz. box of chicken broth
4 oz. can of sliced mushrooms, drained
½ of a 60 oz. bag of frozen California blend veggies (freezer section of the grocery store)
6 chicken bouillon cubes, beef flavored will also work
1 teaspoon each of basil, onion powder, rosemary, and thyme leaves
1 box of Uncle Ben's Wild Rice, fast cook recipe
1½ lbs. of chicken strips

In a large frying pan, pour a drizzle of olive oil. Place chicken in pan and lightly salt and pepper the chicken. Sprinkle a little onion powder on as well. Fry chicken on both sides, until it is cooked through. Set aside.

In a large stock pot, pour in chicken broth, add mushrooms and vegetables. Cook on medium-low, cover with a lid and let simmer. Cut cooked chicken into chunks or use forks to shred the meat. Add meat to the stock pot. Cover with lid and let simmer. Take a coffee cup and fill ¾ of the way full with water and add rosemary. Microwave for a minute to soften the herb. Pour into stock pot and add all other herbs and onion powder, to soup. In a small saucepan, prepare the wild rice recipe according to its directions on the box. When rice is cooked, add to the stock pot mixture. Simmer for 15 minutes to blend ingredients. Serve immediately.

Between Hay and Grass, Green Bean Bundles

Old sayings such as "good food, good company," were meant to compliment a fine meal and the cook who prepared it. Catch phrases, were tongue in cheek statements and witty terms, used in the good ol' days to reference someone's personality or lack thereof, by slowly rolling off the tongue, a timely choice of words. We all grew up with "sayings" and it was typical to ask a worldly adult what they meant. I grew up with "You Bet" and "Well, Yah Know." I am reminded by my daughter how often I use them! Old west "sayings" often referenced someone's character. Here are a few of my favorites: Bunko artist (con-man)...Saddle Bum (drifter)...Bilk (cheat).... Granger (farmer)...Coffee Boiler (shirker or laze person)...Ace High (1st class or respectable).... In Apple Pie Order (tip top shape)....Odd Stick (eccentric person)....Roostered (drunk).... The Whole Kit and Caboodle (entire thing)....Best Bib and Tucker (your best clothes).... Rig (saddle).... Between Hay and Grass (half grown or neither man nor boy).

Bundle up your taste buds, these are fabulous!

This recipe was shared with me, by my friend Teresa Youree, oh so good!

3 cans whole green beans, drained
½ cup brown sugar
1 stick butter, melted
½ teaspoon garlic powder
1 tablespoon soy sauce
1 lb. bacon strips, cut in half

Make sure you drain the green beans before assembling. When placing the individual bundles in the baking dish, make rows of them, down and across. Wrap about 10 green beans with bacon and secure with a toothpick. Place in an 8½ x 11 pan, sprayed with non-stick spray. Mix the remaining ingredients and pour over the bundles. Cover and marinate in refrigerator overnight.

Preheat oven to 400 degrees, bake for 30-45 minutes. Using tongs, turn the bundles over half way through the baking time. Turn broiler on and broil for an additional couple of minutes. Monitor them closely.

Frontier Fries

5 medium yams or sweet potatoes
3 tablespoons olive oil
2 teaspoons salt
1 teaspoon garlic powder
2 teaspoons onion powder
1 teaspoon dried basil
1 teaspoon dried parsley
1 teaspoon dried thyme leaves
½ teaspoon ground fresh black pepper

Sriracha Mayonnaise,
Dipping Sauce

1 cup mayonnaise
½ cup ketchup
1 tablespoon minced garlic
¼ teaspoon lemon juice
1 teaspoon paprika
3 tablespoons sugar
1 teaspoon sriracha or hot sauce
1 teaspoon onion powder
1 teaspoon salt
¼ teaspoon chili powder

Preheat oven to 425 degrees.

Peel and cut sweet potatoes in half and then lengthwise, to make thick fries or slice even finer for thin fries. Place the fries in a large bowl. In a small bowl mix the rest of the ingredients and sprinkle on cut fries, mix well until all fries are well coated. Place fries on pan that has been sprayed with a non-stick spray. Bake for 15 minutes. Remove pan and toss fries over, return to oven and bake for another 10 minutes or until golden brown.

Stir the dipping sauce ingredients in a medium size bowl, cover and refrigerate until the fries are finished baking. Serve Frontier Fries on a platter, with dipping sauce on the side.

 Inside Scoop: I often cut the sweet potatoes in chunks, saving time. *Sriracha* Mayonnaise is also wonderful for burgers, chicken sandwiches, fish tacos, and deep fried veggies!

Cattle Drive, Roasted Veggies

½ teaspoon salt
1 tablespoon onion powder
1 teaspoon garlic powder
½ teaspoon dried thyme leaves
½ teaspoon basil
½ teaspoon rosemary
½ teaspoon dried parsley
2 tablespoons butter, melted
1½ tablespoons olive oil
8 grinds of ground pepper
1 large russet potato
2 cups baby carrots
1 onion diced
Olive oil

Preheat oven to 425 degrees.

Place all spices in a small bowl and mix well. Peel and dice potato, place in a large bowl, add carrots, and diced onion. Pour melted butter and olive oil over vegetables, mix well. Add herbs, stirring well to cover all vegetables. Place veggie mixture on a cookie sheet sprayed with non-stick spray. Bake for 20 minutes, remove and with a spatula turn veggies over, drizzle with an additional 1½ tablespoon of olive oil, return to oven and bake for an additional 20 minutes, or until veggies are fork tender. Size of cut vegetables will determine length of baking time. Turn oven to broil and return veggies to oven for an additional 6 minutes or until golden color. Serve immediately.

Locked and Loaded, Twice Baked Potatoes

1 large russet potato, baked and cooled (see note below)
2 oz. softened cream cheese
1 tablespoon heavy cream
1½ tablespoons fancy shredded parmesan cheese
4½ tablespoons mozzarella cheese
½ teaspoon garlic powder

Note: Before baking potato, I use a sharp knife and cut several slits, then cover in foil and bake at 350 degrees for an hour and a half.

When potato is cooled, scoop out its center into a medium size bowl and mix in the rest of the ingredients with an electric mixer until fully combined. Then spoon mixture into the hollowed potatoes. Bake for 35 minutes at 350 degrees. Serves 2 when cut in half.

Prairie Grass,

Sautéed Brussel Sprouts with Hazelnuts.

½ cup sliced almonds
4 bacon slices, cooked and chopped into small pieces
16 oz. bag brussel sprouts
2 tablespoons olive oil
¼ cup onion, finely diced
2 tablespoons minced garlic
1 teaspoon lemon juice
2 tablespoons maple syrup
1 teaspoon salt
½ teaspoon pepper
½ teaspoon onion powder
2 tablespoons honey

Preheat oven to 350 degrees.

Spread almonds on a baking sheet, and bake for 5 minutes. When almonds are done, cover to keep warm. Shut off oven heat and leave almonds in oven to warm. Cut brussel sprouts in half lengthwise and then slice crosswise making fine slices.

In a large skillet, over medium heat, place olive oil and onion pieces and brown. Cook for a couple of minutes and add minced garlic, stir and add salt and pepper. Now add onion powder, stirring well. Add brussel sprouts, cook for about 5 minutes until tender. Next, add honey and maple syrup, followed by lemon juice. Remove brussel sprout mixture and place on a serving plate, top with sliced almonds.

Inside Scoop: I make a small portion of instant white rice, and grilled teriyaki or sliced tenderloin and serve with the brussel sprouts. Layer white rice first, then brussel sprouts, prepared meat and sprinkle almonds on top.

Keelboats

A. B. Guthrie's novel, "Big Sky" was made into a major motion picture in 1952.[48] A Keelboat Mandan from the movie, now rests on the levee in downtown Fort Benton, Montana. Lewis and Clark and their Corps of Discovery, travelled in keelboats on the Missouri, similar to the movie replica.[49] Keelboat cabins carried a bevy of trading items to garner precious commodities, such as beaver pelts and buffalo hides. Beads and whiskey were popular barter items.[50] The keelboat on the levee in Fort Benton inspired these culinary sides. Any meal will be enhanced with this edible version, its cabin is filled with a cheesy and meaty filling. Enjoy!

Delicious sweet potato boats, baked and filled!

2 large sweet potatoes
½ tablespoon paprika
½ tablespoon cumin
1 tablespoon olive oil
½ teaspoon salt
¼ teaspoon pepper
½ teaspoon chili powder
½ tablespoon onion powder
½ teaspoon garlic powder
1 cup cooked and shredded chicken or other choice of meat
1¼ cup shredded mozzarella
½ cup fine grated parmesan
Kale chips, optional

Clean and dry two large sweet potatoes. Poke holes in bottom and on one side of each potato, and then rub the olive oil on them. Place in microwave for 6-8 minutes, check for tenderness with a sharp end of a knife. While sweet potatoes are cooking, prepare chicken stuffing by mixing remaining ingredients. Heat in microwave for 2 minutes. When sweet potatoes are done, cut a slit from one end to the other, to form a pouch. Do not cut completely in half. With a spoon, push cooked sweet potato center to the inside walls, making room for the chicken filling. Sprinkle a little mozzarella on top of the sweet potato, followed by the chicken filling.

Turn oven to broil. Place keelboats on a cookie sheet that has been sprayed with non-stick spray, broil for 2-4 minutes. Watch to make sure they do not burn. Sprinkle kale chips on top, right before serving.

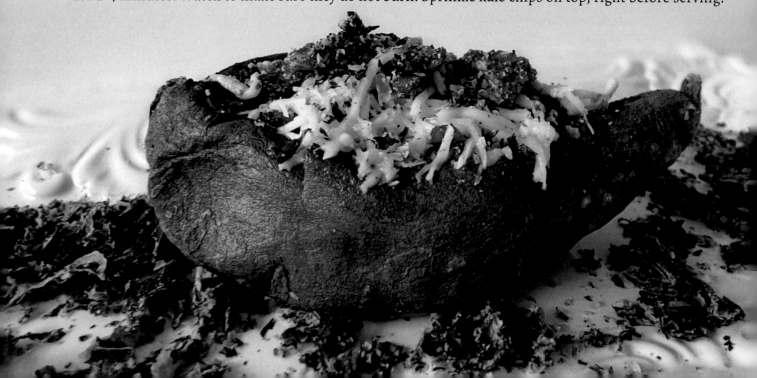

Roundup, Corn On The Cob

¼ cup cilantro leaves, chopped fine
6 ears of cooked corn on the cob
2 limes, juiced
2 teaspoons chili powder
6 tablespoons melted butter
¼ cup Cotija cheese or parmesan cheese, grated

Mix butter, lime juice, and cilantro, set aside. Place grated cheese on a plate. Brush seasoned butter on corn cobs, roll in cheese and sprinkle chili powder on top. Serve when all cobs have been coated

Bust your Britches, Broccoli Casserole

2 tablespoons olive oil
½ cup diced onion
12 oz. package frozen broccoli florets, thawed
10½ oz. can cream of mushroom soup
½ cup mayonnaise
1¼ cup fiesta blend cheese, shredded

1 tablespoon onion powder
½ tablespoon garlic powder
6 grinds of fresh black pepper
½ teaspoon salt
5 oz. bag of New York Bakery, Texas Toast
   croutons (cheese and garlic flavored), crushed

Preheat oven to 350 degrees.

Thaw broccoli, do not cook. In a mixing bowl, add soup, mayonnaise, one cup cheese, salt, pepper, onion powder, and garlic powder. Mix well and add broccoli. Set aside. Place olive oil in a frying pan and sauté diced onion, until it is translucent, then add to broccoli mixture. Place into a 10x6 casserole dish, sprayed with non-stick spray. Sprinkle remaining cheese on top of broccoli, cover with aluminum foil and bake for 30 minutes. While casserole is baking crush croutons with a rolling pin, while still in bag. When timer goes off, remove and add 1 cup of crushed croutons on top of casserole. Bake for 15 minutes more. Serve immediately.

Big Sky, BBQ Beans

1 lb dried Great Northern white beans
1 bottle of beer
½ teaspoon baking soda
2 quarts water
¾ lb salt pork, sliced
1 large onion, finely chopped
¾ cup packed brown sugar
½ cup catsup
1 teaspoon dry mustard
1 teaspoon salt
2 tablespoons Worcestershire sauce
2 tablespoons minced garlic
1 tablespoon onion powder
2 tablespoons liquid smoke

Note: Beans need to soak in beer mixture overnight!

Combine beans, beer, baking soda, and water in a large stockpot, cover and let sit overnight. The next day, drain beans but saving the stockpot water. Cover the stockpot water and set aside. In a large stock pot, add beans and fresh water, almost filling up the pot. Cover, bring to a boil, reduce heat and simmer for 30 minutes. Strain beans.

Preheat oven to 275 degrees.

Mix all ingredients including beans, together, except the pork. In a 3-quart roasting pan or casserole dish, pour beans. Add pork, placing the slices on top of beans. Bake 6 hours. At 2 hour intervals check beans, stirring in pork slices. During intervals, make sure beans are not drying out, stir if necessary. Use a cup of reserved stockpot water, to moisten, depending on how thick you like your beans.

Gunslinger Street Corn

Trust me, when you serve this street corn, your guests will be fighting for the last serving!

16 oz. can of corn (drained)
1 tablespoon olive oil
1 tablespoon butter
2 tablespoons finely diced red onion
1 tablespoon lime juice
1 teaspoon garlic powder
½ teaspoon onion powder
½ teaspoon chili powder
¼ cup mayonnaise
¼ cup sour cream
½ cup cotija cheese, feta will substitute
3 tablespoons cilantro, diced fine
Salt and pepper to taste
¼ cup grated parmesan (in the jar, not fresh grated)
1 lime, cut in wedges for squeezing on corn for individual taste
Baguette of bread

Slice baguette into serving slices, then cut at an angle. Toast and butter with a sprinkle of garlic powder. Cover bread and place in oven to keep warm, until serving.

In a cast iron skillet (preferred pan, although another skillet will work), spray with non-stick spray. Melt butter and olive oil in pan. Place drained corn in skillet and brown corn kernels. While corn is frying, mix rest of ingredients in a medium size bowl, except the parmesan. Once corn has been browned, spoon into the sauce mixture, mixing well. Transfer to a serving container with garlic baguettes on side. Sprinkle parmessan on top of dish, right before serving. Serve immediately.

This pairs well with steaks or tacos and can also be served as an appetizer.

Main
Courses

Montana, What's The Beef?

Ranching in Montana is a cultural and economic staple. Big Sky Country ranks 3rd in the U.S. for having more cattle than people. [51] Locals are vocal and say, "And we like it that way, thank you very much."[52] Hungry miners, eager to make a claim and unearth their dreams of wealth, needed food and lots of it. The mining boom helped encourage cattle ranching in Big Sky Country. Montana beef provided miners a hearty meal, and mining provided ranchers an economic opportunity.[53] The Grant-Kohrs Ranch, a historical, working ranch, located outside of Deer Lodge, Montana, demonstrates ranch life in the 1800s. [54] Kohrs was the ranch's second owner and was referred to as "Montana's Cattle King."[56] The property served as the headquarters for his 10-million-acre empire.[54]

Historical demonstrations are provided, when taking a tour of this remarkable ranch.[57] The Hudson Bay, trading post style home, is filled with nostalgic items from both owners and their families.[55] Kids will enjoy participating in fun activities and learning hands-on ranching skills. [57] The events and hours of operation are listed on their website.

nps.gov/grko ✐ (406) 846-2070 x250 ✐ 266 Warren Lane ✐ Deer Lodge, MT

Rancher Grant-Kohr Filet

1 stick butter softened to room temperature
½ teaspoon garlic powder
⅛ teaspoon dried thyme
⅛ teaspoon dried parsley leaves
(4) 6-8 oz. beef filet mignon

Preheat oven to 400 degrees. Mix butter, garlic powder, thyme and parsley together. Spoon the herbed butter on a sheet of wax paper, then shape and roll into a log. Tie ends with a rubber band or clip, chill in refrigerator for 2 hours. While the filets are cooking, remove butter log and slice into 4 sections. Set aside.

In cast iron skillet, spray with non-stick spray and drizzle olive oil into pan. Sprinkle salt and pepper on each side of steaks. Pan sear steaks on high to medium-high heat, for approximately 2 minutes on each side. Place cast iron skillet in oven for approximately 3 minutes for rare, 5 for medium-rare and 7 for medium doneness. Check by using a meat thermometer, for cooking perfection. Place each steak on a dinner plate and put one butter section on each filet, right before serving.

Hands Down,

The Best Steaks

1 ribeye steak, bone-in
1 tablespoon virgin olive oil
½ teaspoon garlic powder
½ teaspoon onion powder
½ teaspoon salt
1 teaspoon McCormick Grill Mates
   Hamburger Seasoning
4 grinds of fresh ground pepper

In a small bowl combine all dry ingredients. Spoon ½ tablespoon of olive on one side of steak, covering steak completely, then sprinkle half the dry seasoning on the steak. Flip steak over and repeat on the other side. Grill steak according to desired doneness. Right before serving, place a tablespoon of soft butter on steak to melt. Serve immediately.

Teriyaki Chicken

In a large Ziploc bag, place all ingredients in, except chicken. Close bag and shake lightly. Place chicken in bag, zip tightly and shake vigorously to coat chicken. Refrigerate for 24-36 hours, rotating bag from side to side several times, to completely permeate meat.

Grill for 3-4 minutes on each side, test tenderloin for correct temperature with meat thermometer.

Teriyaki Marinade

1½ cups pineapple juice
1¼ cups Kikkoman Teriyaki Marinade
1 teaspoon minced garlic
(2) 5 lb. packages chicken tenderloins
2 teaspoons ground ginger
1 teaspoon onion powder
½ teaspoon garlic powder
½ cup brown sugar

Inside Scoop: I often serve chicken breasts marinated and grilled as a main meat entrée with sides. Be creative and marinate other meats like salmon filet, variety of steaks and jumbo shrimp. I will serve the grilled marinated meats, with a garden salad and Uncle Ben's Fast Cook Wild Rice (box original version). If I am unable to grill because of the weather, I will pan cook the meat. The sugar in the marinade, will caramelize the meat.

Lewis & Clark Ribs,

Short Ribs, Long On Taste

In 1804-1806, The Lewis and Clark Expedition and their Corps of Discovery travelled nearly 8,000 miles in pursuit of gaining knowledge of the Louisiana Purchase. Lewis and Clark were enlisted by President Jefferson to research a possible route to the Pacific Northwest.[58] Approximately 10-20 miles per day were travelled by the commanders and the corps of almost four dozen men. Journals were kept, notating the areas longitude and latitude, climate, soil, native plants, animals, and terrain. These discoveries were highlights in their journals, as was their discovery and naming of new species of plants and animals. Several of these included: bitterroot, sagebrush, Douglas-fir and ponderosa pine, grizzly bears, prairie dogs, and pronghorn antelope. The expedition also named many geographical locations, trails, and waterways after loved ones, peers, and fellow travelers. [58]

Lewis and Clark became diplomats, while learning to communicate with the Native American Indians, convincing them that the expedition crew were indeed friendly, non-threatening and peaceable. Illustrating their exploration finds, were journals, maps, artifacts, specimens of minerals, and plants. These were important articles taken back to President Jefferson. Upon their return to the East, both Lewis and Clark received 1,600 acres for their time and travels, while the accompanying men each received 320 acres. The entire expedition cost $38,000.00. [58] Explore the spicy flavors of these ribs, they will take you down a happy taste trail!

3 lb package country style pork shoulder, butt ribs
8 oz. Original Recipe KC Masterpiece BBQ sauce
8 oz. can tomato sauce
6 oz. can tomato paste
½ bottle of beer
¼ cup brown sugar
2 tablespoons minced garlic
1 tablespoon garlic powder
1 tablespoon onion powder
2 teaspoons paprika
2 tablespoons McCormick Grill Mates Hamburger Seasoning
2 teaspoons chili powder
4 grinds of fresh ground black pepper

Inside Scoop: These tender ribs have a little extra sauce for dipping any bread into!

Preheat oven to 275 degrees.

In large frying pan, drizzle oil and place ribs in pan to sear (I sprinkle a little salt, pepper, and onion powder on them while searing). Only seer for 2 minutes, turning ribs over to cook both sides. Remove from heat. Place ribs on a plate or cookie sheet lined with a paper towel, to remove excess grease. Pat with paper towel to make sure grease is not on the top of the ribs.

In large bowl, mix remaining ingredients. In a large roasting pan, spray with non-stick spray and place ribs in pan. Pour sauce over ribs and cover with foil. Cook for 30 minutes. Remove from oven and turn ribs over, making sure the sauce has covered them thoroughly. Cook for another 30 minutes, remove and turn ribs once again. Cook an additional 30 minutes. Remove ribs once more and cook for 30 minutes. Remove foil and cook uncovered for 30 more minutes.

Wagon Wheel Bites

Often during the holidays, I use leftovers to invent a new bite of flavors. These wagon wheel bites are an example of using leftovers, in a new way.

1 large size muffin tin, sprayed with nonstick spray
1 box of chicken flavor stove top dressing (make according to directions) or use leftover stuffing
Prepared mashed potatoes
Diced turkey
Gravy

Assembly: Place stove top dressing or leftover stuffing in muffin tin, with a spoon, press stuffing/dressing up sides, creating a well. With a cookie scoop or spoon, place mashed potatoes in center of stuffing, scatter turkey around potatoes to edge of the stuffing. Cover and bake for 15 -25 minutes, cooking time depends if items are cold. Serve with gravy.

Inside Scoop: My family loves these wagon wheel bites from leftovers during the holidays, the mashed potato hub, turkey spokes and stuffing/dressing rim are a light and fun way to serve up a quick meal with leftovers.

Coconut Chicken

1 cup Baker's Angel Flake Coconut
½ cup flour
⅛ teaspoon baking soda
¼ teaspoon baking powder
½ teaspoon salt
¼ teaspoon white pepper (ground black will work)
¼ teaspoon garlic powder
¼ teaspoon onion powder
2 eggs, whisked
⅓ cup butter melted
1½ lb. chicken tenders or 1½ lb. shrimp

Preheat oven to 400 degrees.
Mix coconut, flour, baking soda & powder, salt, pepper, garlic, and onion powder. Dredge chicken or shrimp in egg, then into the coconut mixture. Place in a shallow baking pan, that has been coated with non-stick spray. Drizzle the melted butter over the coconut covered meat. Bake 6-7 minutes per side or until golden brown.

Peanut Butter Skewers

1½ cups creamy peanut butter
¼ cup soy sauce
3 tablespoons oil
1 tablespoon onion powder
¼ tablespoon garlic powder
1 teaspoon minced garlic
2 tablespoons KC Masterpiece Original BBQ sauce
1 teaspoon McCormick Grill Mates Hamburger seasoning
1 teaspoon ground ginger
1¼ - 1½ lbs. of skinless and boneless chicken breasts sliced into chunks or
1¼ -1½ lbs. of raw shrimp, cleaned, veins and shell removed.

Note: I have also used cooked shrimp, to prepare dish quickly and serve. They are a little more tough, but nonetheless delicious.

To make sauce, mix all ingredients except meat. Set aside.

Use metal or water-soaked bamboo skewers for grilling. Place meats on skewers, baste with peanut butter sauce and grill. Be sure to check your grilling times for proper temperature, each grill heats differently. Use a thermometer to verify that meat is cooked properly.

This is a great appetizer or meat dish for a meal, served with rice and a salad.

Broccoli Beef

Virginia City, Montana had miners, vigilantes, outlaws, and Chinese residents. America was known as "Gum San," the Land of Golden Mountains, providing opportunities for anyone wishing to make a claim for themselves. However, Chinese were not allowed to stake a claim, but their industrious ways enabled them to line their pockets with gold anyway. The Chinese came to the United States in pursuit of a better life, and doing whatever was necessary to survive and thrive. They worked in back breaking jobs with the railroad, construction, and doing domestic chores, often leading them to open their own laundry services. Upon hearing stories of mines producing great wealth, they tried their hand at mining, by reworking abandoned claims, often in secret. Their tenacity paid off, as their sifting, picking, and panning made them rich. Often they sent more than a million dollars in gold back to China. The Chinese influence in Montana is quite profound. They set up businesses all across the state. Their hard work made railroad travel possible and their domestic contributions created a variety of businesses throughout the state.[65] The Broccoli Beef recipe is deep and rich in flavors. Guests always like it, especially served with my sweet and sour sauce and egg rolls/wontons. Enjoy!

Marinade:

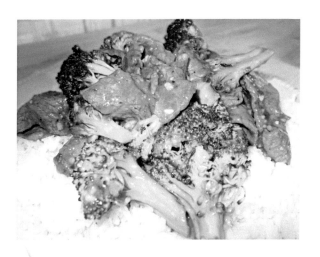

1 tablespoon cornstarch
1 tablespoon oil
1 tablespoon soy sauce
1½ tablespoons minced garlic
1 tablespoon onion powder
3-4 slices of ginger root, sliced
1 teaspoon ginger powder
1 teaspoon McCormick Grill Mates
   Hamburger Seasoning
4 cups of broccoli florets
Minute Rice, for 4-7 servings
1 lb boneless top round or sirloin steak

Follow directions on the rice, to make enough servings for 4-7 people. To make the steak easier to cut, I will freeze it slightly, as this helps the slicing process. I then cut the strips at an angle.

Sauce:

½ cup water
½ teaspoon onion powder
½ teaspoon minced garlic
2 tablespoons oyster sauce
1 tablespoon cornstarch
1 tablespoon soy sauce
1 teaspoon sugar

In a medium bowl, or large Ziplock bag, combine all marinade ingredients, then add meat. Shake or stir the marinade/meat mixture, (ensure the bag is zipped closed) and refrigerate for at least 30 minutes.

In a small bowl, combine sauce ingredients and set aside. In large skillet, heat 1 tablespoon of oil and fry broccoli. Remove and place in a bowl, cover to keep warm. Add another tablespoon of oil and sauté beef (beef only, does not include marinade). Sauté' about 4-5 minutes. Next, prepare the Minute Rice according to directions.

Add sauce to the beef and cook 2-3 minutes, stirring frequently. Next add broccoli and cook until thoroughly heated. Place in a large bowl to serve alongside of rice.

Shep, **A Sheepherder's Best Friend**

Fashioned from a true "tale/tail" and passed through the generations, is the story of Shep. The loyalty of the dog's spirit will tug at your heart strings. The legend of Shep reminds us that a dog can truly be a man's best friend. The four-legged shepherd dog, with a trail of white painting his face, was the beloved companion of a sheepherder in Chouteau County. In 1936, on a farm outside Fort Benton, Montana, Shep's best friend became ill. The sickly sheepherder was hospitalized, leaving behind his faithful companion. Outside the hospital, Shep, the ever devoted canine, waited for his best friend to return to him. The reunion never took place, as the man later died. The man's family requested that his body be returned to the East for burial. Transporting the deceased from the hospital to the train depot, was a final journey for them both. The ever faithful Shep, accompanied his master's body to the train depot, but was not allowed passage. Onlookers witnessed heart wrenching cries from Shep, as the train departed. The best friend stood in despair as his master left on the journey without him. [59]

The determined vigil of Shep, greeting every passenger train, lasted for 5½ years. Everyday, the dog waited for the arrival and return of his best buddy, but to no avail. His vigil...consistent, hopeful, but was nonetheless, a daily disappointment. As each train, made its way into the station, Shep was there to greet the riders, believing that this time he would be reunited with his friend of a lifetime. [59] The dog's bond and love were never broken, however on January 12, 1942, Shep joined his best friend and master, when he was hit by an oncoming train. The dog had slipped while attempting to jump onto the depot platform. The devotion to reunite had finally come...somewhere way beyond the tracks. [60]

The legend of the dog, his patience and his death, is a story that has been told around the world. His devotion touched readers far and wide. The London Daily Express, The New York Times, and Ripley's Believe It or Not, told the story of Shep. Although the despair of the Great Depression was felt worldwide, the story of Shep was a little light of love that brightened the dark days of World War II. The war separated loved ones and best friends. Readers emotionally connected with the story of Shep, as they knew the meaning of waiting for a loved one to return home from war. [61]

The dog's passing made newspapers everywhere. Shep, his loyalty, patience and friendship, became a tale so famous, that even wire services of the Associated Press and the United Press International, published his obituary. His funeral was two days after his passing. Shep's final resting place, is on the bluff overlooking the station. The community of Fort Benton has honored the memory of Shep with a bronze statue, resting on the levee. [61] His story was legendary and his faithfulness was extraordinary.

Shep Memorial

Although this isn't Shep, the picture is reminiscent of the famous and faithful canine. Border collies are very loving, loyal dogs and will often "have an unwavering devotion to their owners."[64] Shep's heart-warming faithfulness to his best friend, remains a powerful love story, even today.

Shep's Pie

1½ cups mashed potatoes (can be made from homemade mashed potatoes, or purchased from the deli or
    frozen food section)
¾-1 cup brown/mushroom gravy
2-3 deli chicken finger strips, sliced
½ cup corn (drained)
¼ cup shredded mozzarella cheese
¼ cup fiesta blend or shredded cheddar cheese

Preheat oven to 350 degrees.

Spray a pie tin with non-stick spray. Spread the mashed potatoes on the bottom and up the sides of the pie tin. Spoon gravy over the potatoes, spread corn on top of gravy, and place the sliced chicken evenly over the corn. Spread mozzarella over chicken, followed by the fiesta cheese. Place in oven and bake for 25 minutes.

Turn oven on broil, bake for an additional 5 minutes. Remove and serve immediately.

Saddle Tramp, Baby Back Ribs

Back in the Old West, cowboys drifted from place to place, never really belonging anywhere or to any-one. Often, they had no family, so this made their nomadic, wanderlust meanderings possible. A saddle and a bed roll were usually their only significant belongings, making roaming easy.[62] These ribs would have made a saddle tramp quit drifting and stay in one place, hoping for more of these wonderful and tasty ribs!

I traditionally make this with huckleberry jelly, however chokecherry jelly really enhances the flavor! If you don't have either, grape jelly is a great substitute.

You Rub Me the Right Way... Rub

¼ cup brown sugar
1 tablespoon salt
½ tablespoon pepper
1 tablespoon cumin
2 tablespoons onion powder
2 tablespoons garlic powder
1 tablespoon paprika
2 teaspoons McCormick Hamburger Grill Mates Seasoning
1 teaspoon chili powder
4 lb. rack of baby back ribs

Huckleberry BBQ Sauce

10 oz. jar of huckleberry jelly (or 1¼ cups grape or chokecherry jelly)
1 cup KC Masterpiece Original BBQ Sauce
½ teaspoon nutmeg
½ teaspoon ginger
1 teaspoon soy sauce
16 oz. can of tomato paste
1 teaspoon onion powder
1 teaspoon garlic powder
1 tablespoon minced garlic
½ teaspoon ground cinnamon

Preheat oven to 250 degrees.
On a large sheet pan, spray with nonstick spray, mix all the rub ingredients and spread on ribs. Place the meat side down, cover with foil and bake for 2 hours.

Heat oven to 350 degrees.
Mix all the sauce ingredients in a large mixing bowl. Set aside. Transfer ribs from original pan, to a clean pan lined with foil and sprayed with non-stick spray. Spoon half of the sauce on ribs, reserving the remainder sauce. Cover extra sauce and refrigerate until ribs are ready again. Bake ribs for 60 minutes, remove from oven and spread remaining sauce on top. Lower oven to 275 degrees and heat for 30 more minutes.

Slick as a Whistle, Chicken Chardonnay

This recipe will satisfy your guests, slick as a whistle! The light wine gravy will have them singing your praises! Paired with the wild rice, this meal is so delicious!

5 lb. package chicken tenders (skinless and boneless)
¼ cup butter
¼ cup vegetable or olive oil
1 teaspoon onion powder
½ tablespoon minced garlic
1 teaspoon salt
½ teaspoon ground pepper
1 cup diced onion
2 cups sliced fresh mushrooms, or an 8 oz. can sliced mushrooms
½ tablespoon thyme leaves
1 cup chardonnay wine
10.2 oz. can chicken broth
2 tablespoons cornstarch in a ½ of a ⅓ cup of cold water (do this at the end of making dish)
½ tablespoon heavy cream, optional
1 box Uncle Ben's Wild Rice (fast cook)

Preheat oven to 275 degrees.

In an extra-large skillet, heat butter and oil, add chicken, then sprinkle with salt, pepper, onion powder, to personal taste. Sauté until golden brown. Remove chicken from pan and place into a large bowl. Add onions to the pan drippings and cook until translucent. Next, add mushrooms and heat thoroughly. Spoon onion and mushroom mixture into the bowl with the chicken.

In the original saucepan, add cornstarch mixture (mentioned in the ingredient list), slowly whisking to make sauce thicker. Add chicken broth, whisk to avoid lumpy sauce. Next, add wine, salt, pepper, thyme, onion powder(from the above ingredient list). Lastly, add the chicken, mushrooms, and onions and minced garlic. Add heavy cream and stir until well mixed. Transfer to an oven safe container, cover and bake in oven for 20 minutes. While chicken is in oven, prepare rice according to directions. Serve chicken with rice and and tossed salad.

Louisiana Purchase,

Cajun Rice And Beans With A Montana Flair

The Louisiana Purchase was the sale of 828,000 square miles of French Territory, sold to the United States for $27,267,622. The purchase from France and Napoleon Bonaparte, was the "greatest land bargain in U.S. history."[63] The land acquisition doubled the size of the United States, creating new and interesting territories, later known as states. The purchase opened up new trade, waterways, agriculture, and the opportunity to build a route to the Pacific. The Louisiana Purchase includes the states of Louisiana, Missouri, Arkansas, Iowa, North Dakota, South Dakota, Nebraska, and Oklahoma. However, the largest states included in the land purchase are: Kansas, Colorado, Wyoming, Minnesota, and of course, Montana![63]

This recipe came to me from my friend, Sherry Fiddler Velarde. We were neighbors and she is a marvelous cook, introducing me to Cajun cuisine. Sherry grew up in the heart of Louisiana and certainly knows her way around a stove! Cajun food is a cuisine based on "neighbors sharing" comfort food, from kitchens that were humble, with cooks who were not financially well-off. Those cooks often improvised from humble pantry staples, creating delicious meals. Sherry kept up the "neighbor sharing" philosophy of her Louisiana, Cajun roots. Rice and beans are a meal staple for my family, and we love them! My version of this delicious beans and rice dish is a family favorite. The heat, helps through long and cold Montana winters. Although I do not have access to andouille sausage, which is a Cajun recipe tradition, I substitute hot Italian sausage. It is wonderful! This version is quick, delicious and hearty! I will always be grateful to Sherry, who shared more than meals. Our friendship grew from being neighbors, to family!

28 oz. can of petite diced tomatoes in tomato juice

14.5 oz. can of petite diced tomatoes in tomato juice

8 oz. can of tomato sauce

6 oz. can of tomato paste

(2) 15.5 oz. cans of pinto beans, drained

¼ tablespoon chili powder, paprika, and cayenne

1 tablespoon onion powder, dried thyme leaves, and dried basil

2 tablespoons rosemary sprigs

½ tablespoon salt

½ tablespoon McCormick Hamburger Grill Mates Seasoning

½ tablespoon garlic powder 1¼ tablespoons chopped or minced garlic

16 oz. (2 cups) cubed and cooked ham

19 oz. hot Italian sausage, remove the casing, cut into bite size pieces and cook thoroughly.

Minute Rice

In a large stock pot, combine tomatoes, tomato paste, beans, herbs, spices and seasonings. Stir well, cover and let simmer on very low heat. Cook sausage in skillet, drain grease. Place cooked sausage on a paper towel and pat to absorb excess grease. Then add to the stock pot mixture. Next, add ham and stir well. Cover and simmer on low, until rice is ready.

Prepare rice according to directions for desired serving amounts.

Inside Scoop: Rice will serve as the bed for the meat/beans and spices. You can adjust seasoning according to personal preferences. If you like a less spicy flavor, cut chili powder, paprika and Hamburger Grill Mates Seasoning measurements in half.

Combine Casserole

This hearty and flavorful casserole is a dinner meal favorite. When I created this casserole, I knew it would have been a harvest favorite. "Combine" these unique pantry staples and make a delicious evening meal, serving it with a side salad.

Chicken prep:
20 oz. package chicken breast tenderloins
3 tablespoons olive oil
½ teaspoon onion salt
¼ teaspoon salt

Rice prep:
3 cups Minute Rice
2 tablespoons butter
3 cups water

Sauce prep:
⅓ teaspoon pepper
1 teaspoon minced garlic
⅓ cup parmesan (in the jar)
½ cup heavy cream
¾ cup sour cream
⅓ cup chicken broth
⅓ cup chardonnay wine
½ teaspoon onion powder

Rice topping:
½ cup plus 2 tablespoons parmesan (jar)

Casserole topping:
¾ cup fiesta blend cheese
1½ cups croutons, crushed

Preheat oven to 350 degrees.

Step 1: In a large frying pan, spray with non-stick spray, place olive oil and place chicken in pan. On medium heat cook chicken and season with onion powder and table salt, cover. Turn chicken over after 3-4 minutes and continue cooking another 3-4 minutes. Take chicken out of pan and put on a plate and cover. Save pan with juices from chicken.

Step 2: To prepare rice, combine with water and butter, cover and microwave for approximately 10 minutes (or until tender).

Step 3: Take pan that chicken was prepared, in and mix in all the sauce ingredients, whisking until well-blended and heated through, on medium heat.

Spray a 9 x 13 x 2 pan with non-stick spray.

Layer the cooked rice evenly in baking dish, spoon half of the sauce over the rice, sprinkle the half cup plus 2 tablespoons of parmesan evenly over rice. Place chicken lengthwise down in 3 rows (makes it easier for dishing up). Spoon remaining sauce over chicken, followed by ¾ cup of fiesta cheese. Cover with foil and bake for 15 minutes. Remove from oven and sprinkle the crushed croutons on top. Return uncovered for an additional 15 minutes. Serve immediately.

Bannack Beans

In 1862, Grasshopper Creek delivered gold and a new Montana town, called Bannack. More than 10,000 miners came to the area in search of riches. Bannack, Montana became a ghost town in the 1940's. The Department of Fish, Wildlife and Parks, protected the town from ruination and made it a state park in 1954. Prior to its ghost town status, the little community was rich with gold, characters, and a notorious sheriff named Henry Plummer. Plummer courted locals and miners. Those in the growing community, trusted their elected sheriff. The abundance of gold and those who possessed it, encouraged the arrival of bandits, known as a secret band of road agents, called "innocents." The road agents robbed and killed more than 100 men. Miners protecting themselves and their pockets of gold, decided to form their own group, called the Montana Vigilantes. Taking the law into their own hands, this group of right fighting citizens hung 24 "innocents," in 42 days, including...Henry Plummer! It seems Sheriff Plummer wasn't so innocent after all, as it was discovered he was the leader of the secret road agents and he met his fate, with a noose. Ghosts are now the only residents of Bannack. Some say Henry Plummer is one of the apparitions who has taken up residency in the ghost town.[70] If you're curious who is roaming around the ghost town, see for yourself.

For information on the park visit:
bannack.org   (406)864-3413

1 teaspoon olive oil
1 lb. hot Italian sausages
1 lb. cooked and diced chicken
1 cup chopped onion
2 tablespoons olive oil
2 tablespoons minced garlic
3 tablespoons chili powder
1 tablespoon onion powder
2 teaspoons cumin
2 teaspoons salt
1 teaspoon pepper
1 teaspoon thymes leaves

1 teaspoon basil leaves
(1) 28 oz. can diced petite tomatoes
(1) 14.5 oz. can diced petite tomatoes
(1) 15.5 oz. can dark kidney beans
(1) 15.5 oz. can pinto beans
(1) 15 oz. can black beans, drained
8 oz. bag of Mexican shredded
   cheese
1 small container sour cream
3 diced green onions
2 tablespoons of chopped cilantro
Bag of tortilla chips

Remove casings of sausage and cut into small bite size pieces. In a large skillet, brown sausage, then drain grease and pat with a paper towel to remove excess grease. Cook chicken and chopped onion, in olive oil with salt, pepper, cumin, and chili powder, drain grease.

In a large stock pot, spray with non-stick spray, and add meats and tomatoes. Drain the 3 cans of beans in a colander, then add to stock pot ingredients. Simmer until nice and warm. Serve with any or all of the following items: shredded cheese, cilantro, sliced onion, tortilla chips, and sour cream.

Stampede Chili, **For A Small Herd**

Charles Conrad was a visionary, not just for establishing Kalispell, building a beautiful and historic home, but also for his conservation efforts and realizing that a preservation area for buffalo/bison was indeed an important concept. Charles started his own buffalo herd that became the core of the National Bison Range herd, of which he was instrumental in establishing.[66] His preservation efforts are not the only area in Montana that bison roam. Yellowstone National Park is home to over 4,000 buffalo. The buffalo roam freely in the park. They are to be respected and not agitated, as they can run up to 35 mph, with a male weighing up to 2,000 pounds, and a female weighing up to 1,000 pounds. A bison's height can reach up to six feet tall. They graze on grass, herbs and shrubs, making their meat lean and desirable.[68] Do not underestimate a buffalo, as they have a keen sense of smell, their vision has great depth, their hearing is impeccable, and their horns can do serious damage to an absent-minded tourist! Yellowstone National Park is the only place in the United States where bison have lived since prehistoric times. The herd is considered pristine in its bloodline, not having mixed with cattle.[67] Bison are seen throughout the park, along the highways, in the valleys, and often along the boardwalks.[69]

These simple ingredients will rustle up your taste buds. An easy to make one pot dish, is perfect on a cold winter's night or to take camping. I make a big pot for camping trips. I grill a couple of hamburger patties over the campfire and then crumbled into the chili. The married flavors are amazing!

16 oz. package of lean ground beef, bison or ground turkey
2 teaspoons onion powder
2½ teaspoons chili powder
½ teaspoon paprika
2 teaspoons McCormick Hamburger Grill Mates Seasoning
(2) 15.5 oz. cans dark red kidney beans, drained
14.5 oz. petite diced tomatoes in tomato juice
28 oz. can of petite diced tomatoes in tomato juice

In a large frying pan, on mediums heat, fry the hamburger with 1 teaspoon onion powder, 1½ teaspoons chili powder, paprika, and 1 teaspoon Hamburger Grill Mates Seasoning, stirring often. When meat is browned and cooked thoroughly, turn off heat and drain excess grease.

Mix into hamburger, 1 teaspoon McCormick Hamburger Grill Mates Seasoning, 1 teaspoon onion powder and chili powder. Add in kidney beans and, diced tomatoes. Mix well and heat until hot. Serve immediately.

Salads

A Party Line of Salads...

When our beige Trimline phone, with its extra-long cord rang, we would all carefully pay attention. We participated in a party line, where we shared the open phone line with a handful of neighbors. We listened for the two long musical rings, assigned to our 733-4744 phone number. We always answered, "Knudson residence," as a courtesy, notifying callers on the party line who they were calling, intentional or otherwise. Once in awhile, an eavesdropper and nosey-information-getter, would be heard clearing their throat or sneezing on the line. No one meant any harm, just curiosity and slow news days had them picking up the line. Once in awhile you heard clicking on the other end, alerting us that our time was up and someone else was waiting to use the line. Fortunately, there wasn't much competition during the winter for phone time, as most of our neighbors lived in Fort Benton during the school year, returning for the summer season only.

The following salads often appear in buffets for my guests, creating a party line of food and making them the talk of the town. Individually, each of these salads make a meal extra special.

Inside Scoop: When needing diced onion for a recipe, slice the top off a whole onion. Then peel the outer layer back. With a knife, score a grid like pattern in the cut side, then turn onion on its side and slice. Small pieces will be diced, and tears will be avoided!

Often for a first course, I prepare a wreath salad, by simply using field greens or cut lettuce and shape around the inside rim of a decorative plate. I use sliced avocado or radish slices to accent the wreath. A large tomato is peeled by using a sharp knife. I then twist the peel to make a rose and place it at the top of the salad wreath. The presentation, while simple to execute, always gets big praises. Bagged lettuce works great, cutting down on assembly time. Use your imagination to create your own personalized "wreath salad."

Note: All salads involving mayonnaise in the recipe should be made in a plastic or glass bowl. Do not store salads in the refrigerator in metal, as there is a reactive process, use only glass or plastic containers!

Karen's Farmhouse Ranch Dressing

This is by far the most requested recipe from my friends and family. It is wonderful for salads, but as a dipping sauce for sides as well. Thinning the dressing can be done with a little bit of milk, as it thickens over time.

1 packet of Hidden Valley Ranch Buttermilk Dressing Packet
1 cup mayonnaise (not miracle whip, it is too sweet)
1 cup buttermilk
1 teaspoon onion powder
1 teaspoon thyme leaves
3 complete grinds of fresh ground pepper

In a bowl, whisk together ranch packet, mayonnaise and buttermilk. Use a soup spoon to scrape the bottom of the bowl, add remaining ingredients. Mix well. Chill in refrigerator, whisking several times before serving.

Inside Scoop: When having a large gathering, I often pour dressing in washed, soda bottles, with a tag or label to identify. The container is easy to pour, and it saves on buying extra containers to serve dressings in.

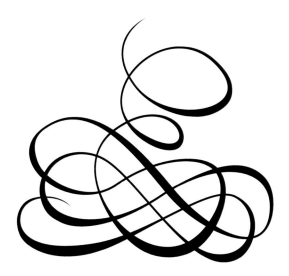

Homestead Cobb

Traditional Cobb salad ingredients get mixed up a bit with the fabulous flavors of my Farmhouse Ranch Dressing and grilled Teriyaki Chicken. These additions will have your guests delighted with the tasteful and beautiful presentation.

I grill chicken for this when I want it to be a dinner. Refer to the Teriyaki Marinade recipe on page 91. The marinade works for all meats. The grilled chicken on top of this salad, served on a large platter with small slices of green onion for garnish, is a lovely and lighter meal.

Chicken, grill right before serving
2 cups iceberg lettuce, chopped
2 cups romaine, chopped
2 cups red leaf lettuce, chopped
1 cup red cabbage, chopped
2 medium tomatoes, cut into pieces
3 medium avocados, peeled and sliced
8 peppered bacon slices cooked, drained and chopped
4 hard boiled eggs, sliced or chopped
3 tablespoons chopped green onion

Follow Teriyaki Chicken Recipe (page 91) and serve with my Farmhouse Ranch Dressing (page 107). On a large platter or plate, creatively display the above ingredients. I recommend tossing chopped lettuces in a large bowl first. Place the lettuces and spread evenly on a platter. I will decorate the lettuce bed with items mirroring each side of the platter, leaving the center open. Place grilled teriyaki chicken, avocados and bacon in the center.

Inside Scoop: This salad is a wonderful ladies' luncheon meal. I have also heated 1 cup of pecans and sprinkled on the edges of the platter. Cupcake carriers work wonders to carry muffin tins of individual salad toppings. The muffin tins are easy to pass to guests or make a picnic table bright and colorful.

Potato Salad

No summer barbecue or picnic is complete without potato salad. I usually boil several extra eggs for dressing the top of the salad, adding thin slices of green onions for additional garnish. See photo for design.

3 slices cooked bacon crumbled
2 lbs. or 5 medium russet potatoes
3 hardboiled eggs

Sauce:
1½ cup mayonnaise
1½ tablespoons yellow mustard
½ cup diced onion
⅓ cup diced celery, optional
1 teaspoon paprika
¼ teaspoon ground pepper
⅛ teaspoon salt
½ teaspoon onion powder
2 tablespoons raw horseradish

Note: Cook potatoes and boil eggs, a day before and refrigerate, works great!

Cook bacon and drain grease on a paper towel on a plate. (Use cooking shears and cut bacon slices into small pieces and cook.)

Wash and peel potatoes, slice into cubes and place in a large saucepan with boiling hot water. Water needs to be boiling first, then add potatoes, boil 10-15 minutes until fork tender. Drain, and place into container to cool, then cover and refrigerate.

Boil eggs covered in water, approximately 15 minutes. Drain water, place eggs in a container and refrigerate. Once cool, peel and slice. Mix sauce ingredients and add potatoes, mix well. Add bacon and two sliced eggs. Mix well.

Spoon salad into a clean serving dish and slice remaining egg. Place on top, to decorate salad. I will also slice thin strips of the green stalk of an onion and lay on top of the salad. Sprinkle a light dusting of paprika, if desired. Cover and refrigerate for at least 4 hours, unless the sauce was made in advance and it is well chilled.

Inside Scoop: During Easter celebrations, I shape the potato salad in the shape of an egg, I use thin strips of the green end of an onion and make a zig zag formation, resembling stripes. Sliced eggs also make a fun decoration on the egg-shaped potato salad.

Broccoli Salad

Oh my goodness, I could have this salad every single day! For gatherings I often serve it in individual jelly jars or large ramekins. For a festive twist, I have tied a fork on the side of the individual container. Guests love this presentation and convenience, while making their way through a buffet line.

8 oz. bag shredded cheddar cheese
½ red onion diced finely
1 broccoli brunch, diced
1 lb. bacon, cooked and chopped into small pieces
¼ cup roasted sunflower seeds, I like the honey roasted
½ cup finely chopped red cabbage
4 radishes sliced fine

Dressing:
1 cup mayo
2 tablespoons apple cider vinegar
½ cup sugar

Mix dressing, set aside. In a large bowl prepare salad items, tossing to mix well. Add salad dressing and mix well. Refrigerate for at least 2 hours, toss before serving.

Inside Scoop: During Christmas, I make a double batch of this salad. I use a large platter and shape the salad into a Christmas tree shape. Sliced carrots serve as the tree trunk, cherry tomatoes can be used as a tree topper or ornaments, and a sliced red or yellow pepper can serve as a star topper. I serve this "vegetable tree salad" with a baked ham and cheesy potatoes.

Spinach Salad

At Christmas time or other holidays, I have used a salad plate and arranged the spinach leaves to make them look like a wreath. To shape the wreath, circle the spinach leaves around the outside rim of the plate/platter. Then slice 2 eggs, fanning them on top of plate, to create a mock bowtie. Place fresh raspberries in the center, about 2 or 3 raspberries. Serve the croutons on the side.

2 bunches of spinach or ready bag of spinach
4-6 hard boiled eggs, dice 4, slice 2, set aside
1 lb. cooked bacon crumbled
1 pint raspberries, sliced in half
⅛ cup of walnuts
1 bag of rustic French bread croutons
16 oz. bottle of Paul Newman's Raspberry & Walnut Salad Dressing

Slowly pour most of the oil off the bottle of dressing. I know you are thinking this is a waste, but it reduces the calories and creates a lighter dressing, not weighing down the salad. Then warm the dressing for about 20 seconds in the microwave and checking it at 10 second intervals. Careful not to overheat. (Heating the dressing intensifies the flavors of the dressing.)

Option 1. In a large bowl, mix spinach that has been torn or sliced into smaller bite size pieces, with diced egg, bacon, walnuts, and raspberries. Top salad with sliced remaining eggs and an edge of croutons, creating a wreath inside the bowl. Serve warmed dressing in a gravy boat/small bowl with ladle.

Option 2. Plate individual servings, from the large bowl of mixed salad ingredients. Place sliced egg rings on salad with a serving of croutons. Dressing is served the same as in option 1.

Asian Salad

This recipe has a bounty of infused flavors and textures, making it a dinner or party staple. I often create a salad bar, which is a variety of salads, feeding my herd of guests. This salad always starts the "party line." Call your friends and family, the party's starting with this delicious salad starter!

1 napa cabbage, finely sliced
½ cup red cabbage, finely chopped
½ cup shredded carrots

Dressing:

½ - ¾ cup oil
¾ cup sugar
1 teaspoon onion powder
¼ cup of vinegar
1 tablespoon soy sauce
3 tablespoons mayonnaise
1½ tablespoons Miracle Whip
½ tablespoon Dijon mustard
6 grinds of fresh ground black pepper
½ teaspoon garlic powder
⅛ teaspoon salt

Salad Topping:

2 (3 oz.)packages Maruchan Ramen Noodles, chicken flavor crushed
½ cup melted butter
¼ cup slivered almonds
2 tablespoons sesame seeds

Inside Scoop: When making this salad as a meal, prepare my Teriyaki Chicken recipe on page 91 or buy 4-5 chicken strips from a deli, serving sliced and warm on top.

Dressing:

Whisk the dressing ingredients together, 15 minutes before serving. Lightly dress the vegetables, mixing with thongs right before serving. Pour remaining dressing in container, for your guests to access.

Topping:

Preheat oven to 400 degrees.

To prepare topping, add noodles, butter, almonds, and sesame seeds, in a medium sized bowl and mix well. On a cookie sheet, sprayed with non-stick spray, evenly spread the noodle mixture. Bake until golden brown, about 5-7 minutes, watch the time, as all ovens heat differently. Broil if you need to, but watch very carefully. Remove from heat and let cool. Once cooled add topping to the cabbage and carrots, stir well. Then add dressing, right before serving.

Sandy's Tuna Salad

No summer is complete without this marvelous salad. Often my friend Sandy serves this poolside, signaling summer is here! It is great for a picnic at a park, or for a potluck dish. I often make a batch to serve with ham sandwiches after Easter or alongside a BBQ'd hamburger. Your friends will ask you for this recipe, be prepared!

3 cups cooked elbow macaroni
1 large can tuna, drained
4 hard boiled eggs, sliced
2 cans sliced black olives, drained
2 tablespoons sweet relish
1 teaspoon onion powder
½ teaspoon salt
⅛ teaspoon pepper
1 tablespoon celery seed
½ cup mayo
½ cup Miracle Whip

Blend together onion powder, salt, pepper, celery seeds, and relish. Mix well. Set aside.

In a medium size bowl, mix macaroni, tuna, eggs and olives, mix well. Add dressing ingredients and spices to macaroni. Cover and refrigerate or serve immediately.

Mediterranean Salad

There is so much to say about my veggie Mediterranean salad. Delicious, colorful, and artful are just a few. The Italian dressing is lite, flavorful and does not weigh down the veggie flavors. Often, I add sliced chunks of cheese, sometimes buffalo mozzarella or Swiss cheese. I also include slices of hard salami, as the flavors enhance the already fabulous salad. It can be made into a meal when served with an array of artisan breads or my Lodgepole Twists! (page 60)

1 bunch of radishes sliced (approximately 6 radishes)
1 bunch of broccoli, cut into small bite size pieces
Small bag of baby carrots, chopped
4 Roma tomatoes, diced
1 red onion, diced
1 large cucumber, peeled and diced
12 oz. bag of Wacky Mac veggie spiral pasta
6 oz. zesty Italian dressing packet

Cook pasta according to directions. In a large bowl assemble all cut vegetables, add cooled pasta. Prepare the Italian dressing according to directions on packet. Pour over salad, one hour before serving.

Spring Salad Bouquet

Frequently, I have had to think of imaginative ways to serve individual salads. For a French inspired birthday party (page 164), I served an array of soups in gorgeous tea cups, followed by the the tulip salads.

Fresh tulips with the stamin removed, cleaned and dried, work wonderful for the stuffed salad. Artificial flowers will work as well, they can be done in advance. Wrap the stuffed flowers with plastic wrap and store in refrigerator until ready to serve. An elegant ribbon bow accentuates the creative presentation of the tulip salad. The artful display of a tulip salad will wow your guests!

That's a Pizza! Pizza, Cookie?

Birthday treat memory...My daughter, Savannah's second grade year was a difficult one. We moved away from her beloved childhood home, to Billings. In the new school, cliques had already been formed and she struggled to make friends. As a Mom, I wanted to make her class birthday treats extra special. I found myself scrambling for a unique idea. The usual cupcakes, cookies, or other snacks would just not do. I created this recipe, while letting her believe I would deliver cupcakes. Instead, a pizza box was delivered with mock mini pizzas! Savannah was thrilled. I received a note from her teacher, stating that in her 35-year teaching career, no celebration treat had ever created such excitement! Sometimes you just have to think outside the box and into a pizza one.

Crust:
16.5 oz. roll of Pillsbury refrigerated sugar cookie dough

Sauce and toppings:
5 oz. box cherry Twizzler bites
6 oz. box Mike and Ikes original fruit candy
16 oz. white candy melting discs
16 oz. container creamy white/vanilla supreme frosting
1 oz. red food coloring
2 teaspoons almond extract

Preheat oven to 350 degrees. On 13½ x 15 cookie sheet, spray with non-stick spray coating.

Open the boxes of candies, take out two plates: one for Twizzlers and one for Mike and Ike's. Slice the candies so they resemble pepperoni and colored peppers. Cover, and set aside. Open frosting container and stir well. Add almond extract and red food coloring. Mix well, cover and set aside.

Slice refrigerated cookie dough according to directions. Take one slice at a time, roll into a ball in the palm of your hand, and place on cookie sheet. When you have 8 balls on the sheet, place cookies in the oven and bake for about 12 minutes or until lightly browned on edges.

Immediately after removing cookies from oven, take a small spoon and slightly flatten the center of the cookie down. Continue to work outwards, leaving a rim to resemble a pizza crust and repeat until all cookies are shaped.

When cookies are cooled, gently frost the center of each pizza cookie with a spoon, making it look like sauce on a pizza. Sprinkle the colorful mixture of Mike and Ike candies (which equates to 12 small pieces). Then take 6 Twizzle bite pieces and place in center of cookie to resemble pepperoni. Chop, grate, or slice, 1½ white candy discs over the top of each cookie, to resemble mozzarella cheese. Microwave decorated cookies for just a few seconds to melt the pretend cheese.

Serve cookies from a pizza box.

Note: I have either purchased a pizza box or received donated boxes from our local pizzeria.

Pansy Shortbread Cookies

1¼ cup flour
¼ cup of sugar
2 oz. cream cheese, room temperature
½ cup butter, room temperature
¼ teaspoon vanilla
1 tablespoon dried egg whites or meringue powder (following package directions)
2 tablespoons water
Pansies, pesticide free, rinsed and patted dry
Sanding sugar
Edible pearl sprinkles

Preheat oven to 325 degrees.

In a large mixing bowl, mix flour and sugar, add cream cheese, vanilla, and butter, mixing well. Sprinkle flour on a cutting board. Take dough and roll out, on board. Turn it over and roll again, until the dough is ¼ inch thick. Use a cookie cutter and cut dough. Place cookies on a baking sheet and bake for 20 minutes or until brown. Check cookies when timer goes off and bake additional time if necessary.

Brush the prepared meringue powder on cookies, using it as a glue for the pansies. Then brush more egg mixture on top of the pansy/cookies. Sprinkle sanding sugar on top, randomly place the edible pearls. When all cookies are finished being decorated, place in oven for 5 more minutes. Let cool and serve when desired.

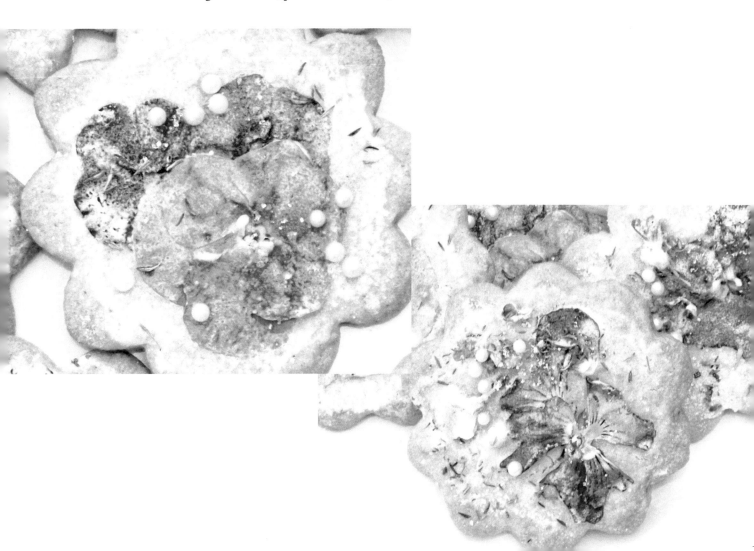

Gramma Knudson's Chocolate Sandwiches

I was blessed with two wonderful grandmothers. Both loved their families, God, and a crochet needle. Gramma Knudson had a vegetable garden with perfect rows and no weeds. During the summer, her kitchen always had a freshly made pie, with impeccably made lattice crusts. She is a treasure of my heart! You will treasure these yummy chocolate sandwiches.

2 cups flour
½ teaspoon baking powder
1½ teaspoon baking soda
½ cup cocoa
½ cup butter, softened to room temperature
1 cup sugar
1 egg
1 teaspoon vanilla
1 cup milk

Preheat oven to 375 degrees.

In a bowl, combine flour, baking powder and soda, and cocoa. Set aside. In large mixing bowl cream butter, sugar, egg and vanilla, and milk, mixing well. Then add flour mixture and mix until dough is smooth. On greased cookie sheet, drop spoonfuls of cookie dough, about 2 inches apart and bake for 7 minutes.

Marshmallow Filling For Sandwiches

½ cup Crisco shortening
2 cups powdered sugar
1 cup marshmallow cream
1 teaspoon vanilla
3-4 teaspoons milk

Cream shortening and powdered sugar, mixing well. Add remaining ingredients and mix well. On cooled cookies, spread filling on one cookie, placing another on top to make a sandwich. Continue until all cookies have filling.

Snowballs

When I created these cookies, I needed some thoughtful, but not expensive birthday gifts, as I had several birthdays in a row for acquaintances. I found vintage teacups and saucers and placed a few cookies inside them, with an assortment of teas. I wrapped the filled cups in cellophane, with a lovely ribbon and gift tag/recipe card. The presentation and functionality was a dual hit!

1 stick margarine softened
7 tablespoons powdered sugar
1 teaspoon vanilla
2 teaspoons almond extract
1¼ cups of flour
2 oz. cream cheese softened
1¼ cup of chopped pecans
Powdered sugar

Preheat oven at 350 degrees.

On a plate or low profile bowl, place powdered sugar for rolling baked cookies. Set aside.

Cream margarine and powdered sugar, add vanilla and almond extract, mix well. Now add flour and mix well. Next add cream cheese and mix again. Dough will be sticky, don't worry. Blend in chopped pecans. Spray a cookie sheet with non-stick spray. Take a dinner spoon and scoop out dough, roll into small balls and place on cookie sheet. Bake for 8-10 minutes. When cookies are slightly warm, roll in powdered sugar. Re-roll if the cookies were too warm and absorbed the sugar. My family prefers these cookies chilled.

Inside Scoop: My daughter does not like nuts, I would make a batch without them, calling them "snowman poop!"

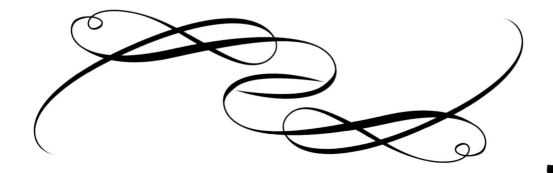

Montana, Setting Records

Approximately 30 miles from the farm of our youth, is Loma, Montana. The small community made big news on January 14th and 15th, in 1972. The mercury in local thermostats were in for a wild ride in the small community of Loma. A 103 degree temperature swing had locals talking, so was the nation. Area residents were freezing in their boots with -54 degrees below zero temperatures. Within those 24 hours, Chinook winds blew into Lorna, raising the mercury to 49 degrees above zero. The roller coaster ride of temperatures, set a national weather record.[77] January 20, 1954 the temperature dropped to 70 degrees below zero at a mining camp near Lolo, Montana. The dip in temperature is the coldest official temperature recorded in the Continental U. S.[78] Another tongue in cheek weather reference from Jeff Foxworthy says, "Montana has 4 seasons... "almost winter, winter, still winter and road construction."[79] Setting snowfall records for Montana is commonplace. However, one particular snowfall set a record of a different kind. The largest snowflake ever recorded was in Fort Keough, Montana, the size of it measured 15 inches! The historic "flake" was located at the fort, located on the western edge of Miles City, where Army personnel, witnessed and recorded the size of the enormous snowflake. It is still listed as the largest flake, in The Guinness Book of World Records. Soldiers at the fort, reported seeing many extremely large snowflakes. There is a scientific phenomenon, where several flakes bond together to create one enormous flake. Typically a large snowflake is considered to be 3 inches, Fort Keough's record is 5 times that. A local area rancher was interviewed regarding the sizable flake, claiming it was "larger than a milk pan."[80] History has lost his name, or perhaps he wished to be anonymous. However, a cowboy's reputation was his badge of honor and his word a testament to his character. Perhaps the rancher did not want to be known as the "crazy flake" who believed a snowflake was so big it was the size of his milk pan![80]

Pudge

Decadent peanut butter fudge! This recipe is always on my Christmas "must make" list. One holiday season, as I was preparing gift boxes of homemade goodies, my 4-year-old daughter misunderstood the name and innocently asked for a piece of "Pudge." Need I say more?

1¾ cups semi-sweet chocolate chips
1 bag peanut butter chips
1 can sweetened condensed milk

Spray a microwave-safe bowl with non-stick spray. Place chocolate chips in bowl and microwave for about 3 minutes. Stir well and add sweetened condensed milk, stirring until smooth. Add peanut butter chips and heat in microwave for 2 more minutes. Stir again. Pour in a small glass baking dish, sprayed with non-stick spray, smoothing evenly in pan. When it is cooled, cut into squares and serve.

Bunkhouse Brownies

The bunkhouses of days long gone, were sparsely furnished, but provided solace to many a weary ranch and farm hand. They were often drifters, without family. Working on a spread, often gave them the family they never had and friends of a lifetime. Riding the range, tending to the cattle, and having a horse of your own, was a hand's dream. A bedroll was a constant companion, as hands often had to sleep on them until they made their way back to the bunkhouse. Bunkhouse bars were created to celebrate the memory of my bunkhouse playin' days and to the men, who long ago called it home. Our old bunkhouse range, while tired and weary, was a workhouse for my pretend meals and desserts. The creative bunkhouse play of my youth, inspired the dessert creations I am known for. These delicious treats represent a "bed" of chocolate brownie and a lofty white "blanket" of cream cheese topping. You will not have to pretend that these are fabulous. If you have tired and weary 'hands' who need a little comfort, give these delicious bars a try!

Brownie Bunk Bed
12 oz. bag of semi-sweet chocolate chips (2 cups)
½ cup sugar
¼ cup butter, room temperature
2 eggs
2 teaspoons vanilla
½ teaspoon salt
⅔ cup of flour, sifted

Blanket Covers, Cheesecake Topping
8 oz. package of cream cheese, room temperature
½ cup sugar
3 tablespoons butter, room temperature
3 eggs (3 small or 2 large/jumbo eggs)
2 tablespoons milk
1 tablespoon flour
1½ teaspoons almond extract
¾ cup chocolate chips

Set aside ¾ cup chocolate chips for the blanket cover topping.

Preheat oven to 350 degrees. Spray a 9-inch baking pan with non-stick spray.

In a double boiler or in microwave melt chocolate chips. Stir until completely melted and silky, set aside. In a large bowl combine sugar, butter, and cream together. Add eggs, one at a time, mixing well in between each egg. Add vanilla and salt mix well, then add melted chocolate and flour. After batter is combined, pour into baking pan and spread evenly. Set aside.

In a large bowl combine cream cheese and sugar, beat well. Add butter and mix again until smooth and creamy. Add eggs, one at a time, mixing in between each, add milk, flour and almond extract. Beat well. Carefully pour evenly over brownie base and sprinkle chips on top of cream cheese. Bake for 35-45 minutes until top is golden brown. Check baking time at 35 minutes, as ovens vary.

Note: If you are using a 9-inch rectangular pan, it will be thinner than a 9-inch square pan.

Annie Oakley

✤ ANNIE OAKLEY, ✤
(LITTLE SURE SHOT.)

J. WOOD, PHOTO.   208 BOWERY, N. Y.

Photos courtesy of US National Archives

The West was legendary with figures bigger than life. Tall tales surrounded many a table and campfire conversation. Outlaws, trappers, vigilantes, and discoveries of gold, were among the stories swirling the Big Sky Country. However, a few good women created their own stir. One such woman, was Annie Oakley. Born in a log cabin in the Ohio frontier, Annie began shooting guns at the age of 9. Her widowed mother struggled to support and feed her children. Fortunately, Annie quickly proved to be an accurate shot and provided wild game and birds for her hungry family.[71] During my research of Annie, I discovered that a general store, owned by the Katzenberger Brothers was the first business to purchase the wild game that lost their battle between Annie and her rifle. The brothers reportedly paid a handsome price for fresh game, making little Annie an up and coming business. [72]

At the age of 16, Annie entered a shooting competition. Her accuracy gave her a notable reputation. Frank E. Butler, was an accomplished marksman who wowed audiences in his Vaudeville act. Rumors of Annie's ability made their way to Frank and soon a competition was planned. Annie won the contest by only one point! Not long after the friendly sporting event the entranced Frank Butler married her. Annie became his partner in life and in his traveling shooting act. Frank soon recognized that his wife was more talented than he, and truly the real star of the show. Personal manager, husband, and promoter became Frank's career. The frontiersman and showman, Buffalo Bill Cody, didn't need much convincing that Annie was show material and in 1885, they joined the Buffalo Bill Wild West Show.[72]

Let the show begin! Pistol, rifle, or shotgun, it didn't matter, Annie became famous for using all the guns in her shooting act, in the Wild West Show. Her craft became legendary on both sides of the Atlantic, drawing enormous crowds to the show.[73] She was lovingly named "Little Sure Shot", by Chief Sitting Bull, the famous Indian chief, who defeated General George Armstrong Custer, at the Battle of The Bighorn. The two met while she wowed audiences for 16 years, as the pistol packing powerhouse of the Wild West Show. The famous Indian Chief adored Annie and the depth of their relationship provided a father figure for her.[74]

Annie's reputation in the show, gained her international recognition. The spitfire sharpshooter soon found herself across the Atlantic, performing stunts for audiences who greeted her with roaring applause. It is there that she famously shot the ashes off a cigarette, from the mouth of Kaiser Wilhelm II, of Germany.[73] Additionally, a Broadway musical hit "Annie Get Your Gun," and major motion picture, of the same title, honored Annie's legacy.[75]

What is the connection of Annie and Montana? Although, I cannot substantiate the rumor that Annie and Frank lived in the state, it does seem likely, with the close proximity of Cody, Wyoming and Billings, Montana. Years ago, I was told through an old timer by the name of Tom Frye, that Annie had taken ill in Cody, and was brought to Billings, for medical attention. Traveling from Cody, proved taxing, therefore a decision was made for them to stay in Billings. Annie's recuperation took her through the late months of fall and into the early days of spring. It was rumored that she and Frank were guests on a friend's property, which is now the location of the Billings Zoo. [76]

Whether or not the tale is a true one, she represents a long list of pioneer women, who like her, took a skill, perfected it and made a show stopper out of it! Many of these show-worthy examples, were proudly displayed at a county fair, garnering a ribbon, and a reputation, for "Best in Show." Annie, like many women before me, used good old-fashioned-know-how, to create a life they dreamed of. Often these women faced hard times, which made everyday existence a challenge. Fearlessly, these women targeted their dreams and established themselves as winners in life. I have created an "Old Faithfully" good recipe to honor the woman, who so many years ago, walked into a man's world and stole the show. My "Annie Oat-ley" cookies, are blue ribbon worthy. They are a little legendary in their own right, at least in my circle! Enjoy!

Annie Oat-ley Cookies

These are as memorable as a blue-ribbon winner or Annie's sharp shootin' ways. Just sayin'!

1 teaspoon cornstarch
1 ½ teaspoon cinnamon
½ teaspoon nutmeg
1 teaspoon baking soda
1½ cups flour
½ teaspoon salt
2 sticks softened butter, at room temperature
½ cup white sugar
1½ cup brown sugar
2 eggs
1 teaspoon vanilla
4 cups quick minute oatmeal

Inside Scoop: Use a scoop of huckleberry ice cream or flavor of your choice, to make an ice cream sandwich with two cookies!

Preheat oven 350 degrees.

In a small mixing bowl combine the cornstarch, cinnamon, nutmeg, baking soda, flour, and salt. Mix and fluff with a fork and set aside.

In a large bowl mix butter, sugars, eggs, and vanilla, until combined. Then add the dry ingredients. Once thoroughly mixed, add uncooked oatmeal. Use a cookie scoop or small spoon and place rounds onto a cookie sheet and bake for 9-11 minutes, until lightly golden brown.

Charlie Russell

From the playground, on the prairie and inside the walls of the bunkhouse, I dreamed of a life filled with the stories delivered by returning ranch hands off the range. Watching the staples of westerns, on either of our two television channels, were the blueprints for my imagination. Saddlebags, bedrolls, a riding duster, boots, and a hat, were a cowboy's personal inventory. Possessions, minimal as they were, were time-worn and full of character. They had memories of the cowboy's life, written all over them.

"A Quiet Day in Utica," painted in 1907, was one of Charlie Russell's most popular works. The talents of Russell, highlighted his life in Montana. The painter did not grow up in in the Treasure State, but in Missouri. He journeyed to Montana and found employment on a working cattle ranch in Judith Basin County.[85] Like the ranch hands in my imagination, he too, made friends for a lifetime, from his time on the prairie and the range. The painting of "A Quiet Day in Utica," depicted Russell and his friends of a lifetime; general store owner, Charles Lehman and an ex-slave, Mollie Ringgold, standing in front of the mercantile. The setting in Central Montana and Judith Basin County were inspiration for many of Charlie's paintings and where Russell called home for many years. The sunrises and sunsets were his family, while animals, cowboys and Indians were his partners in crime. Charlie was a storyteller. His narrative spoke through his skillful hands, a quiet conversation of his heart. He chose to record history as it were, one sketch, bronze, or painting at a time.

While working as a ranch hand on the Judith Basin spread of Jake Hoover, he received a letter from its owner. It was the dreaded winter of 1886 - 1887. The ranch proprietor, while living in Helena, wanted the run down from Russell about the toll winter had on his herd. The news was not good. The skillful "hand" sent a postcard-sized drawing of a starving cow. Words did not accompany the sketch, as the exposed ribs, said it all. The rancher showed the "story" to several of his wealthy city friends and wrote back to Russell, that he could probably sell a few of the drawings. A career was born, history was made and a record set, that winter of '86 -'87. The harshest winter in Montana proved to be a career changer for Charlie. [86] Montana suffered through the difficult winter, but the severe cold, traveled as far as San Francisco. The "City by the Bay," had a little of the white stuff too. On February 5th, 1887, 37 inches of powder, lay inch upon inch, on the famous bay.[87] Russell's love of Montana, its lifestyle and its inhabitants, were canvas worthy. Central Montana influenced his creative genius. He captured stories of the Old West, the hard-fought war between man and beast, and cowboys vs. Indians.

Later, his wife Nancy, became his manager, promoter and studio model. She was a motivated advocate for her husband's art and possessed great business savvy. Her insight and skill in public relations, helped him become one of the highest paid artists during his time.[88]

In 1926, the artist was called to his home, up yonder. Upon Charlie's death, all school children in the "Electric City," otherwise known as Great Falls, Montana, got the day off. Their school absence allowed them to pay their respects. His coffin was placed in a glass box, driven by four black horses during his funeral procession.[89] The world famous Charles M. Russell Museum located in Great Falls, has Russell's original homestead cabin. The museum also boasts a vast collection of curated Western art and Russell originals. [90] These are all a must see! In early spring the museum hosts their renowned Western art auction. Refer to their website for further information.

400 13th Street North ✎ Great Falls, MT
cmrusell.org ✎ (406) 727-8787

Charlie Russell Brownies, An Artist's Palette

19.9 oz. box of Betty Crocker dark chocolate
    brownie mix
¼ cup water plus 1 tablespoon water
½ cup vegetable oil plus 1 tablespoon oil

2 large eggs
Wilton's assorted candy melting discs
Plastic artist's palettes

Preheat oven to 350 degrees.

In large mixing bowl, add brownie mix, water, oil, and eggs. Mix well, stirring or whisking by hand. Spray a 9 x 13 inch baking dish with non-stick spray. Pour prepared brownie batter into pan and spread smoothly. Bake for approximately 25 minutes, test with a knife and bake for 5 more minutes if necessary.

Cool brownies before decorating.

Next, cut 5 pieces of brownies and placed on the painter's palettes. Cut a small slit towards the back of the brownie and place the brush handle in the slit. (I used 5 different sandwich bags, with 20 discs of different colors in each bag. I melted each bag, one at a time in the microwave for 30 seconds. Turn the bag over and microwave an additional 30 seconds. Cut a corner off and pipe down the brownie. Repeat until all colors are used and all brownies have been decorated with the disc paint.) Use sprinkles or other cake decorating gems to sprinkle on the palette boards.

Note: I purchased a set of two plastic artist's palettes in a package, from the art supply section of Hobby Lobby. Trace a portion of a paintbrush, five times on a piece of paper. Over the tracing, place wax paper. Melt 30 light brown melting discs in a small sandwich bag. Once melted, cut off the tip of the bag and use it to fill in the paint brush outline. Then use a table knife and spread the chocolate smoothly over the pattern.

Caramel Runs Thru 'Em Bars

For the love of family and fishing...

These bars are a baking delight, inspired by Norman Maclean's 1976 novella, "A River Runs Thru It." The book was a reflective masterpiece that drew readers to the deeply moving story of the author and his family. Maclean's work, celebrated the relationship of a father and his sons, their love for one another, and the passion of fly-fishing that bonded them. The artfully told story, cast from the water's edge, shared the pursuit of man vs. fish, and the conflict between them all. The novella inspired the award-winning motion picture, "A River Runs Thru It," where audiences witnessed the intertwining of family, faith, and fish. Life's hard choices and fragile moments were on display in the beautiful movie, cinematic moments highlighted the beauty of Montana. Upon the movie's release, fly fishing in Montana surged. Maclean's tribute to his family, and the sport he loved, reached both reader and viewer alike.[91]

Once you cast your eyes on these "Carmel Runs Thru 'Em Bars," and savor their gooey, tasteful flavors, you will drop a line, that these are your favorite thing ever!

6 tablespoons butter
¾ cup brown sugar
1 egg
1 tsp vanilla
1 cup all-purpose flour

½ teaspoon baking soda
⅛ tsp salt
1 tablespoon milk
7.6 oz. bag of Rolo candies

Preheat oven to 340 degrees. Grease or spray a 9 x 11 glass baking dish.

Unwrap 36 Rolos and cut in half, set aside. Cream butter and brown sugar until light and fluffy. Add milk, egg, and vanilla, mix well. In a small bowl mix flour, soda, and salt, fluff with a fork to make sure it is well mixed. Add to wet ingredients and mix well. Spoon batter into the baking pan and spread evenly. The batter is very sticky, be patient while spreading. Take Rolo slices with caramel side down and make 9 rows across, with 8 rows down. Do not push Rolo's thru the batter, they will melt to the bottom of the pan and it is difficult getting them out. Bake for 16 - 18 minutes, until lightly browned.

Note: Always use a glass baking dish. Metal and aluminum pans cause the bars to be crispy rather than chewy.

Inside Scoop: This is the number one recipe of mine that everyone wants! The light brownie, paired with the caramel, is absolute perfection. I always have this on hand during the holidays, but it makes regular appearances year round.

Hay Bale Trail, What The Hay?

Central Montana hosts the yearly Hay Bale Festival in early September. The first Saturday after Labor Day is a bale of fun in Central, Montana. Neighbors create hay bale attractions for 22 miles, meandering through the highway by Windham, including Hobson and all the way to Utica. Hay bale sculptures are imaginative, clever and artistic. The "bale of fun festival," in 2003, became Montana's Tourism Event of the year, however, Utica offers more events and activities during the festival. [92]

This is Charlie Russell country. His painting passion got its start in Hobson and Utica, which provided much of the artistic background for Russell's most famous works.[85] I think Russell, would appreciate the artistic nature of using bales to create roadside sculptures. Russell country is the canvas, bales the medium, and locals the field artists. Come join the fun in Central Montana, "hay" what do you have to lose?

(406) 423-5234 ✍ montanabailtrail@gmail.com ✍ montanabaletrail.com

Hay Bales

These rice krispie treats come from the recipe box of my Gramma Heintz. She made homemade desserts daily, as there was always impromptu company coming to visit. The Greatest Show on the Prairie's concession stand, sold out of these rice krispie treats, lickety split! Gramma Heintz spelled love, with the letters f-o-o-d! Her abilities as a hostess, were only surpassed by the love she poured into each and every delicious meal or dessert.

5 cups Rice Krispies cereal
3 tablespoons butter
1 package regular marshmallows or 4 cups miniature marshmallows

In a large saucepan, sprayed with non-stick spray, melt butter over low- medium heat. Add marshmallows and stir until melted. Remove pan from heat and add cereal, stir until well mixed.Spray a 13x9x2 pan, with non-stick spray. Spoon krispie mixture and lightly pat to smooth. Cover with foil or plastic wrap, cut into bales when cooled.

Dirty Hay Bales

1 cup white sugar
1 cup white corn syrup
1½ cup smooth peanut butter

4 cups rice krispies cereal
1 cup semi-sweet chocolate chips
1 cup butterscotch chips

In sauce pan, sprayed with non-stick spray, add the sugar and syrup. Cook on medium heat, stirring constantly. Bring to a boil and boil for 2 minutes until sugar is completely dissolved. Remove from heat, add peanut butter and mix well. Add cereal, mixing well. Pour into well sprayed or buttered 13x9x2 baking dish. Melt chocolate and butterscotch chips, mix well, pour over Krispies, and spread evenly. Place in refrigerator to cool. Cut into bars and serve.

Very, Bearly Lemony Bites

Black bears have a diet of fruits, nuts, insects, greens, berries and meats.[82] Their close-up vision is excellent and they see in vivid color, which helps them see small instincts and berries.[81] A grown male bear weighs between 130-660 pounds, while a female weighs between 90-175 pounds. A bear cub's birth weight is between ½ to 1 pound. Cubs stay with their mother for approximately 2 years and often live to be 33 years old.[83] Black bears were known as "beggar bears" in Yellowstone National Park. The bears would hang around the roadsides waiting for visitors to feed them. Visitors fed the bears from their cars, by garbage sights and campsites. Laws were enforced to ban bear feeding in 1970, no roadside feedings are allowed.[84] Feed your little cubs these "beary" delicious cookies, but beware, they will be beggin' for one more!

1 box 18.25 oz. lemon flavored cake mix
3 teaspoons lemon juice
2 oz. cream cheese, softened at room temperature
1 egg

4 oz. Cool Whip
½ of 5 oz. box of Lemon Drop Candy
Powdered sugar on a plate, about ¼ cup

Preheat oven to 350 degrees. Spray cookie sheet with non-stick spray. Place lemon drops in a bag and crush. I use a rolling pin, then pour crushed candies on a plate

In a large bowl, combine cake mix, egg, lemon juice, and cool whip. Batter will be stiff. With a dinner spoon, scoop out a ball of dough, roll in the palm of your hand. Then roll it lightly in candy and then in powdered sugar. Cookies should be 2 inches apart on the baking sheet. Bake for 8-10 minutes until the bottoms are light brown. I use a spatula and look at the bottom of the cookies at the 8 minute mark, to assess if more baking time is required

Church Social, No Bake Chocolate Oatmeal Drop Cookies

During Easter celebrations, I have made these cookies. I spoon them on waxed paper and use a spoon to shape a well in the center, so that they look like a nest. Once they are cooled, I put Jelly Bellies or jelly beans in the center.

2 cups sugar
½ cup cocoa
¼ cup margarine or butter
½ cup milk

½ cup peanut butter
2 cups quick oatmeal
¼ cup chopped walnuts or pecans, optional

Combine sugar, cocoa, margarine/butter, and milk in a pan. On stovetop, bring to a boil on medium to medium-high heat, for at least 3 minutes, stirring constantly. Remove from heat and add the following ingredients in order: peanut butter, oatmeal, and then nuts. Mix well. Using 2 small spoons, scoop and drop cookies on waxed paper. Once cookies are cooled and set, remove from paper and serve.

Date Night with Dori Bars

Every Friday night, Dori and I have a date to discuss life and all the week's events. When we were growing up on the farm, Mom made Date Bars for Yahtzee game nights or for treats during harvest. When my daughter was little I made them for Friday night at the movies. A store box kit was used when we were growing up, but the mix has since been discontinued. However, Mom and I came up with this recipe as a reminder of those good old days. I hope you make a date to have these wonderful bars and many memories to go along with them!

Crust and Topping:
1¾ cups quick minute oatmeal
1½ cups all-purpose flour, sifted
1 cup brown sugar, packed tightly in measuring cup
1 teaspoon baking soda
½ teaspoon cinnamon
½ teaspoon salt
1 cup cold butter, diced into small pieces
½ cup finely chopped pecans, optional

Filling:
2½ cups chopped dates, chop very fine
¾ cup sugar
¾ cup water
⅛ teaspoon cinnamon
1 teaspoon vanilla
1 teaspoon almond extract
2-3 extra tablespoons melted butter to mix in the last half of crust

Preheat oven to 350 degrees.

In a large bowl, combine dry crust/topping ingredients, then cut in butter, mixing until crumbly. Next add pecans, if you are using them in the recipe. Set aside.

In a medium saucepan, place filling ingredients on medium heat, until bubbly. Reduce heat to low and cover. Simmer on low for 10 minutes, stirring occasionally.

Spray a 13 x 9 x 2 glass baking dish with nonstick spray, use ½ - ¾ of the crust/topping mixture and press into the bottom of the pan and up the sides just slightly, making a bed. Spread date filling evenly in pan. Add the 2 -3 tablespoons of melted butter into remaining oat topping and mix well, spreading evenly on top. The extra butter in the crust, makes the topping chewy and not dry. Bake for 25 minutes or until golden brown.

131

Desserts & Cakes

Custard's Last Stand, **A Trifle Too Late**

Custer's Last Stand Reenactment & Little Big Horn Days, occurs each summer in Hardin, Montana. The battlefield is 6 miles west of Hardin.[93] The reenactment portrays the events of June 25, 1876, where Lieutenant Colonel George Armstrong Custer and his U.S. 7th Cavalry were defeated by the Plains Indians. Chief Sitting Bull, a medicine man of the Hunkpapa Sioux Tribe, led warriors from the Cheyenne, Arapaho, and Sioux Nations.[94] The Indian warriors claimed victory over the 7th Calvary and the "yellow-haired" military leader, known as Custer. [95] The reenactment pays tribute to the events of the bloody battle and the historical impact of adversarial cultures. The authentic nature of costumes, characters, and location, offers audiences the opportunity to have a visual glimpse into history and observe this infamous battle. Little Bighorn Days offers a variety of events reflecting the historical period of 1876. A parade, grand ball, quilt show, living history, and historical book fair, are all part of the event's line-up.[96] Shoppers will delight in the art and craft show in the center of downtown. Hardin's community members work tirelessly, presenting a wonderful event and offering locals and tourists alike, the opportunity to look back in time. The events are a celebration of the Old West, cultural heritage, and the famous Battle of the Bighorn.

Big Horn County Historical Museum 🖉 1163 3ʳᵈ Street East, Hardin MT
(406) 665-1671 🖉 bighorncountymuseum.org

---

1 lemon sliced thinly, with a slit on one side to center (to be twisted)	6 oz. frozen container of cool whip
½ cup lemon juice	1 lemon cream cake (bakery section in store)
½ cup sugar	10 crushed Nilla wafers
2 small boxes instant lemon pudding mix	1 box of Dream Whip
¼ cup powdered sugar with 2 tablespoons lemon juice	3 cups cold milk
	Can of spray whipped cream (aerosol type)

Note: The dish will be served in a trifle bowl or large footed compote dish. I strongly recommend that a clear glass container is used, to display the beautiful layers of ingredients.

Cut the lemon pound cake into 1-inch cubes and cover with plastic wrap, so it does not dry out. In a small saucepan, heat sugar and lemon juice together, on medium heat. Stir and heat until the sugar is completely dissolved, then set aside. In a mixing bowl, whisk 2 envelopes of dream whip and 2 cups of cold milk, until soft peaks are formed (approximately 5 minutes). Next, add the packets of lemon pudding, and milk, to the whipped cream mixture. Whip for an additional 2-3 minutes or until thick. Add powdered sugar and mix well.

In a compote or trifle bowl, assemble the following: half of the cubed cake on bottom layer, then drizzle half of the lemon syrup, top with half of the lemon pudding mixture, and half of the cool whip. Repeat this for the next layer, with the remaining lemon cake, lemon syrup, lemon pudding mixture, and cool whip. Next, spray the whipped cream decoratively on top in circles. Then sprinkle the crushed Nilla wafers on top and place twisted lemon slices for a garnish on top or on the sides of the trifle bowl. Serves 6-8.

Inside Scoop: I have made this in individual servings, using jelly jars, tying a ribbon holding the spoon upright. This serving style is great for buffets or BBQs!

Pink Lemonade Dessert

This recipe came to my grandmother from Merle Wilhelm. She was such a special friend, neighbor and downright wonderful woman. Hardworking Merle could hang a fresh load of laundry faster than a gunslinger at the O.K. Corral! She attached those wooden clothespins to a laundry line, quicker than "pudge" went to my thighs. She was simply amazing. I remember her making her own soap in the kitchen. Who did that? Merle did that, and so much more. As you make this dessert, realize that it won't last long! Be prepared for your taste buds to sing like a meadowlark in spring.

Crust:
60 Ritz crackers, crushed
¼ cup powdered sugar
½ cup butter, melted

Filling:
1 can sweetened condensed milk
1 large container of cool whip
6 oz. can of frozen pink lemonade, thawed

Spray a 9 x 13 pan with non-stick spray. Mix together crushed crackers and powdered sugar. Stir in melted butter. Set aside 1/3 cup of the crust mixture. Spread remaining crust mixture evenly into the bottom of the pan. Mix together filling ingredients and pour over crust. Sprinkle reserved crust mixture on top. Cover and refrigerate. Serve when filling is set.

Call Out the Calvary,

Espresso Yo' Self Cupcakes

15.25 oz. box devil's food cake mix
1 chocolate pudding snack cup
3 tablespoons brewed espresso
Cupcake liners
Muffin tin

Follow directions on the back of the cake mix. Stir in espresso, mixing well, followed by chocolate pudding cup. Pour batter into muffin liners and bake for 19 minutes. Check a cupcake by inserting a toothpick in the center. If the toothpick comes out clean, they are done. An additional 2 minutes might be needed to thoroughly bake, depending on the size of the muffin tin. Makes 18 cupcakes.

Make Ganache with the espresso added, lightly spoon on cupcakes (page 159).

Chet Huntley

Newscaster. Visionary. Outdoorsman. Montanan. Chet Huntley, born in Cardwell, Montana, became co-anchor of NBC's evening news program, called The Huntley-Brinkley Report. Huntley also gained notoriety, as the "Founding Father of Big Sky."[98]

Big Sky Resort, opened in 1974, is located in Gallatin County, 45 miles from Bozeman, Montana. The resort, which resides at the base of Lone Mountain, was Huntley's vision. Skiing at Big Sky includes 5,800 acres of breathtaking terrain. Views from its 11,166-foot vertical peak, spans four different mountain ranges, two national park ranges, and three different states.[99] Perhaps Chet Huntley's comment, "Maybe where there's clarity of air, there's clarity of thought." was inspired by the beauty, of what was to become, the resort of Big Sky.[100] The Montana native's personal collection, of his typewriter, roll top desk, and other memorabilia can be seen at the Visitor Center, at Big Sky's entrance.[101] Chet's popularity as co-anchor of the nightly news, made him a household name. Huntley's vision of Big Sky has created a personal legacy.

The resort attracts tourists and locals year-round. It's reputation for amazing ski conditions with vistas to match, puts Big Sky on many people's "must do list." His statement, "Just as important as working for the good life, is finding a place to enjoy it." reflects his love of Montana and his vision for the resort.[102] Make time to see and enjoy Big Sky. Come see, what Chet saw! This recipe, like Chet Huntley, is award winning. When you serve this delicious cake, the oohs and ahs will be broadcast louder than any nightly news report! My recipe for this cake, is another one of my "Old Faithfuls", and is one that is often requested.

Chet Huntley Cake

15.25 oz. box yellow cake mix
7 oz. almond paste
3 eggs
1½ cups coconut
1½ cups brown sugar
½ cup chopped pecans
1 teaspoon nutmeg
2 teaspoons cinnamon
1 teaspoon vanilla
2 tablespoons plain yogurt
1 cup water
½ cup oil

Preheat oven to 350 degrees. Spray a fluted or Bundt pan with non-stick spray. A 9 x 13 greased pan may also be used instead of the Bundt pan.

In a large mixing bowl, stir cake mix, and add eggs one at a time. Mixing well after each one. Add yogurt and mix thoroughly, add water and oil, mix again. Add brown sugar, nutmeg, cinnamon, and vanilla, mixing well. Next, add in coconut, stirring until blended.

In a small microwave safe bowl, cut almond paste into small slices. Place in microwave, long enough to soften the paste. Remove and beat slightly, then add to the batter mix. Pour batter into cake pan of your choice and bake for 32-35 minutes. Check doneness by poking a knife or skewer into center of cake. Check every three minutes, until completely done.

Note: Fresh slices of peaches, strawberries, or raspberries, sweetened to taste, with whipped cream on top is delicious. I have also used frozen fruit and added ¼ to ½ cup of sugar to sweeten.

Berry Lovely Mascarpone Filling

8 oz. container of mascarpone, room temperature
4 oz. cream cheese, room temperature
1 teaspoon vanilla
⅔ cup powdered sugar
¾ cup of frozen blackberries, thawed
¼ cup huckleberry jelly, (any other berry jelly/jam will work fine)

In a large mixing bowl, cream the mascarpone and cream cheese. Add vanilla, mix again. Next, add powdered sugar, mix well. Add the mashed berries, mix well, then add the jelly of choice, with a final mixing. Refrigerate the filling. When cake has cooled, spread the mascarpone on baked cake, or cover and chill.

Inside Scoop: This topping is easily scooped and placed on an individual cake serving. You can also add fresh berries, flowers, and leaves, to adorn the top of a cake, making it a very festive treat!

Tudie's Rhubarb Crunch Cake

½ cup butter softened
1½ cups brown sugar
2 eggs
1 teaspoon vanilla
1 teaspoon baking soda
1 cup cultured sour cream.
2 cups all-purpose flour
½ cup chopped nuts
1½ cups chopped rhubarb, cut into ¼" pieces

Topping:
½ cup sugar
1 teaspoon cinnamon
½ teaspoon nutmeg
2 tablespoons melted butter

Preheat oven to 350 degrees. Spray with a non-stick spray, a 9 x 13 x 2 inch pan.

Cream together butter and brown sugar. Add eggs, vanilla, baking soda, and sour cream to the batter, add alternating scoops of flour and nuts, until well mixed. Then add rhubarb, mix well.

Pour batter and spread evenly into pan. Combine the topping ingredients, mixing well. Sprinkle on top of batter. Bake 40 minutes. Serve sliced plain, with whipped cream or ice cream.

Gussied Up and Ready to Go Cake

Store bought angel food cake works wonderfully for this recipe!

3 tablespoons brewed coffee
10.2 oz. jar of mini Nutella, (you will only use half)
⅓ cup powdered sugar
10 crushed Nilla wafers
2-3 bananas, sliced bananas
Angel food cake, purchased or homemade

Brew coffee as follows: ¼ cup of coffee grinds and ½ cup water. When finished brewing, set coffee aside.

Mix Nutella, powdered sugar, and brewed coffee, together in a medium sized mixing bowl. Place a slice of angel food cake on a plate. Drizzle the Nutella sauce over the slice of cake, then place banana slices on top. Lastly, sprinkle crushed Nilla wafers over bananas. If desired, place a dollop of Glacier Whipped Cream (page 155) on top!

Inside Scoop: The Nutella sauce is wonderful on ice cream, with or without the bananas, whipped cream and crushed Nilla wafers!

Yogo Sapphire Crepes

5 oz. bag of ready-made crepes, 10 crepes

Filling:
8 oz. cream cheese, softened to room temperature
7 oz. jar of marshmallow cream
4 tablespoons powdered sugar
4 tablespoons sour cream
4 teaspoons lemon juice
2 teaspoon vanilla extract

Blueberry Sauce:
2 tablespoons sugar
1 tablespoon cornstarch
¾ cup water
1 pint fresh or frozen blueberries, thawed
1½ tablespoons lemon juice

In a medium size bowl, place cream cheese and beat with an electric mixer until smooth. Add marshmallow cream and mix well. Add lemon juice, vanilla, and sour cream, mixing wel. Then add powdered sugar and beat until smooth. Cover and refrigerate.

In a medium saucepan, heat water and sugar over medium heat. Stir until boiling, add cornstarch, stir well and then add blueberries. Mixing well and boil until thickened. Remove from heat and cover, keeping filling warm.

Fill each crepe with filling, about 1½ spoon-full. Spread on crepe like frosting and fold in half and then half again, making the crepe into a ¼ piece. Repeat until all crepes have been filled. Place on individual plates or a platter. Serve blueberry topping warm, either on the side or on top of crepes.

Celebration Cake

This cake is my favorite summertime treat! Every 4th of July, it makes an appearance. I surround the cake with a colorful bounty of berries. Their colors pay tribute to "Old Glory." For extra impact, I place small American flags and sparkling birthday candles around the perimeter. As seen in the picture, a reproduction gold miner's pan, serves as the cake platter. Celebration or not, this cake will wow your guests! The presentation is just as memorable as any fireworks display. Whenever you choose to make and serve this luscious cake, it will be cause for a celebration.

Angel food cake, (either a premade, purchased cake or one that is homemade)

Pink Lemonade Glaze:
1 cup powdered sugar
½ can pink lemonade concentrate, thawed (in frozen food section)
1 teaspoon of red food coloring
1 tablespoon heavy cream
Raspberries, blackberries and blueberries, approximately ½ pint of each

Mix all glaze ingredients well and drizzle over angel food cake. Decorate cake and/or platter with berries, alternating the different varieties, around the edge of cake.

Sapphire Village Coffee Cake

Batter:
½ cup vegetable oil
½ cup milk
1 egg, beaten

¾ cup sugar
1½ cups flour
2 teaspoons baking powder
½ teaspoon salt
2 tablespoons plain yogurt
1½ cup blueberries

Topping:
½ cup sugar
1 tablespoon flour
½ teaspoon cinnamon
2 tablespoons butter, melted

Preheat oven to 375 degrees. Grease a 9 x 12 inch baking pan.

Combine oil, milk, and yogurt, until well mixed. In a medium size mixing bowl, add ¾ cup sugar, flour, baking powder, and salt. Fluff with a fork and add to the liquid mixture. Gently fold in blueberries mix well. Pour batter into baking dish.

In a small bowl combine the topping ingredients. Mix well and sprinkle over batter.

Bake for 25-30 minutes, use a sharp knife or toothpick to check for doneness.

Catch a Cowboy, **German Chocolate Cake**

A cake so good, it will bring you to the altar! I propose you make this delicious cake, if you're looking for a compliment or a commitment. Just sayin'!

15.25 oz. box of dark chocolate cake mix
1 chocolate pudding snack cup
¼ cup sour cream
2 tablespoons plain yogurt
3 eggs
½ cup vegetable oil
1¼ cups water
¾ cup semi-sweet chocolate chips, chopped

Preheat oven to 350 degrees. Spray a 9 x 13 inch glass baking dish with non-stick spray. In a large mixing bowl, place cake mix, pudding, eggs, water, oil, and mix well. Add sour cream and yogurt and mix until well blended. Fold in chocolate chips, mixing well. Pour batter in the baking dish. Bake for about 30 minutes. Check to see if a knife comes clean, testing for doneness. Bake at 5-minute intervals and recheck for doneness.

Note: Since the cake is so light and airy, I refrigerate it before frosting. It is much easier to spread the gooey frosting on the cold cake. I also prefer to keep it chilled, even when serving.

Coconut Pecan Frosting:
1½ cups evaporated milk
1½ cups sugar
4 egg yolks, whipped
1½ teaspoons vanilla
2 teaspoons almond extract
2 cups sweet flaked coconut
1½ cups chopped pecans
¼ teaspoon salt
12 tablespoons butter

In a medium size saucepan, melt butter and stir in milk. Add in salt, vanilla, and almond extract. Slowly whisk in eggs, careful to cook on medium-low, as to not scramble the eggs. Once the liquid starts to thicken (and is well incorporated), add sugar. Continue cooking, stirring constantly, approximately 10 minutes. Remove from heat. When frosting base is warm but not hot, add coconut and pecans. Let cool and frost on a chilled cake.

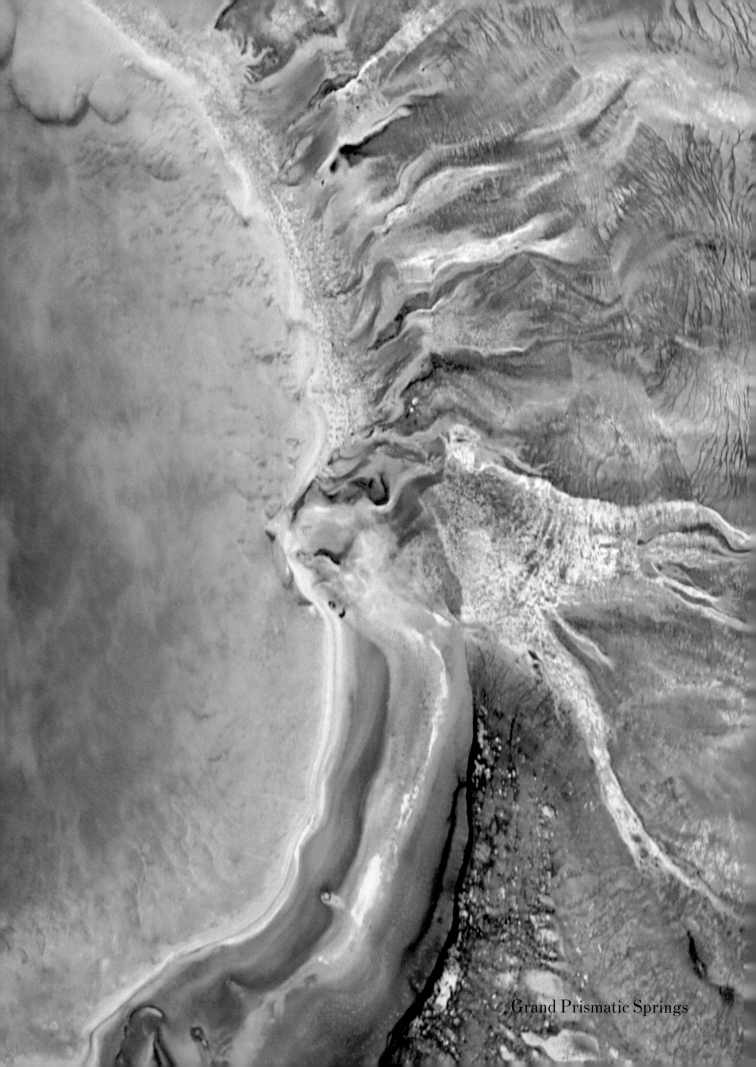

Grand Prismatic Springs

Yellowstone Hot Pots

The Grand Prismatic Springs, located at Midway Geyser Basin, is the largest hot spring in the U.S. It is a boiling lake of vivid colors, which represents the prisms of the rainbow. The beautiful Prismatic Spring, is the third largest hot pot in the world! Hot pots and the famous Prismatic Spring are located in Yellowstone National Park. Minerals contribute to the array of colors seen at the various hot pots.[97]

My edible version of nature's hot pots, will bring a lot of curiosity seekers too! When guests realize the beautiful pot is edible, they are amazed. The Grand Prismatic Springs, was the inspiration for these delicious treats. What will inspire yours?

Several bags of candy melting discs, colors of your choice
Sandwich bags
Wilton shot glass mold, with 8 cavities (I purchased mine at Walmart in the wedding aisle)

Choose melting discs of your choice, you can do individual colors in separate bags or place a mixture of colors and mix when melted. I used approximately 15 discs in 4-5 colors. Melt discs in microwave, in 30 second intervals, turning bag over every 30 seconds, until you feel the discs have melted. Swirl, by pushing colors into one another. Then snip a corner of the bag off and pipe into each Teflon cavity. Let stand to cool, peel back the Teflon form to release the pot. Do not put in direct sun, as they can melt.

Inside Scoop: I have used these as flower vases for events, at individual place settings (do not place in direct sun or they will melt). As individual desserts, I have placed scoops of ice cream inside each hot pot. Alternately, I have filled the hot pots with a homemade mousse using the recipe for "A Tisket a Tasket, A White Chocolate Mousse Basket", page 154. A lovely option is to top it with Glacier Whipped Cream, page 155.

Pies, Toppings, & Sweet Sauces

Huckleberries

In late July, the Flathead Valley, Kootenai National Forest and Glacier National Park area are full of huckleberries. Local stands and restaurants cater to recipes featuring the coveted, purplish colored berry. Huckleberries are a distant relative to the blueberry. Both berries have antioxidant properties and top the list of healthy berries. These berries love an acidic mountain soil and an elevation of 3,500-7,200 feet above sea level.[19] A wild patch of berries, are an attractive find for bakers/cooks and a soon-to-be hibernating bear. In the fall, a third of a bear's diet for winter hibernation is huckleberries.[103]

Huckleberries make their way into memorable summer dishes and desserts, but they have also played a part in Montana history. In August 1805, Captain Meriwether Lewis, of the Lewis and Clark Expedition, made a journal notation stating he had wild huckleberries for breakfast. In addition, Native American Indians used salmon bones to remove the berries from bushes and dried them for pemmican, a meat/berry mixture, much like jerky. Berries were also used in "cake" that they used to snack on while traveling.[103] Chokecherries and huckleberries, once juiced, served as a stain for Native American Indians to color their faces and decorate animal hides.[104]

The wonderful flavors of huckleberries enhance barbeque sauces, jellies, jams, syrups, and baked desserts. The delicious and distinctive flavor of huckleberries are as memorable as the big sky from which they are grown. This is our favorite berry pie! It is delicious!!

Dori's Huckleberry Pie

1 prepared pie crust
¾ cup sugar
½ teaspoon salt
1 cup huckleberries
⅔ cup water (with 2 tablespoons lemon juice, optional)
2½ tablespoons cornstarch
2 tablespoons butter
2 cups fresh or frozen huckleberries
Whipped cream
Ice cream

In a medium size saucepan, place sugar, salt, one cup of huckleberries and mix well. Stir over medium heat until it reaches a bubbly boil. Mix cornstarch and water together, then whisk into berry filling. Stir well, until incorporated and thick. Remove from heat and add butter. Mix until butter is melted into berry filling. Stir in remaining 2 cups of huckleberries.

Pour filling into prepared crust, cover and refrigerate. Whipped cream or ice cream may be served with the pie. My family prefers this pie slightly warm, with ice cream.

Been There, Ate That, Huckleberry Crisp

Filling:
4 cups huckleberries
½ cup of huckleberry jelly or jam
¼ cup flour
1 cup sugar
2 tablespoons heavy cream
1 teaspoon vanilla
1 teaspoon almond extract
3 tablespoons butter, diced or sliced

Topping:
⅓ cup melted butter
¼ cup flour
1 cup quick oatmeal, uncooked
½ cup brown sugar
½ teaspoon cinnamon
⅛ teaspoon nutmeg
¼ cup finely chopped pecans

Optional toppings:
Huckleberry syrup
15 Wilton white chocolate candy melting discs

In a small mixing bowl, combine the filling ingredients (except diced butter), stir well. Set aside. In a large bowl, mix the topping ingredients and stir well. Then add the melted butter and combine.

In a 9 x 13 baking dish, spray with non-stick spray. Evenly spread the filling on the bottom of the pan. Then sprinkle the topping mix on top of filling. Place sliced/diced butter randomly on the topping. Bake for 25-30 minutes, until golden brown.

Before serving, if available, drizzle heated huckleberry syrup over crust in a zig-zag pattern. Next, place white chocolate discs in a Ziploc bag, put in microwave for 30 seconds, turn bag over and heat for another 20 seconds, until soft and melted. Massage bag, to make sure all discs are melted. With scissors, cut a narrow tip off one corner of the bag. Drizzle in zig-zag pattern, opposite of the pattern that you did with syrup. Serve with Glacier Whipped Cream (page 155) or vanilla ice cream.

Banana Cream Pie

In the picture, the banana cream pie is sitting next to a No. 5 can, that I decorated as a multi-use container. The photos are special moments of my daughter growing up. I photocopied the images and used double-sided tape to adhere them to the can. Then I used crystal, pearls, and shabby chic embellishments to decorate and highlight photo edges and the can borders. At my daughter's graduation party, the decorated can served as a vase with fresh cut flowers from the garden.

I have also used similarly decorated cans for other functions. They have served as cake stands, with a platter resting on the top, a gift card receptacle, and gift "can" instead of a gift basket. I have also used them as other types of gift baskets. For example, I would fill the can with treasures, thoughtful items, and personalized gifts. Then cellophane would be wrapped around the can with a large bow. I made these for Christmas for gifts and they were a hit! Let your imagination take over!

2½ cups milk
(2) 14 oz. cans sweetened condensed milk
2 boxes 3.4 oz. banana cream instant pudding and pie filling
6 medium bananas
2 teaspoons vanilla
3 teaspoons banana flavored extract
2 pie crusts, prepared or homemade

In a medium size bowl, mix milk and sweetened condensed milk, then add the pudding packets and mix again. In a small bowl, place 2 bananas and beat until smooth, add to the pudding mixture, blending well. Add vanilla, banana extract and mix again.

Slice remaining bananas and place slices on the bottom of pie crusts. Pour the custard mixture over the banana slices.

Place plastic wrap over the custard, to prevent a film from forming when cooled. Cool pies in refrigerator for at least 2 hours. Serve with whipped cream or a meringue topping.

Gramma's Original Frosting or Milky Way Bites

2 cups white sugar
1½ cubes chocolate, from a 4 oz. box of Baker's semi--
    sweet chocolate bar
1 cup butter
½ cup white corn syrup
½ cup evaporated milk
1 teaspoon vanilla

For Milky Way Bites:
½ cup semi-sweet chocolates chips
1 box of premade chocolate cups or boxes
Turtles original bite sized candies

In a medium saucepan, mix sugar, cubes of choco-late, butter, corn syrup, and evaporated milk. Bring to a rolling boil. Boil for one minute. For a firmer frosting, continue to boil 1½ minutes. Remove from heat and add vanilla, beat until it becomes a creamy spreading consistency.

Inside Scoop: Add ½ cup semi-sweet choc-olate chips to the frosting, mixing well. Spoon the filling/frosting into the choc-olate cups. Top off with a ¼ slice of a

149

Savannah's Chocolate Derby, Mousse Pie

One Easter, my daughter Savannah and I decided it was time to create a new dessert. This mousse pie is the result of our creative endeavor. For a lovely Derby luncheon, I provided beautiful spectator picture hats for my guests, complete with Savannah's Derby Pie. Chopped Andes Mints decorated the top of the derby dessert, giving a nod to the legendary mint juleps. When I was researching the famous "Run for the Roses," I discovered a Montana connection. Noah Armstrong, from Twin Bridges, Montana, raised a copper-toned stallion who raced in the 1889 Kentucky Derby.[105] This was also the same year as our statehood.[106]

Noah named his treasured and winning race horse, Spokane.[105] The stallion grew up grazing on Montana grasses, in the arid climate of the Tobacco Root Mountains. The Derby favorite Proctor Knott had odds of 2-1 to win, while Spokane came in with 10-1 odds. The pride of Montana and for that matter, the west, had a surprising performance. It is reported that a shocking silence was felt in the grandstands, when Spokane completed the mile and a half race in a record time of 2:34.5 minutes. Fans, sportswriters, and people in the know, referred to the win as pure luck. After the unexpected victory, Spokane ran in the famous Clark Stakes and the American Derby. Armstrong's instincts of his horse's ability were proven accurate when Spokane won those races as well. Today, those three races are comparable to winning the Triple Crown. Spokane's derby record was held up until 1896, at which time the race was shortened to one and a quarter mile. Therefore, his record has never been broken![107] Spokane was retired in Twin Bridges, at the Doncaster Barn where he was raised.[105]

The beautiful Doncaster Round Barn now accommodates, parties, celebrations, and weddings. The barn is in close proximity to the location where the Lewis and Clark Expedition camped along the river. Captain Clark named the majestic area, the Jefferson Valley/River.[105]

While researching the derby, I also discovered that horse racing in Louisville, has another connection to Montana. Meriwether Lewis Clark, Jr., the grandson of William Clark, was instrumental in starting the

Kentucky Derby. It seems that the Clark men were on the hunt for new adventures and discoveries. William Clark, the famous grandfather of Meriwether Lewis Clark, Jr., inspired the younger Clark to seek his own adventures. In 1872, the younger Clark travelled to Europe and became fascinated with racing history across the Atlantic. He was eager to follow European tradition, so he established a jockey club in Louisville. In 1874, land owned by his uncles John and Henry Churchill, became the property for the famous Churchill Downs, home of the Kentucky Derby. [108]

2 Oreo cookie crusts (found in the baking aisle)
4 tablespoons melted butter.
1 quart of mint chocolate chip ice cream
1 small bag of Andes Mints
8 oz. cream cheese, room temperature
7 oz. jar marshmallow cream
2¾ cups heavy cream
1½ cups semi-sweet chocolate chips
Springform cheesecake pan, 10-inch size

Chill a large mixing bowl and beaters in freezer for 10-15 minutes before using.

Remove Oreo cookie crusts from pie tins, forking them into a medium-sized bowl. Add melted butter and mix well. Then pour into, a greased cheesecake/springform pan. Pat crust on bottom and up sides to create a shell for mousse. Refrigerate. Combine cream cheese with marshmallow cream in medium bowl. Set aside.

In a double boiler, melt chocolate chips and ½ cup heavy cream. Mix well, stirring until completely melted, then turn off heat. Leave pan as is, to keep mixture warm.

In a chilled bowl with chilled beaters, beat remaining heavy cream until soft peaks are formed. Add the marshmallow/cream cheese mixture and blend well. Fold in the chocolate and heavy cream mixture. Mix well. Pour into refrigerated crust and place in freezer for 2 hours.

Release springform pan and run a knife around edges. Remove band from pie, then run a long knife under the crust and between the pan bottom. Slide a knife around entire base. Place pie on a serving platter or cake stand.

Before serving, place scoops of mint chocolate chip ice cream around edges, with Andes Mints on top. You can also add chocolate curls, or whipped cream. If plating individually, a dollop of whipped cream and graded chocolate works well, followed by a drizzle of chocolate syrup.

Pumpkin Pie

15 oz. can pumpkin pie filling
4 oz. can sweetened condensed milk
2 eggs
⅛ teaspoon nutmeg
⅛ teaspoon cloves
½ teaspoon ginger

½ teaspoon salt
1½ teaspoons pumpkin spice
1½ teaspoons cinnamon
½ cup white sugar
¼ cup brown sugar
9½ inch pie crust

Preheat oven to 415 degrees.

Spray a 9½ inch pie plate with non-stick spray. Lay pie crust in dish, spread evenly and crimp edges on pan.

Note: I usually make enough dough or use a second pie crust and cut leaves. Then bake them until golden brown, on a cookie sheet that has been sprayed with a non-stick spray.

Mix the remaining ingredients, blending well. Pour pie filling in the uncooked pie crust. Bake for 15 minutes. Then lower oven temperature to 350 degrees and bake for 40-45 minutes, until a knife inserted in the pie comes clean. Cool to room temperature and refrigerate until ready to serve.

When I plate up slices of the pie, I top with Glacier Peak Whipped Cream (page 155), adding the cooked pie crust leaves last. The presentation is always as good as the taste.

Inside Scoop: If your pie pan or tin seems quite full, place on a cookies sheet, lined with foil to catch any bubbling over. I also prefer using a glass pie plate when baking the pie.

Fleur Pizza

1 package almond bark
Bowl of edible flowers, washed and patted dry, stems off
Rosemary sprigs
Dried thyme leaves
Pizza pan, with parchment paper cut to fit

Following the package directions, melt ¾ of the bag of almond bark, in a microwavable safe container. Check bark a couple of times, to make sure it does not burn. When bark is completely melted, evenly spread on the parchment paper. Place edible flowers on top of bark, lightly pressing flowers down. Sprinkle the herbs randomly, for interest. When the bark is cooled, use a large knife to cut into pizza slices. Plate and serve.

Inside Scoop: For a bridal shower, party favor, I made this edible bark. I used alphabet shaped cookie cutters. I cut the bark using the first initial of each guest's name, wrapped them in a cello bag, decorated with ribbon and placed them on the dinner plates. They served as a visual extension of the table decor, but also a guest favor. The favors were gorgeous, and the compliments were abundant.

I have also cut the bark into squares and inserted them into small, square vases (purchased at the Dollar Store), filled with silk flowers. Do not add water for real flowers or sit them in the sun. For Mother's Day, I prepared gift baskets, with tea, the edible bark, pansy cookies (page 119), bouquets of flowers, gardening gloves, knee pads, and a digging spade. These were so fun! They made a beautiful presentation, and did I mention...unforgettable?

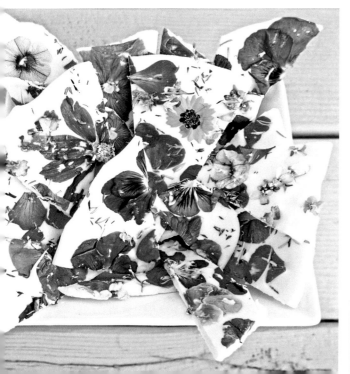

A Tisket, A Tasket,

A White Chocolate Mousse Basket

8 oz. package of cream cheese, softened
7 oz. jar of marshmallow creme
3 cups heavy cream
3 boxes of 4 oz. Baker's white chocolate squares
2 teaspoons vanilla
16 oz. bag frozen raspberries, thawed
1¼ cup sugar
16 oz. package of phyllo dough,
   thaw only 1 sleeve (8 oz.)
Muffin tin

Preheat oven to 350 degrees. Spray muffin tin centers with non-stick spray.

In a small bowl, stir 1 cup sugar into thawed raspberries and refrigerate. Remove phyllo dough from freezer and let thaw for 15 minutes at room temperature.

Unwrap all the boxes of the white chocolate squares, then break into small pieces. In a microwaveable safe container, mix ½ cup cream and white chocolate squares. Melt in microwave for 1 minute. Remove container and stir, until well melted, do this in 30 second intervals, watching carefully, as to not scorch or burn the chocolate. Stir and set aside.

In a large bowl, use an electric mixer and beat cream cheese until smooth. Add marshmallow creme, mix together, then mix in vanilla. Set aside. In a medium size bowl, beat remaining whipped cream until soft peaks are formed. Softy whip together the cream cheese/marshmallow creme mixture, and melted white chocolate/heavy cream ingredients. Cover and refrigerate for 4 hours.

Take one phyllo dough sleeve and slice the sheets in half. Place a single cut sheet in a muffin tin, press into the inside bowl of tin and up and over the edge. Place another sheet in the opposite direction of the first one, press down, making a basket. Alternate creating baskets in every other tin, allowing the dough to overflow, over the muffin cup. Spray dough with non-stick spray and sprinkle remaining sugar lightly on the top of "baskets." Bake for 4-5 minutes, until golden brown.

Right before serving your guests, place a basket on a plate or bowl, add 2 soup spoons of mousse to each basket and spoon raspberries on top. Use a licorice strand or two candy canes to make a handle. Place the handle in mousse right before serving.

Inside Scoop: During Christmas, I use two candy canes as the basket handle, I place chocolates wrapped like mini presents on the plate, chocolate foil wrapped kisses or nonpareils. At Easter, I place shredded coconut in a Ziploc bag with green food coloring. Close the bag and massage color into coconut. Place the basket on the coconut, so it looks like grass, sprinkle jelly beans, malted milk eggs or Jelly Bellies on the side, with a licorice handle.

Glacier Whipped Cream

Glacier whipped cream is a family favorite, as is Glacier National Park, for whom it gets its name. Montana's second national park has rugged snow-covered peaks, glacier-carved valleys, sparkling waters, and vistas for miles. The park is known as the "Crown Jewel of the Continent," as its peaks topped with snow, is often seen year-round. In 1910, the park was declared the 10th national park by President Taft.[109]

The famous actor Robin Williams, was in Glacier National Park while filming the movie, "What Dreams May Come." He said, "If it isn't God's backyard, he certainly lives nearby."[110] There is so much to say about Glacier, but I think Williams sums it up quite nicely. If you haven't made a trip to see this magnificent park, I recommend it as a bucket list priority!

Glacier has been nicknamed, "America's Switzerland." The lodges in the park have gabled roofs, expansive balconies, and exposed beams, all reminiscent of Swiss architecture. There are 375 historic buildings and structures scattered throughout the park.[111] The scenic "Going to the Sun" highway is around 50 miles long and considered an engineering feat. Travelers can expect the route to take about two hours, without stopping. The highest point of the famous road is Logan Pass at 6,646 ft. Along this scenic highway, bighorn sheep and mountain goats are often seen. Wildflowers, waterfalls, and epic mountain scenery makes travelling the highway extraordinarily memorable.[112]

⅓ cup powdered sugar
⅔ cup heavy cream
1 teaspoon vanilla extract
1 teaspoon almond extract

Place heavy cream in a bowl and beat until soft peaks are formed. Add powdered sugar, vanilla, and almond extract. Whip until peaks can stand when mixer blades are removed. Chill until ready to serve.

Note: For a sturdy cream that does not separate after a day or two in the refrigerator, make sure to whip the cream first, then add the powdered sugar.

Lake McDonald-Glacier Park

Missouri Mud Pie, with Continental Divide Topping

The Missouri River is North America's second longest river, starting in western Montana and ending north of St. Louis, Missouri. The Gallatin, Madison, and Jefferson Rivers in Montana, all flow into the Missouri. During the Expedition, Lewis and Clark were the first people to explore its entire length.[113] The famous river, laden with heavy silt, has been nicknamed the "Big Muddy" or "Muddy Mo."[114]

The Continental Divide runs along the crests of the Rocky Mountains from Canada to Mexico, literally dividing the waters of the North American Continent. Montana is known as the headwaters of the divide and is the only state with a triple divide, allowing water to flow to the Pacific, Atlantic, and Hudson Bay.[115]

This delicious mud pie with the Continental Divide topping, is by far the best mud pie you will ever make! The mountain rich candies, white water cream topping, and dirty cookie crust, will leave your taste buds on a Rocky Mountain high! Your guests will be thrilled that you have made them this gooey and delicious "muddy dessert."

Crust:
(2) 6 oz. Oreo crust pie shells
4 tablespoons melted butter
10 or 12-inch springform pan

Filling and Topping:
1 half gallon of Wilcoxson's Chocolate Runs Through It ice cream, softened
1 half gallon Cream & Coffee Fudge ice cream, softened
12.25 oz. jar caramel topping
1 king size Heath Bar, crushed (I break bars into quarters and place in a small plastic bag and hit with a rolling bin to make them finer pieces)
1 king size Turtle Caramel Candy (contains 3 turtles), cut into small pieces (I use kitchen shears)
¼ cup slivered almonds
1 can of aerosol whipped cream, optional
1 prepared recipe of ganache (page 159) or remaining ½ jar of caramel topping

Preheat oven to 350 degrees. Line a cookie sheet or pizza pan with foil.

Remove the Oreo crusts into a medium size bowl, use a fork to make the cookie crumbles soft. Add melted butter and mix well. Pour into springform pan that has been sprayed with non-stick spray. Use your fingers to evenly pat the crust on the bottom and up the sides of the pan. Place pan with crust, on foil-lined pan and bake for 7 minutes. Remove from oven and let cool, or place in freezer on a towel and freeze until chilled.

Remove crust from freezer, spread chocolate ice cream evenly on bottom. Next, spread half the jar of caramel topping on top of ice cream, followed by the coffee ice cream. Take a large piece of plastic wrap and place over ice cream. With palms of hand, pat the ice cream making it smooth and even, cover and place in freezer. Freeze for 24 hours.

Remove ice cream pie from freezer and unsnap pan. Run a table knife in between sides of pan and ice cream to release pan from pie. Drizzle remaining caramel topping or prepared ganache over pie. Sprinkle candy bar toppings and almonds on top.

Inside Scoop: An optional decoration, is to swirl aerosol whipped cream circles around outer circumference of pie, then freeze for two hours. Another option is to cut slices of the pie, top each with whipped cream, then sprinkle slivered almonds on top. Serve immediately and return extras, to freezer.

Missouri Headwaters

Tipi Treat Topping,

for the Missouri Mud Pie

For a birthday party, I re-invented my Missouri Mud Pie recipe and created edible "tipis" to coordinate with a tipi-themed birthday party. Refer to photos for decorations, placement and helpful ideas, to execute your own tipi inspired dessert.

1 box of Nutty Buddy Bars ice cream treats (in sugar cones)
Bag of chocolate melting discs or chocolate chips
Pocky chocolate cream covered biscuit sticks (usually located across the aisle in the candy section in Walmart) or Pretzel sticks will also work. Break pretzel sticks into smaller sizes.
River rock candy
Slivered almonds
Confetti edible decorating pieces, used for cakes or cookies
Mud Pie, page 156

Slice the ice cream mound from the Nutty Buddy sugar cones, with a warmed kitchen knife (run under hot water). Freeze all ice cream pieces until firm. Take ice cream mounds from freezer and slice into quarters and freeze until firm. Break pretzels or Pocky sticks and set aside. In a microwave safe bowl, melt 30 chocolate melting discs or 1 cup of chocolate chips, for 30 seconds. Remove and stir. Repeat for another 30 seconds if necessary, to completely melt discs.

Take the Nutty Buddy cones out of freezer and carefully snip the tip off, making enough room for 3 pretzel or Pocky sticks. Take ice cream cone and dip both bottom and top of the cone in melted chocolate. Sprinkle edible confetti around the edges of the top and bottom of the cone (refer to photo for decorations). Dip the ends of the pretzel or Poky pieces in melted chocolate and glue them into the "tipi top." Place all Nutty Buddy tipis on the Missouri Mud Pie.

Use the ice cream quarters as boulders by dipping them in the melted chocolate, place on mud pie, randomly sprinkle slivered almonds and scattered edible river rock on top of ice cream pie. Freeze for at least 24 hours.

Ganache

The butter gives the Ganache a slight gloss and extra richness. Spoon on cupcakes, over ice cream or dip Biscotti cookies in the delicious ganache. I often drizzle it on cheesecakes or on my Missouri Mud Pie.

8 oz. semi-sweet chocolate chips
½ cup heavy cream
1 teaspoon vanilla
2 tablespoons butter
2 teaspoons brewed espresso, optional

In a medium saucepan, over low heat, combine all ingredients. Mix well and bring to a soft boil. Remove from heat.

 Inside Scoop: Take cooled ganache and place in a standing mixer or in a large bowl. Mix for several minutes on medium speed. Add ½ to 1 cup sifted powdered sugar and mix until well blended and stiff. Use it to pipe onto cupcakes.

Cream Cheese Frosting

Lemon extract or other flavors can be added to change this frosting up!

8 oz. brick of cream cheese, softened
2 tablespoons butter, room temperature
2½ cups sifted powdered sugar
1 teaspoon vanilla
1 teaspoon almond extract
Pinch of salt

In a large bowl, whip cream cheese with an electric mixer. When smooth add butter and continue to mix. Then add vanilla, almond extract and blend until well incorporated. Add powdered sugar, mixing until smooth. Refrigerate until ready to use.

 **Inside Scoop:** If you want a stiff frosting, add another ½ cup to 1 cup powdered sugar.

Party Themes

Party Themes, **Bring them on!**

When my daughter was growing up, we determined that she would have only milestone birthday celebrations. Those parties were quite memorable. They involved themes and costumes. A February birthday in Montana, presented limited outdoor options, so indoors it was! The themes set the party stage. I soon discovered that the costume idea was a hit in more ways than one. Parents were able to recycle old Halloween costumes and the children loved playing dress-up.

One particular birthday theme that stood out, was the *Oscar/Academy Awards*. Complete with "awards" and a red carpet. I contacted the mothers of the guests, learning which Halloween costume their daughters would wear and created an award category to coordinate with each costume. The categories included best actress nominations; in a romantic comedy, a made for television program, a sci-fi movie, etc. Dad, the master of ceremonies, announced the nominees in all the categories, as well as the winners. Each guest received a "Silver Slipper Award." To create these, I found wooden stars, painted them silver and glued glitter on. A clear glass slipper from the bridal section of the Dollar Store, was glued to the top of the star. I printed out each child's name, with the category for which they *would* win and decoupaged it, on the underside of the star. An envelope was designed to match the category and inside was the winner's name. During the awards ceremony, the envelope was given to the recipient.

Eighteen years ago, party decor was limited, as was my budget. I stretched my imagination for ways to replicate an inexpensive version of the pricey and extravagant "real Oscars." I used red felt for the red carpet. I made director's reels from old Christmas ribbon rolls. An Oscar replica was used for the top of the cake and reserved for the birthday girl. I used melting discs and poured the chocolate into molds shaped like stars and miniature shoes. Edible metallic paints and dusting sugars decorated the stars and shoes, which were then used to decorate the cake border. Glittered stars with each guest's name, served as place settings. I found a wooden replica of a "director's take" and all the kids had their closeup picture taken with it. Streamers were created from plastic tape, to look like old fashioned camera film. The decor was staged to resemble a glamorous Oscar party. I recycled glittery Christmas branches and crystal vases. I used Colorfil, which are crushed plastic beads to fill the vase bottoms and highlight the glow of LED votives. Crystal wine glasses, fine china, and silver flatware upped the atmosphere. Gift bags were not the caliber of the Academy's, but they were met with exuberance. There were samples of nail polish and other girlie stuff, filling the bags.

Life's A Beach, was my daughter's 6th birthday theme. The windchill had been 30 degrees below zero. We laid a tarp down in the basement with a kiddie pool, filled it with sand, and treasures. I wrapped all the treasures in Ziploc bags, which included: candies, small toys, shells, turtle eggs (malted milk eggs, wrapped in cellophane baggies), and coins. All the Ziplock gift bags were buried in the sand, like real pirate booty. We had a child-size bucket and shovel and the children took turns digging for treasure at our pretend beach. Although the kids came in snow suits, underneath they were clothed in shorts, tank tops, and sun dresses. One memorable guest came in a two-piece swimming suit!! Record snowfall and wind chill had been upstaged, by the bikini-wearing 6-year-old.

The beach party decor, started with LED tiki torches stuck in sand dunes (snow piles). Each guest received a lei, a matching wristlet, and a homemade grass skirt. To make the skirts, I used ribbon and glued strands of raffia all around, with simple ties in the back. Besides the activity of digging for treasure in our pretend beach, the guests also enjoyed beach ball games and hula lessons. A tabletop S'mores bar station was set up, alongside an ice cream birthday cake, decorated to look like a beach ball. The gift bags had a collection of starfish, seashells, miniature beach balls, and stickers with beach themes.

Under the Big Top, became another birthday party theme. The pretend circus tent was made of white twin sheets, with stripes of red duct tape going down the sides, attached to a hula hoop frame. To make the Big Top Tent, I cut an oversized circle from polka dot fabric. I repeatedly traced the perimeter of a bowl, to create scalloped edges. I finished the edges by turning them under and sewing them. Fabric glue could be substituted, if you prefer not to stitch the edges. Heavy-duty ribbon was attached to the top of the hula hoop/tent to hang from a sturdy tree branch. A buffet table sat underneath to house the food items. I swung each sheet/panel (fabric Big Top Tent) over the table edge, creating a pretend Big Top. Circus food sat on the table under the circus tent and corn dog pops sat in cupcake liners with a circus theme print. Hamburgers and hotdogs were also available, as were chips and soda.

The circus confetti birthday cake had frosted circus animal cookies lining its side, along with confetti sprinkle dots. The cake topper was a Christmas ornament, from Pier 1 Imports. However, a small milk carton, could be painted and decorated to resemble the ornament instead. I also made caramel corn and placed it on the plate, to surround the cake. The gift bags had an admission ticket

for a future play date, candies and small toys. The toys consisted, of small bottles of blowing bubbles, and master of ceremony batons (glow sticks). Concession stand treats (party favors), were mini tubs of cotton candy in cello bags (cotton candy in clear plastic cups), cracker jacks, and of course...animal crackers.

A master of ceremonies, complete with top hat and moustache, helped with activities for the little circus performers (guests), who once again, came in circus act costumes! There were clowns, tigers, bears, trapeze artists, a mini master of ceremonies, and a tiny white kitten, made her way to the circus. An adult clown created balloon art, giving each little circus performer/guest something else to take home.

Très Jolie Birthday

La Vie en Rose, was my friend's favorite song, so I created a party around the song and her love of all things French. She requested my "Sac Lunch" croissant sandwiches (page 71), her favorite. I also included other finger sandwiches and a buffet of soups. The soups were served in vintage tea cups, while a two-tiered caddy was used for the sandwich selections. I used my Great Grandmother Anna Heintz's wedding dress, as a nod to Marie Antoinette. An antique screen was positioned by staged desserts, while the back-side served for photos. I drew a Marie Antoinette likeness and positioned the likeness three ways on the folding screen and on gift bags. I used beautiful bracelets as napkin rings, while a custom mask was made for each guest and staged on their place setting. I used antique bed springs to house the signage, while painter stir sticks held up the individual words, which I had sprayed and glittered on to them. I made and purchased cookies for the dessert side of the party. My friend loved the French bee, but I was unable to find one in the dead of winter, however I found a lovely crystaled lady bug pin to give as a gift to her and placed it on her personal cupcake. This party

was one of the best of my career as I got to use my imagination in ways that were not typical for a function. She was thrilled, the party was a huge success and the compliments lived on for days!

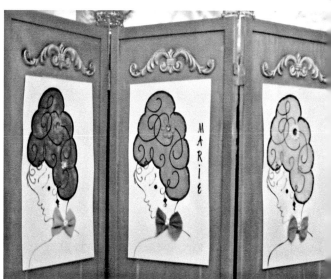

Tipi–Boho Birthday

I was contacted by a mother whose daughter was turning 10. We arranged a meeting time to discuss the birthday girl's party vision. During the interview I discovered that the child's bedroom was being repainted. While talking with the mother and daughter, I soon realized there was potential for a birthday/bedroom redo combination.

The birthday girl desired a boho design, for her bedroom makeover. I decided it would be budget friendly to incorporate it into her birthday party theme. I took notes on her party wishes and told them I would call the mother with some party ideas. Unbeknownst to the birthday girl, I suggested to the mother that we collaborate on birthday gifts, and use them as part of the party decor. This would stretch the budget and be a fun way to celebrate.

I used her new drapes to create a tipi. The wrapped gifts were staged around the party site and also used to elevate the party foods, creating a beautiful and colorful tablescape. I selected pillows as cushions for the young guests, setting them around an aged wood palette, for a tabletop. A taco bar, complete with my salsas (pages 52 & 56), and other party foods were displayed on and around the presents. I coordinated canned beverages to match the party decor. The little details, make a big difference!

The bedroom was going to have a tipi reading nook, so I found a sign which said, "This Is My Happy Place" to hang in the nook. I found a chicken coop box to sit on the daughter's desk for school papers and incidentals. Additional decorative pillows were set inside the tipi, and extras would be used for her bed. A dream catcher, also a nod to the boho-chic design, was used near the food table where guests would find fruit "arrows," complete with my Huckleberry Dip (page 52).

Adults were treated to a chili bar, as well as tacos. My Missouri Mud Pie (page 156) was topped with a Tipi Top decorations (page 158), substituting as a birthday cake. Cupcakes were also made available. I painted tipis on gift bags, filled with goodies including Indian beaded bracelets. The young guests also got to decorate a giant tipi sugar cookie.

A Whoville Party

One year my daughter ice skated to the song "Where Are You Christmas," from the movie The Grinch Who Stole Christmas. I created a costume which made her look like Cindy Lou Who. She was darling in her outfit and so was the party created around the Grinch theme. The guests were to arrive in pajamas and we would provide the finishing touches. Upon arriving each guest was given, battery operated necklaces, with vintage strands of Christmas bulbs that would light up. I purchased pipe cleaners, pom poms, ornaments, headbands in red and lime green, and anything that looked like "Whoville." All guests were adorned with elaborate hairdos, creative face paint, and finger nail polish decorations.

Using masking tape, I wrapped the table surface in a candy cane-striped wrapping paper. An artificial/dummy cake, sat atop a Patience Brewster cake stand for the tablescape eye candy. I created cupcakes with edible embellishments and fashioned Chinese takeout containers in the coordinating theme colors, filled with over-the-top candies.

Platters of pizza sat on top of the paper mache boxes I painted to match the "Whoville" theme, decorated with fabulous coordinating trims. Polka dot straws matched the mugs the kids drank their "Grinch Hot Chocolate" from. I also made green Glacier Peak Whipped Cream, (page 155) for the top. Lime green nonpareils were served on the side. The kids watched

167

the Grinch Who Stole Christmas movie, while eating cinnamon popcorn.

Gift bags were substituted with small popcorn tubs. They contained bags of the cinnamon popcorn, hot chocolate packets (with a recipe for Grinch Green Whipped Cream), lime green and red nail polish, and a Grinch mug. The party was magical, colorful and so much fun!

A Candyland Birthday

Candy, cookies and gingerbread, were the theme of a December birthday party for a young girl who wanted something festive but still birthday-ish. Collaborating on winter, existing Christmas decor and a December birthday had me thinking, candy...cookies and gingerbread. Brown lunch bags (used as treat bags for party favors), were decorated with felt, that was cut in the shape of ornaments, then embellished and glued onto the bags. A craft table was set up with items for the guests to decorate their bags and felt ornament. The ornament was detachable with a double-sided tape, so the guests could have a gift bag, as well as an ornament for their tree. I precut the ornament and hot glued a satin ribbon hook on

to it and the children did the rest of the decorating.

A large burlap gingerbread character was staged above the tablescape and was later used as part of a game. I made a large red heart with a sticky back. The kids were blindfolded and spun and attempted to place the heart where it belonged on the gingerbread character.

The tablescape was under a burlap-draped wall. Kissing balls were attached to the table corners, with ribbons, pennants, and an assorted sizes of ornaments draped along it.

I made gingerbread cookies and used muffin tins for all the decorating items to be set in. The tins were easy to pass around for the guests, while they were decorating. Many of the items on the dessert table were prizes for the games that were played. (See photo for the prizes used as props.)

I rolled out brown butcher paper and used masking tape to adhere to the floor. Each guest's body was traced on the paper and later they drew on faces and decorated the life-sized gingerbread. The self-portrait gingerbread doll, was to be hung on their bedroom door for the holidays.

I also made felt, hand puppets resembling the top half of a gingerbread doll. The puppets became dancers to music for the party. They were darling and the girls danced their hands off! A December birthday so close to Christmas can be a challenge, but repurposing the items used to decorate the party, also became gifts for the birthday girl, as well as keepsakes for the years to come. Reinventing, repurposing, and reusing was a thoughtful way to execute this Christmastime birthday.

Weddings & Celebrations

Creative Cakes

Wedding Cakes are *'thee* thing!' Opulent and beautiful, but pricey. Not all budgets can include the high price tag of a wedding cake showpiece. I have often substituted dummy cakes, as they are much easier to work with and cheaper. Fondant draped over polystyrene forms, or paper mache boxes, with beautiful embellishments, served as a custom bakery alternative. I typically elevated the artificial cake with clear glass containers, surrounded by silk petals, greenery, and real flowers, making them look very grand. Dec-

orated wood palettes, crates, slabs, and stumps also made nice displays, as well as traditional cake stands. For the first anniversary cake, a small bakery cake would be purchased and used for the cutting ceremony and saved for later.

New traditions are always on the rise, so individual cakes, with various flavors are currently trending. Dessert bars are also in vogue. In lieu of the high-priced custom cakes, sheet cakes are another affordable option and have numerous assorted flavors.

Here are a few samples of my dummy cakes, made from paper mache boxes. I created all three for under fifty dollars. I painted the sides to resemble a "naked cake," then glued doilies and cardboard cake rounds, to the bottom. The cakes can be embellished with items resembling what a bakery would do. Candle stick holders can elevate the cakes to various heights. I suggest you hot glue the bottoms, to the candle sticks for sturdiness.

For several weddings and bridal showers, a purchased bakery cake that would serve eight guests, was staged as part of the guest table centerpieces. The dual-purpose of staging a table and providing a dessert, helped stretch the budget and the edible centerpieces eliminated long lines for cake. If you are having a dessert bar, intersperse dummy cakes for extra impact. **Note:** Grocery store bakeries can fill orders for individual cakes, without having custom bakery prices.

Bridal Shower Bling

I was working with a bride who loved bling, crystal, and shabby chic decor. She was a novice cook, who was passionate about creating meals for her soon-to-be-husband. As I interviewed the bride and her extended family about the wedding, my mind was swirling with ideas. I presented the group

with creative concepts and rental items, that I thought would work for the wedding day.

The mothers of the bride and groom were hosting a bridal shower and also enlisted my services. I created a specialized recipe card that served as a shower invitation. Included, was a request for the guests to bring a family recipe as a gift. A special notation was added, asking the guests to bring a piece of used costume or vintage jewelry. Single earrings, bracelets, brooches, sweater clips, pins and old-fashioned hair pins were among the bling gifts. The donated items were going to be repurposed in the wedding decor. Charming brooches were fastened with a jeweler's weld, to the cake cutting serving pieces and some of it was also used in the bridal bouquet.

I also collected jewelry from the mothers of the bride and groom. With some of the pieces of their jewelry, I created a personalized recipe book to coordinate with the shabby chic theme. I also decorated picture frames (that had lovely photos of the bride and groom inside), adding the bling to embellish them. Beautiful ribbons, with jewelry items in the center of the bow, adorned the frames. The decorated frames were then used as part of the centerpieces at the guest tables.

After the guests enjoyed food and refreshments, I explained the purpose of the additional gift surprises. The bride opened the custom recipe book first, then the recipes, each chosen carefully for the bridal couple, followed by the jewelry gifts. Each guest then explained the history of their recipe and jewelry.

When I showed the bride the frames, I suggested that the bridesmaids, grandmothers, and both mothers each receive one of the blinged reception photos as a personalized thank you gift. After they returned from the honeymoon, the bride presented the embellished photo frames to the intended recipients. I must add, that guests commented on how fun it was to clear out jewelry boxes or hunt for jewelry to contribute! Personalizing a theme with family treasures and making new memories from old things, became my business tradition!

Note: Used wine bottles became vessels for a variety of coffee flavorings.

The 5 Mile Ranch Wedding

Beth (Degenhart) and Dale Arlon (Cookie) Koch

The June wedding of Beth and Cookie, had three areas requiring staging. The ceremony site was creek-side, on the family's 5 Mile Ranch. A cowhide rug was displayed under a wooden arch built by the groom, adding trophy antlers to the top. I made aisle flags from dowels, with heavy-duty cardboard cake plates, vintage papers, and ribbon. Vintage clothespins held burlap ribbon in place, to cordon off reserved seating. The bride and groom's brands were married together at the top of the aisle entrance using spray paint. To do this, string was draped in the brand configuration, to make a pattern. Then paint primer was sprayed over string. The string was removed and several layers of paint were sprayed over the pattern. The ring bearer's rode stick horses down the aisle, while a pipe cleaner held the rings in place. Beth, arrived in a horse drawn buggy and Dually, her best buddy, was "best dog."

The wedding tent was decorated with remote controlled Edison lights, strung high in the ceiling with kissing balls, chandeliers, and large paper flowers. Ornate picture frames were embellished with lace ribbon, pearl strands, and even larger paper flowers, which hung high above the guests. Old tablecloths and doilies were cut and draped on lamp frames, embellished with vintage pins, repurposing them as chandeliers. An old desk, vintage typewriter, and antique window, gave guests a peek into some classic photos of the bride and groom. Custom paper lunch bags, with a variety of designs, representing the bride and groom's brands were place settings. Guests were offered cold water bottles, with custom labels honoring the occasion.

Centerpiece arrangements were made using sangria/water bottles, small coffee drink glasses and number 5 cans, embellished with shabby chic trims, papers, and crystals. Randomly placed throughout, were zinc buckets filled with river rock These were used to stabilize the enormous white roses that bridged the gap of table top to tent ceiling height. Battery lighted branches were nestled among the flower stalks and twisted tissue paper hid the bucket necessities. A popcorn bar was set up using decorated mayonnaise jars filled with popcorn kernels, to hold the sign, "Thanks For Poppin' By!" Vintage drawers held the scoops, while decorated large metal bins held caramel and white cheddar popcorn. A barn wood lemonade stand was also available for guests (page 26).

The barn was repurposed with rope trim, as well as saddles and bridles belonging to the bride and groom. Vintage paper pennant swags, tissue paper kissing balls, and a "Love Is Sweet" sign for the cupcake area hung high in the barn. I also used crystal cloche containers, tier metal stands, and birch stumps, to create a beautiful tablescape on an enormous fiber optic cable spool which housed the assorted cupcakes. An old hog feeder was repurposed with two card table tops, for the Charcuterie (appetizers) station. Large rice krispie bar/hay bales had small Montana shaped chalkboard signs, sitting on the station, to notify guests about the various dips and items served. (See recipe for detailed list of items served in the charcuterie station, page 51).

The tablescape focal points on the buffet tables consisted of old wood milk benches, vintage china, lanterns, antique corbels, and flowers. I made "Begin Here" signs, for the buffet line. Old rusted sections of bed springs, were adorned with ribbons and crystal buttons, to stabilize the signs. Basic serving utensils, were enhanced with vintage earrings and jewelry. A jeweler can weld them for a small fee, however, I simply used wire and hot glue on some and had a local jeweler do the others.

I would like to acknowledge Debbie Hamilton of D. Hamilton Photography, who graciously allowed me free use of some of the photos shown in this wedding!

bitterrootequinephotos.smugmug.com
(406) 360-2668

Romantic Bliss… In Black, White & Fuchsia

Allison Anderson and Brad Sternberg

The lovely and etheral wedding ceremony for Alli and Brad was held in a beautiful, uptown Butte church. The use of white roses, hot pink/fuchsia accents, and tulle, transformed the stately church into a romantic setting. I made very large rose kissing balls/pomanders, to hang from the church pews. Large styrofoam balls became the pomander center, while a large silk ribbon was glued around its center, with a loop to hang. Corsage pins and glue, were used to adhere individual roses to the sphere. Tulle was then draped along the pews, creating an elegant effect. 3M hooks made the attachment and removal easy. To stage the wedding alter, long, clear vases were filled with silk rose petals and rose pomanders resting on top. I also made matching wreaths for the church doors and decorated the stair handrails with paper kissing balls and matching ribbons.

The reception took place in the historic Front Street Station. I provided a dummy cake for the cake cutting

ceremony. The bride's mother, did the cake decorating and made a small cake for the cutting ceremony. The dummy cake consisted of a styrofoam base with layers of fondant covering it. I placed the cake on clear glasses to elevate it and cascaded silk petals all around the base. The Station's original arrival and departure sign for the trains, was used as the backdrop for a dessert bar. I used apothecary jars, vases and buckets to hold candies. The candy/dessert bar serving vessels were elevated on flocked damask boxes, crystal platters, and boxes wrapped to match the wedding decor.

Guests were served cheesecake in lieu of traditional cake. I made an assortment of cheesecakes for the guests to enjoy, and were staged under the arrival/departure sign. I created additional decorations from scrapbook paper pinwheels, by folding and embellishing them, then attaching each to bamboo skewers (found in the kitchen aisle of stores). They were placed in water softener salt, (a large bag is around $6.00) so they would stand upright. To personalize, square vases from the Dollar Store, had adhesive bling letters attached. An LED light was placed at the bottom of each vase and Colorfil plastic crystals were layered on top.

The centerpieces and tablescapes were coordinated with the wedding color palette, with an eclectic mix, to make the Station more colorful and interesting. I created silk floral arrangements in vases filled with water softener salt. The salt hid the silk flower stems and weighted the vases, making them stable.

I wish to thank the husband and wife team, Samantha and Reid of Orange Photographie, in Bozeman, Montana, for the free use of the photos shown in this wedding

orangephotographie.com
(816) 516-1540

Whatever your color scheme or theme, any of the decor shown in both weddings would be easily interchangeable. (Refer to the wedding photos for interchangeable ideas for the day of your dreams.) Enhancements could vary with a change of color, papers, buttons instead of crystals, a variety of cans instead of glass vases, or even scrap pieces of wood for table numbers.

Colored LED lights will add a subtle color hue to the Colorfil and give it a softer, romantic look. Paper lunch bags can be redesigned for housing silverware/napkins, party favors or for treat bags. I made adhesive labels, stating, "Life is Sweet, Take a Treat." Folded polka dot, cocktail napkins became bowties to decorate the bags. To make them, I used a paper punch to create two holes and used florist wire to adhere the bowtie to the napkin. Assorted buttons embellished the front of the bag. I used an old bushel basket to hold the treat bags, which were stationed next to the dessert table. An extra napkin was folded inside for the guest to use. The treat bag made carrying the edible party favor home, much easier!

The popcorn bar is easy to use for many different types of events. I have used the idea for "He Popped The Question," for an engagement party, "She's Ready To Pop," for a baby shower, and "Pop On Over" and Celebrate (substitute name), for a birthday or graduation party.

Thanks For

Poppin' By

Valentine Bridal Shower

Cherubs and Victorian decor were the themes for a bridal shower in February. Blush pink was the bride-to-be's favorite color, so it was incorporated into her shower decor. I painted paper mache hat boxes in blush and embellished them with pearls, feathers, lace, and cherub appliques. These were used as items to stage the party. Pink wine glasses were also used to drink with my Highfalutin' Punch (page 27), while a cherub statue draped with pearl strands, was positioned nearby. Lace fans and umbrellas were hung for a Victorian flare, as were paper doilies alternating in pink and white colors. Crystal cylinder vases had pink LED lights in the base, with bouquets of pink flowers crowning the top. Lace tablecloths set the stage for guest tables, while pink tulle was wrapped around the chairs and tied to the side. The bride-to-be's pink chair cover, had pearl strands draped on the back, like a woman's necklace. Cherub ceramic plant holders had miniature rose plants in them. Pink taper candles were placed in candle-abras, adorned with pearl strands dripping down and attached with pink satin bows. This lovely and romantic shower was highlighted by various textures, using elements of repurposed indoor and outdoor items.

Mother's Day Breakfast

Lilacs were the inspiration in the color palette for a Mother's Day Celebration. A festive table of purple and lime green was staged outside, for my guests to enjoy a lovely May morning. I made my Motherlode Casserole (page 42), as the main dish, while store bought pastries filled in the sweet side. Fresh fruit was served in May baskets, with lilac bouquets and lavender polka dot plates and mugs to match. The fragrance of the lilacs in my yard and their corresponding color, made my Mother's Day very special. My guests took bouquets of lilacs home, as well as leftovers for another breakfast. Supplementing home cooking with store bought items is a time saver, and sometimes a necessity for a busy working woman!

An Easter Celebration

When you live in Montana, you can usually expect snow for Easter. A lovely springtime color palette makes the Easter tablescape feel like spring. The following is an example of an Easter celebration.

The adult table had a hostess gift, and jeweled, hand painted eggs, resting on each place setting. For the kid's place settings, I cut egg shapes from poster board. Each one was decorated and their name was written on it. A "yummy" scrapbook pennant hung above the dining room mirror, reflecting where the guests would eat.

The festive Easter meal included a potato salad, that was shaped like a large egg, decorated with garnishes, resting on a large platter, see page 109 for recipe. A country ham was baked, Locked and Loaded Twice Baked Potatoes (page 82), were also served. For the sides I made Green Bean Bundles (page 80) and Broccoli Salad (page 110), which were served in large plastic egg halves. Assorted cookies were served, including the Sunday Church Social no bake cookies which were formed into nests with jelly bellies inside (page 130). A plastic wheelbarrow from the dollar store held a "dirt" dessert with gummy worms, both inside and out. Oreo cookie crumbs served as the dirt, while pudding was the filling. The miniature shovel was used as the spoon. The wheelbarrow dessert sat on artificial grass, next to a foiled bunny statue, complete with assorted Easter candies.

I made large bunny feet from vinyl tablecloth fabric. I placed the feet in a path, to greet the guests inside my home and outside on the patio to the game area. I took a poster board and cut it into a large egg-shape for each of the children to decorate. Once the children had decorated them, I gathered all the enormous eggs and stapled each one onto a large garden stake. I made a large golden egg for the finish line. Since the weather was beautiful and warm, all the egg stakes became an obstacle course for games in the backyard. The egg obstacle course was very entertaining and each child took home their original poster egg stake. Games included eggs on a spoon race, rolling a paper mache' egg with a rolling pin to the finish line, and the adults got in the action by having a hard boiled egg positioned between their backs, making their way thru the egg course. I also assigned specific egg colors to age groups for the egg hunt, so that the smaller children would have a chance, without the older children getting all the eggs. It was an egg-stra special day, celebrating a beautiful spring day and Easter in Montana!

Fall In Love, With Baby

Fall, inspired a baby shower complete with polka dots, baby ducks, and a matching dessert bar. A large plush duck (baby shower gift), was set in my vintage wicker, baby buggy and staged under the gazebo for guests to be welcomed by. It later strolled its way onto my patio, with the other baby gifts.

A mum plant was a hostess gift for the mom-to-be. The gift would be planted and bloom year after year, in honor of the baby. The duck theme was found throughout. Dessert picks, baby clothes, and a larger duckie was used as the cake topper. Yellow melting discs were turned upside down, to make large polka dots on the cake. A popcorn bar was created, in honor of the mom-to-be, with a sign which read *She's Ready to Pop!* A salad and sandwich bar were made available for guests.

Party favors were placed in polka dot boxes, to accent the theme. My pond had a very large rubber duckie floating next to budding tissue flowers glued to clear plastic plates, allowing them to float. I made polka dot table runners, highlighted with sunflower bouquets in mason jars and matching polka dot ribbons. Everyone fell in love with the duck/polka dot theme, as there was no gender reveal. The fall atmosphere was a perfect backdrop to this baby shower theme.

For years, I always decorated in red and green for Christmas. Doing holiday parties and Christmas weddings, had me decorating at home, early in November. When my daughter settled into her own apartment, I saw an opportunity to gift her, all the Christmas decor of her childhood, allowing me the chance to depart from the red and green traditions of the past. Utilizing a neutral palette, made it possible to incorporate an accent color, bringing interest to the monochromatic tone. This works very well, as the winter wonderland to New Year's Eve seasons, can be decorated without having to take down Christmas.

An artist's canvas was wrapped in linen, with a beaded trim-shaped Christmas tree, allows extra ornaments to be placed into it. This is a wonderful way to give a child their childhood ornaments. It works especially well for a college dorm room or a small apartment (see photo for craft idea).

The advent calendar was created with birch bark squares, along with thoughtful sentiments printed on papers, then attached with double-sided tape. Each day, the bark square is removed, and the thoughtful statement read. Some sentiments included: what are you thankful for this holiday season, call someone you haven't talked to and let them know you love them, do a random act of kindness, make a new holiday tradition, etc.

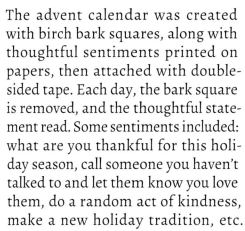

I also made stockings for my French doors, from poster board. To do this, I actually sewed them and then glued birch bark strips on top, accented with gorgeous brooch embellishments.

An oversized reindeer was staged on my kitchen table. I placed glittered tulle in a cloud-like formation underneath. Serving containers were interspersed in the *cloud billows.*

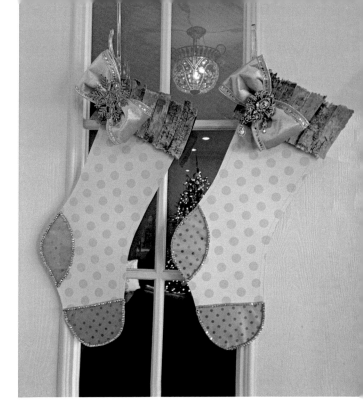

I also made bands, to change the basic accent-pillows into a festive feel. Simple modifications, with ribbon or pillow covers, will accent the neutral palette changing it from one year to the next, for minimal investment. I painted my fireplace to match a purchased mirror. Extra Christmas ornaments were hung from the center of the mirrors above the headboard.

The chair next to the fireplace was a thrift store find. I painted the fabric, and saved money by only upholstering the chair cushion. The cushion was reversible, coordinating with the changing seasons. See photos for decorating ideas and let your imagination create a *wintery dreamland* of your own!

During the holidays I add progressive decorating items, transitioning from November to New Year's Eve. Large crystal icicles and a variety of ornaments adorn my dining room chandelier. A faux fur throw became a tablecloth, complete with silver antler napkin rings, a gift from my daughter Savannah.

Darling snowmen appear and stay around until January. Layers of glittery branches, pinecones and candles are placed throughout my home. Beaded and crystal pillows accent seating, while Montana's snowfall creates the backdrop for a dreamy winter wonderland.

Mansions of Montana

Mansions of Montana

My decision to highlight the mansions of Montana in this book, was to recognize the efforts of so many, who have dedicated time and effort to rescue and restore these homes to their former glory, giving all of us a glimpse into the past. Supporting these mansions is so important to their survival. I hope you will take the opportunity to tour one or all of the mansions of Montana, to see for yourself, how the wealthy families who once called Montana home, had lived. History is a teacher of the past. The glorious homes of yesteryear are insights to an era long gone. However, I often wonder what their 406 table conversations were like....we can only imagine.

The former homes of the Daly, Conrad, Clark, Lehrkind, Moss, and Bair families are opulent and grand. The elite list of wealthy families, whose homes are available for tours and/or lodging are architectural masterpieces dating back to the turn of the century. The businessmen of those families built stately homes which showcased their financial empires and sent a visual message of their wealth to the communities they called home. The mansions represent a time when grandeur was paramount. Artisan skills were the best money could buy, as can be seen in the details of stained-glass windows, woodwork, and furnishings curated from around the world. Each mansion has details of exquisite craftsmanship, which is very rare today. I can only envision the parties, food, and entertainment hosted from within the grand halls of those 406 mansions.

These beautiful homes are open to the public for overnight stays, tours, and weddings. Tour guides are versed in each mansion's family history. The guides describe the impact the wealthy families had on the growth of Montana, their financial backgrounds, and how the owners amassed their fortunes. The wealthy elite were trendsetters, risk takers, and entrepreneurs. Their homes hosted famous artists, politicians, newsmakers and their own families' events, making memories from their own 406 table.

The Lehrkind Mansion

The Lehrkind Mansion is a beautifully painted, Queen Anne style home. Built in 1897, the stately Victorian now operates as a bed and breakfast inn. Julius Lehrkind was born in Germany, where, as a young man he learned valuable skills, while working in a brewery. Later, he fled his native country to England. From there he and his brother became stowaways, which brought them to the U.S. Julius attended the Milwaukee Brewery School, earning credentials as a Master Brewer. Eventually, Julius came to Bozeman, Montana where he used his people skills, brewing roots, and business savvy to open Bozeman Lager Brewery.[116] The brewery was the largest building in Gallatin County, until the field house was built at Montana State University, 70 years later.[117]

Fresh mountain water and ample crops of barley were the perfect pairing, for Julius to make his brewery dreams possible. Montana's barley crops helped produce a lager that would have made "stout" competition

for Lehrkind's German brewing roots. The streams flowing from the mountains of Montana, supplied perfect water for the locally harvested barley. The marriage of mountain water run-off and local barley made Julius's reputation as a brewer, as grand as the massive home he built. [117] As a generous boss and progressive thinker, Julius created an unconventional 40-hour work week and paid time-and-a-half for his employees. The brewery's success lined Lehrkind's pockets, but also had him dreaming of new business opportunities. He expanded his breweries to include the towns of Livingston, Red Lodge, and Silesia. Unfortunately, prohibition closed all the breweries, but the resilient Lehrkind added more to his business profile. He ventured into dairy, ice, and Coca-Cola. [116.]

Situated next to the brewery, the home of Julius Lehrkind and his family, is a true treasure of the Gallatin Valley and the community of Bozeman, Montana. The bed and breakfast furnishings are quite remarkable. The comfortable atmosphere of the grand inn has charming grounds, lovely gardens, and a beautiful reflection of the Bridger Mountains. Old Baldy is framed via the front door window, appearing as a portrait (Refer to the mansion photo below, to see the reflection in the front door window).

A massive, elegantly carved hall tree in the foyer, once used to store hats and other outerwear, begins the unveiling of antique treasures found throughout the home. Behind one of three pocket doors was a treasure I have never seen before, a Regina music box, built in 1897, the same year of the home's completion. The seven-foot historic music box created with German technology, was built with enormous metal discs, allowing melodies to flow from the upright music box. I was entertained with *The Blue Bells of Scotland*, emanating from the antique device.

The home's huge, beautiful stained-glass windows, sit high above, nearly reaching the floor to the ceiling. They illuminate the room's high ceilings and elegant decor. Photos of the Lehrkind family are scattered throughout, paying tribute to the original family of the home. Atop the fireplace, sets an original bottle from the brewery, apparently the only one known to exist.

The beautiful bedroom furnishings reflect the time period of the home. The large rooms easily accommodate massive carved oak, walnut, and ash beds, along with their suite of furnishings. Millwork is original to the home. A lovely fretwork piece extending between the first and second parlor, showcases the wood craftsmanship in the home. Douglas fir harvested from local forests, provided much of the lumber used in the mansion. Claw-foot bathtubs are in the original home, as well as in the guest house. The home had indoor plumbing, electric lighting, and a coal powered heating system, which were all innovative for the time.

There are intimate and charming stories regarding purchases of the items selected to furnish the home. Chris Nixon, shared a wonderful story of a painting of poppies hanging in the stairwell wall. Be sure to ask Chris about this when you visit the Lehrkind.

There are many rooms to choose from when booking a stay, each is thoughtfully decorated with period appropriate furnishings and delightful touches. The guest house located behind the mansion, has a grotto, four additional rooms for sleeping/relaxing and garden views.

Contact Chris Nixon for rental information and see the jewel of Bozeman!

bozemanbedandbreakfast.com
Lehrkind Mansion
719 N. Wallace Ave.
Bozeman, Montana
(406) 580-6932

The Daly Mansion

Photo courtsey of the Daly Mansion

Nestled outside the lovely community of Hamilton, Montana is the stately Daly Mansion. The stunning Bitterroot Valley, inspired Marcus Daly to build a summer residence that was lovingly referred to as *Riverside*. The three-story, 24,000 square foot mansion has 50 rooms, 25 bedrooms, 7 fireplaces, and rests on 46 acres of the pristine Bitterroot Valley.[118]

A tree-lined entrance creates a canopy of foliage, escorting tourists and visitors to the breathtaking Georgian-Revival styled home. In the fall, the trees change to any array of diverse colors, making the mansion look akin to 12 Oaks, in Gone with the Wind. The background of Montana's Big Sky and the gorgeous Bitterroot Valley, illuminate the unique mansion, artistically painting the perfect setting for a wedding, party, reunion, or celebration of any kind.

Marcus Daly, an Irish immigrant, was known as one of "The Copper Kings". He was famous for his contributions in the copper industry and personal political agendas. His life's journey in mining made him a very rich and powerful man. His business ventures included breeding race horses, where success followed him to the track. Funded by George Hearst in many successful business acquisitions, Daly amassed much wealth. At the time of his death in 1900, his Montana business/land holdings were worth a reported $75 million dollars. [119]

Daly was instrumental in creating the town of Anaconda, where he built a smelter to process copper thus, creating more notoriety and wealth. [120] He was strongly opposed to the political viewpoints of William Clark, another mining magnate and "Copper King," who later became a Montana senator. Daly used his paper, printed inAnaconda to express his many views, including political ones. He hired the best printing operations from New York, staff, writers and made his otherwise quiet voice... heard! He was a vital powerhouse in Montana's history, creating jobs, communities, and helped light the world with his copper discovery and smelting plant. [121]

The Daly Mansion is rich in history, with splendid gardens and elegant grounds. This Montana State owned home has had over 2.5 million dollars worth of restoration funded by the Daly Mansion Preservation Trust that manages the home. It has approximately 80% of it's original furnishings. The gorgeous setting of the mansion in the beautiful Bitterroot Valley is very breathtaking. The grounds and flowers of the estate are a perfect complement to the Montana scenery.

Tour guides are well-versed in the life of Marcus Daly, as well as his business and political life. Intimate and charming stories of Daly and his family are recanted in the mansion tours. In season, there are daily tours, but activities and events take place year-round. I have referred to the mansion as "The Tara of Montana." It is a must see! Missoula, Montana is only 45 minutes from the mansion and the small quaint community of Hamilton is just minutes away.

For further information visit the mansion's website or contact the staff directly.

dalymansion.org
The Daly Mansion
251 Eastside Highway
Hamilton, Montana 59840
(406) 363-6004

The Conrad Mansion

Photo courtesy of Patrick Booth, Mystic Creek Studios

Charles Edward Conrad left the "Birthplace of Montana," with full pockets, high hopes, and big dreams. He and his brother had created a shipping and freight empire along the banks of the Missouri, in Fort Benton, Montana. The brothers were originally from Virginia, growing up on a large plantation, amongst their eleven siblings. The plantation could not sustain the large family, so the brothers set out west, in search of fortunes. Destiny brought them to Fort Benton, Montana where they lined their pockets and their bank accounts with rewards from their risk-taking endeavors. [122.]

Once the brothers arrived in Fort Benton, they flipped the only coin in their possession. Charles lost the toss and stayed, while his brother moved to Helena. Charles proceeded to make a name for himself while working at a local mercantile. He later bought the business and allowed his brother to return and become a partner. The brother's business prowess gave them the wisdom to sell their business to the famous Hudson Bay Trading Company. After the sale, the brothers looked for a new community to call home and another business investment to pursue. [123]

With his entrepreneurial spirit and drive to conquer new business ventures, the Conrad's went on a scouting mission. Destiny led him to a townsite, currently known as Kalispell. Immediately, they knew this was going to be their new home. The landscape, vistas, and wildlife filled their spirits. Conrad has been credited as the "Founding Father of Kalispell."[123]

A proper residence, befitting such an important community figure, was paramount for the family. With business ventures in banking, real estate, and commerce, the Conrad's new home and its grandeur, was to be the talk of the town. Abundant financial resources enabled them to hire a worthy and compatible architect. [124]

Kirtland Cutter's reputation as a notable architect, and whose vision was in sync with the Conrad's, proved to be a wise choice. Cutter had designed the beautiful Davenport Hotel in Spokane, Washington, the Lake McDonald Lodge in Glacier National Park, as well as the Kootenai Lodge on Swan Lake, Montana. [124]

The original estate was 72 acres, that overlooked the Swan Mountain Range and the Kalispell valley. Cutter designed the beautiful Victorian-era, Norman inspired mansion. The home has beautiful stained glass windows that illuminate the gorgeous, quarter sawn oak paneling. Diamond-leaded glass panels are beautiful additions, not to mention the eight sandstone fireplaces. The mansion consists of 13,000 square feet, encompassing three floors. There are 26 rooms that still have 90% of the family's original furnishings. [124]

On Thanksgiving in 1895, the Conrad's served the first of many holiday meals in their new home. Charles M. Russell, the famous western artist and frequent dinner guest, was considered a close family friend. Theodore Roosevelt, also a guest and family friend, shared Conrad's enjoyment of the great outdoors and its many sporting activities. Conrad's vast firearms collection is quite impressive. [124]

Creative events take place at the mansion in the off-season. They are worthy causes and memorable experiences. Book a tour and see a part of history, with an authentic perspective of life in a bygone era.

conradmansion.com
The Conrad Mansion
330 Woodland Avenue
Kalispell, Montana 59901
(406) 755-2166

The Copper King Mansion

The Copper King Mansion is a cultural heirloom, resting uptown Butte, Montana. The Northern Rockies on the Continental Divide, is home to the mining community of Butte, famously known as the "Richest

Hill on Earth." William A. Clark chose to build his lavish residence here. Leaving a visual entre' into the life of Clark and his family. [125]

Clark, "Butte's Copper King," was involved in every detail of the construction of his mansion, overseeing even minute details. It is reported that construction materials were an approximate $200,000, [126] but the overall cost to build the beauty on the hill, was $260,000. [127] Enduring cold, hard winters, and traversing the hilly location, took craftsmen four years to bring the mansion to life. Its completion occurred in 1884. [126]

What a beauty she is! The red brick Victorian mansion is trimmed with a French mansard roof and dormer windows. [128] Impressive as it is on the outside, wait until you see the interior! An array of the finest woods were used to create the intricate details, showcasing Clark's vision. Rosewood, birds-eye maple, Philippine mahogany, and beautiful oak, are woven throughout the mansion, reflecting the fine craftsmen and their exemplary skills. [126]

Photo courtesy of the Copper King Mansion.

Stained glass windows, ornate carved fireplaces, and a vast collection of antiques and artifacts, accentuate the life of Clark. Thirty-four rooms filled with nostalgia, provide a glimpse into the successful world of the Copper King. In addition, painted frescoes on the ceilings, a 64-foot ballroom, and painted plaster swirls embrace the details, that William had envisioned.[126]

The mining mogul, who later became a Montana senator, had a life story as rich as his bank account. Banking records showed at the height of his career, he had a monthly income of 17 million dollars.[127] The price he paid for the construction of the mansion, was less than half a day's income for him!

Clark's masterpiece, the Copper King Mansion is open May-September. During the off-season, tours are given by appointment only. Imagine waking up in one of the Clark family bedrooms, feeling like an heir to the mining magnate! The mansion has guest bedrooms for rent and are also available year-round. The beauty on the hill, is waiting for you to visit. You will thoroughly enjoy her history and appreciate her elegance.

thecopperkingmansion.com
The Copper King Mansion
219 W. Granite St.
Butte, Montana 59701
(406) 782-7580

The Charles M. Bair Mansion

Photo courtesy of PJ (Paula) Beezley

The 11,000 square foot, Charles M. Bair Mansion, is located outside of Martinsdale, Montana. The Bair daughters, Alberta and Marguerite had quite the discerning eye for collecting. The 20-room mansion holds replicas of the original paintings placed in the same locations where Marguerite once hung them. Bair family collections of silver, porcelain, exquisite keepsakes and original furniture remain in the family residence. The new museum built in 2011, holds vast amounts of curated artifacts from Europe, including an extensive fine art collection. Famous artist's paintings are on display, along with Bair's treasured selection of Native American artifacts. [129]

The dining room is beautifully staged with acquisitions of London's premiere silversmith, Paul Storr. The dining table is of English origin and the chairs are Chippendale style. These pieces make a formal statement in the Bair's dining room, while a gorgeous chandelier overhead illuminates the elegantly decorated room. [129]

The living room is rich in antique furnishings with a formal fireplace centered in the room, with two rare Louis XV commodes, one of which is signed. A wedgewood shell holds a Sèvre porcelain urn, obtained from a summer palace in the Netherlands, known as Het Loo. Upon seeing the urn, a museum conservator stated, "The museum world had been wondering what happened to these urns. Wait until I tell them they are in a ranch house in Montana!"[130]

The bedroom furnishings are exquisite and rare, including a bed once owned by Marie Antoinette. Porcelain figurines are displayed throughout the house, their provenance is quite impressive. Tour guides are very informed about the figurine's origins. One particular bathroom was a tour highlight for me, as it was quite unexpected for the Montana location. Gold fixtures were a surprising discovery in the bathroom, as most rural Montana homes built in that era, had chamber pots and out houses. They were certainly not furnished with fixtures made of gold!

Bair's success story is as interesting as the mansion. Charles arrived in Montana via the Northern Pacific Railroad, as a conductor. He made his initial fortune, while investing in a thawing device for mining. He then took those proceeds and invested in oil and mining. Bair also purchased real estate, giving him a vast amount of Montana range. The massive land he acquired, allowed Charles to purchase numerous sheep. His extensive grazing land enabled his sheep herd to flourish. The herd expanded, along with his reputation. Charles was given the title, "The most successful sheep rancher in the world." His herd of 300,000 sheep was larger than the population of Montana at that time. [131]

With its enchanting surroundings, there is so much to see, learn, and enjoy at the Charles M. Bair Mansion. Guided tours, allow visitors intimate insight to the lifestyle of the Bair's and their personal treasures, including my favorite, the golden bathroom. Contact the museum for current hours of operation. Photo courtesy of the Bair Family Museum.

bairfamilymuseum.org
The Charles M. Bair Museum and Home
2751 Mt. Hwy. 294
Martinsdale, Montana 59053
(406) 572-3314

The Moss Mansion

Preston Boyd Moss was instrumental in building the historic Northern Hotel and had business investments that included large herds of cattle and sheep. He developed an electric company, telephone exchanges, and many diverse businesses that made good use of the partnership desk, still displayed in his office.

In 1903, the red sandstone home was designed by the famous New York designer, Henry Janeay Hardenbergh.[132] The Waldorf Astoria and The Plaza are also created by the vision of Hardenbergh. The cost of the home was $105,000, while most average homes during that time cost $5,000.[133]

Numerous details in the mansion provide insight in to the lives and times of the home and its occupants. Upon entering, you are greeted by a Moorish archway, providing a dramatic entrance into the home. Moss's office, also known as the library, is to the left. His office includes original furniture, as well as his partnership desk. Mrs. Moss (Mattie Woodson Moss), was an artist who painted china and lovely oil paintings, which are on display in various rooms. It is reported that she was the fun one in the family, as well as the first woman in Billings who learned to drive.[132] Apparently, that task made her even more popular.

Six beautiful tiled fireplaces and modern amenities (that were quite remarkable for the time), can be found throughout the home. There are 28 rooms and a beautiful glass solarium, also known as the Conservatory. Astonishingly, about 95% of the mansion's furnishings and fixtures displayed today are original.[132]

Every Christmas I try and tour the Moss Mansion in Billings, Montana. Clubs, non-profit organizations, and local businesses try their hand at decorating a room, complete with a themed Christmas tree. The Christmas decor is delightful, with contributions from local Billings volunteers, creatively reinventing old traditions. This year, I was particularly aware how "old is new again," as I revisited the home, seeing burlap, subway tiles, and marble throughout. I love the French Parlor with its columns, French furniture, spectacular light fixtures, gorgeous appointments, and luxurious draperies. The Billings sympohony and dozens of Melville Moss's music students use to play regularly on the mansion's main floor. I can only imagine the parties and celebrations, highlighted with glorious sounds of music coming from the open main hall and grand staircase landing. As I ascended that wide staircase, after my tour at Christmas, it made me think of the joy that the Moss children must have had growing up in such a lovely home.

The Mosses made Billings, Montana home, leaving Missouri in search of the west and unchartered territory. Mr. Moss upon his arrival to Billings, wrote his wife a letter stating, "There is more happening in Billings, Montana at midnight than at noon in Paris, Missouri." [133] I think the Moss family would be thrilled to know that there is a lot happening at the Moss Mansion still today.

The mansion has had a movie career as well. *Son of the Morning Star* and *Return to Lonesome Dove*, made the home visible on the silver screen.[134] The Mosses would probably be thrilled that tours, weddings, themed parties, and events take place all year long.

There are guided tours, or you can personally take charge of your sightseeing adventure. A video is made available for guests to have background information, pertinent to the mansion. For further information contact:

mossmansion.com
The Moss Mansion
914 Division St.
Billings, Mt. 59101
(406) 256-5100

Montana Facts and Trivia

Montana Facts and Trivia

1. "Treasure State" is the official nickname for Montana.[135]

2. Montana means "mountain" in Spanish. [135]

3. The highest point in the state is Granite Peak at 12,799 feet. [135]

4. Montana's Big Sky country spans more than 147,000 square miles, making it the 4th largest state in the U. S. The states of Virginia, Delaware, Maryland, New York and Pennsylvania can fit in the borders of Montana and still have enough room for the District of Columbia. [135]

5. "The distance from southeast Montana to Texas is 587 miles, the distance from southeast Montana to northwest Montana, is 626 miles." [136]

6. Flathead Lake, in Northwest Montana contains over 200 miles of water, 185 miles of shoreline and is considered the largest natural freshwater lake in the west.[18]

7. Glacier National Park has 250 lakes within its borders. [135]

8. The Treasure State has two national parks, Glacier National Park is known as "The Crown Jewel of the Continent," while Yellowstone National Park has the honor of being the first United States National Park. [135]

9. Butte, Montana is known as the "Richest Hill on Earth," due to its long and profitable mining history. [135]

10. The world's shortest river is the Roe River outside of Great Falls, Montana. "The Roe River flows 200 feet between Giant Springs and the Missouri." [137]

11. Frontier counties are those which have 6 or less people living per square mile. In Montana, 46 out of the 56 counties are defined as frontier counties.[138]

12. Montana's state flower is the Bitterroot, 'Oro y Plata' means gold and silver, and is the state's motto. The Western Meadowlark is the official state bird. The Grizzly Bear is the state animal. Agate and Sapphire are the state gemstones. The Cutthroat Trout is the state fish. Ponderosa Pine is the state tree. Bluebunch Wheatgrass is the official state grass. [135]

13. Cattle outnumber people in Big Sky Country. [135]

14. Montana has the largest grizzly bear population and golden eagles in the lower 48 states. [135]

15. The nation's largest migratory herd of Elk is located in the Big Sky Country. [138]

16. Moose herds were once thought to be extinct in the Rockies, but the Treasure State now has over 8,000 moose. [135]

17. Located near Choteau, Montana, is Egg Mountain. Dinosaur eggs have been unearthed there, and their discovery has elevated the theory that some dinosaurs were more similar to mammals and birds, than reptiles. [136]

18. Freezeout Lake Wildlife Management Area, hosts up to 300,000 snow geese and 10,000 tundra swans

during the migration season. [138]

19. North of Missoula, is home to the biggest population of nesting common loons throughout the western United States, in addition to the largest population of trumpeter swans in the lower portion of the nation. [138]

20. Spring mating rituals of more than 100 sage grouse carry out their mating dance near the Pines Recreation Area. [138]

21. The eastern community of Ekalaka, was named for the daughter of the famous Sioux Indian Chief, Chief Sitting Bull. [135]

22. Seven Indian reservations call Montana home, with the first inhabitants in Montana being the Plain Indians. [138]

23. The Battle of the Little Bighorn or Custer's Last Stand took place on June 25th, 1876. The bloody massacre took the lives of almost 200 of Custer's men, in less than 20 minutes. [139]

24. In 1965, the first luge run in North America was built at Lolo Hot Springs on Lolo Pass. [138]

25. Montana elected the 1st woman to Congress in 1916, Jeannette Rankin was born outside of Missoula, Montana, when the Treasure State was still a territory. [135]

26. Helena, Montana in 1888, had more millionaires per capita than any other city in the world. [135]

27. The cornflower blue gem pride, known as the Yogo Sapphire, is the only North American gem included in the Crown Jewels of England. [138]

28. Harry Landers has almost a mile of fence posts topped with over 300 boots, travelling down highway 59. [140]

29. Montana had the first placement of a Gideon Bible, placed in a hotel. [140]

30. It is technically illegal for an unmarried woman to fish alone. [141]

31. The Montana Vortex and House of Mystery in Columbia Falls, Montana is a "quantum or gravitational anomaly" that seems to defy the laws of physics and nature. [142]

LIVING IN MONTANA

Montanans have a certain understanding of what living in the Treasure State is really like. Comedian Jeff Foxworthy's take on "You might just be from Montana, if...." is a humorous slant on what Montanans know to be true. The following are excerpts credited to Jeff Foxworthy.

You might just be from Montana if..."you had a lengthy telephone conversation with someone who dialed a wrong number. Vacation to Montanans means going south of Missoula for the weekend. Distance is measured in hours, not miles. You know several people who have hit a deer more than once. You install security lights on your house and garage, but leave both doors unlocked. You carry jumper cables and your wife knows how to use them. You design a kids Halloween costume to fit over a snowsuit. Driving is better in winter because the potholes are filled in with snow." [143]

You also might be from Montana if...."you know all four seasons, almost winter, winter, winter, road construction. You find 0 degrees a little warm, and are proud that you make the national news because you live in the coldest spot in the nation. When parking your car for the night, you just might be from Montana, because it involves an extension cord. You're family vehicle is a crew cab pick-up and the largest traffic jam centers around a high school basketball game. If your town has an equal number of bars and churches" [144] and you know how to correctly spell, Butte, [145] you might just be from Montana. "If you see people wearing hunting clothes at social events, you notice 7 empty cars running in the parking lot at Walmart, there are more people at work on Christmas Eve Day than opening day of deer season, you might just be from Montana." [144]

MONTANA'S MOVIE CAREER

Montana is a bit famous for being on the big screen. She has hosted many film crews and several famous actors. The beauty of Glacier National Park made the cutting room floor and landed on the big screen. The cinematic work, "What Dreams May Come," starring Robin Williams, highlighted scenery from 'The Crown Jewel of the Continent,' otherwise known as Glacier National Park. [146]

The following is a list of movies made in Montana: [146, 147, 148]

Cattle Queen of Montana	A River Runs Through It
A Plumm Summer	Forrest Gump
Rancho Deluxe	What Dreams May Come
The Untouchables	Hidalgo
Always	The Missouri Breaks

The Patriot
Don't Come Knocking
The Revenant
A Fork in the Road
Layover
Taking Chance

Nebraska
Legends of The Fall
Thunderbolt and Lightfoot
Heartland
The Chronicles of Narnia, the Lion, the Witch and
    the Wardrobe

We have come to a close, with the last pages read. It is my hope that there has been something learned and *The 406 Table* has indeed served up some memories, history, and opportunities for some meaningful meals and celebrations. The Lakota Indians have no word for good-bye. I like that idea. Perhaps we will meet one day under the Big Sky, by a park or near a mountainside. Thank you for supporting my book dream, it means so much!

The coffee's always on, Montana's doors are always open and in case you're running late, we'll leave the light on….

Our farmhouse lamp, complete with crafted metal fisherman, handmade by Skid.

What do you do with a collection of vintage salt and pepper shakers, an old frame, and some paint? Create a one-of-a-kind chess game table! I painted the center of the picture frame with chalkboard paint and then used chalk to create a grid. The frame was painted in a shabby chic style. The collection of salt and pepper shakers rest on each end, while the game board sits on an old table (for inside use). When the weather is good, I will make a pitcher of lemonade and we will sit outside under the Big Sky, and enjoy a game of chess.

ENDNOTES

1. Tempel, Jessamyn. If You're Lucky Enough to Live in Montana, You're Lucky Enough. The Odyssey. [Online] January 30, 2017. [Cited: January 22, 2019.] https://www.theodysseyonline.com/if-youre-lucky-enough-to-live-in-montana-youre-lucky-enough.

2. N.A. Montana Territory Created. History.com. [Online] A&E Television Networks, July 21, 2010. [Cited: January 5, 2019.] https://www.theodysseyonline.com/if-youre-lucky-enough-to-live-in-montana-youre-lucky-enough.

3. Brown, Kellyn. Steinbeck's Short Stay. Flathead Beacon. [Online] November 7, 2014. [Cited: January 28, 2019.] https://flatheadbeacon.com/2014/11/07/steinbecks-short-stay-2/.

4. N.A. Tombstone Pizza Corporation History. Funding Universe. [Online] 2018. [Cited: January 22, 2019.] www.fundinguniverse.com/company-histories/tombstone-pizza-corporation-history/.

5. N.A. Harvey's Wagon Wheel Saloon & Gambling Hall. Facebook. [Online] 2018. [Cited: January 16, 2019.] https://www.facebook.com/pg/HarveysWagonWheel/photos/?tab=album&album_id=645334388896378.

6. N.A. Little Mondeaux Lodge: Where's the pizza? Reno Gazette-Journal. November 21, 1990, p. 18.

7. Reports, Staff. Genoans remember businessman Ron Simek. The Record-Courier. January 22, 2015.

8. Staff. Headless Bride Ghost of Old Faithful Inn. My Yellowstone Park. [Online] September 27, 2013. [Cited: January 19, 2019.] http://www.yellowstonepark.com/park/yellowstone-old-faithful-inn-ghost.

9. N.A. Old Faithful Geyser Frequently Asked Questions. National Park Service. [Online] July 6, 2018. [Cited: January 4, 2019.] https://www.nps.gov/yell/learn/nature/oldfaithfulgeyserfaq.htm.

10. Reinhart, Karen Wildung. Old Faithful Inn. Yellowstone Science. Spring 2004, Vol. 12, 2.

11. Vanuga, Jeff. Old Faithful Inn in Yellowstone National Park. My Yellowstone Park. [Online] December 12, 2018. [Cited: January 15, 2019.] www.yellowstonepark.com/where-to-stay-camp-eat/historic-old-faithful-inn.

12. Staff. No More Lunch Counter for Yellowstone Bears. My Yellowstone Park. [Online] June 11, 2011. [Cited: January 4, 2019.] http://www.yellowstonepark.com/things-to-do/yellowstone-bears-no-longer-get-garbage-treats.

13. Club, Highwood Woman's. Trails and Tales of the Highwoods 1964. s.l. : Highwood Woman's Club, 1988.

14. Charles M. Russell. Sid Richardson Museum. [Online] 2018. [Cited: January 24, 2019.] https://www.sidrichardsonmuseum.org/gallery.php/art/russell.

15. N.A. Sacagawea. History.com. [Online] A&E Television Networks, April 5, 2010. [Cited: January 20, 2019.] https://www.history.com/topics/native-american-history/sacagawea

16. Dippie, Brian W. The Imagery of Sacagawea. Jackson Hole History. [Online] 2018. [Cited: January 8, 2019.] https://jacksonholehistory.org/the-imagery-of-sacagawea-by-brian-w-dippie/.

17. N.A. The city of Helena, Montana, is founded after miners discover gold. *History.com*. [Online] A&E Television Networks, December 13, 2018. [Cited: January 4, 2019.] https://www.history.com/this-day-in-history/the-city-of-helena-montana-is-founded-after-miners-discover-gold.

18. N.A. Flathead Lake. *Visit Montana*. [Online] 2018. [Cited: January 7, 2019.] https://www.visitmt.com/listings/general/lake/flathead-lake.html.

19. Horowitz, Ellen. Huckleberry Hounds. Montana Outdoors. [Online] July 2004. [Cited: January 11, 2019.] http://fwp.mt.gov/mtoutdoors/HTML/articles/2004/Huckleberries.htm

20. Wallenfeldt, Jeff and Di Certo, Joseph. Pony Express. Encyclopedia Britannica. [Online] 2018. [Cited: January 19, 2019.] https://www.britannica.com/topic/Pony-Express.

21. Spreeman, Russel. Pony Bob. American Cowboy. [Online] September 11, 2012. [Cited: January 17, 2019.] https://www.americancowboy.com/ranch-life-archive/pony-bob.

22. N.A. Boot Hill Cemetery. Visit Montana. [Online] 2018. [Cited: 7 January, 2019.] https://www.visitmt.com/listings/general/landmark/boot-hill-cemetery.html.

23. N.A. Fort Benton. Fort Benton. [Online] 2013. [Cited: January 28, 2019.] http://www.fortbenton.com/.

24. Roddam, Rick. 50 Things You Probably Didn't Know About Montana. KMHK. [Online] July 17, 2014. [Cited: January 24, 2019.] http://kmhk.com/50-things-you-probably-didnt-know-about-montana/.

25. N.A. Grand Union Hotel. Visit Montana. [Online] 2018. [Cited: January 14, 2019.] https://www.visitmt.com/listings/general/hotel-motel/grand-union-hotel.html.

26. N.A. Hotel History. Grand Union Hotel. [Online] 2014. [Cited: January 16, 2019.]

27. N.A. Lewistown Chokecherry Festival. Lewistown Chokecherry. [Online] 2018. [Cited: February 2, 2019.] http://lewistownchokecherry.com.

28. Reichard, Sean. Yellowstone History: President Theodore Roosevelt's 1903 Trip. Yellowstone Insider. [Online] April 18, 2016. [Cited: February 3, 2019.] https://yellowstoneinsider.om2016104/18/yellowstone-history-president-theodore-roosevelt-1903-trip/.

29. N.A. Yellowstone History: Laying the Roosevelt Arch Cornerstone. Yellowstone Insider. [Online] April 28, 2016. [Cited: February 3, 2019.] https://yellowstoneinsider.com/2016/04/25/yellowstone-history-laying-the-roosevelt-arch-cornerstone/.

30. N.A. An Overview of Underwear. Tudor Links. [Online] 2003. [Cited: February 5, 2019.] http://www.tudorlinks.com/treasury/articles/viewvictunder1.html.

31. N.A. History of Hats for Women. Vintage Fashion Guild. [Online] March 19, 2012. [Cited: February 6, 2019.] https://vintagefashionguild.org/fashion-history/the-history-of-womens-hats/.

32. N.A. Sacagawea Biography. The Biography.com. [Online] A&E Television Networks, April 2, 2014. [Cited: February 11, 2019.] https://www.biography.com/people/sacagawea-9468731.

33. Hafen, LeRoy Reuben and Lecompte, Janet. French Fur Traders and Voyageurs in the American West. Lincoln: First Bison Books, 1997. p. 79.

34. N.A. Sacagawea Gives Birth to Pompey. History.com. [Online] A&E Television Networks, November 16, 2009. [Cited: February 12, 2019.] https://www.history.com/this-day-in-history/sacagawea-gives-birth-to-pompey.

35. Malby, Andy. Long-awaited Sacajawea Statue Arrives in Three Forks. Belgrade News. [Online] April 1,

2005. [Cited: February 12, 2019.] http://www.belgrade-news.com/news/long-awaited-sacajawea-statue-arrives-in-three-forks/article_77f7ee27-a2fd-5f57-9057-584831770479.html.

36. Hill, Pat. Autumn in Livingston. Outside Bozeman. [Online] Fall 2008. [Cited: February 12, 2019.] http://www.outsidebozeman.com/fall-2008/autumn-livingston.

37. Tracey. The Native American Cradleboard, More Than Just a Baby Carrier. Prairie Edge. [Online] June 14, 2011. [Cited: February 12, 2019.] https://prairieedge.com/tribe-scribe/the-native-american-cradleboard-more-than-just-a-baby-carrier/.

38. N.A. History. Friends of Pompey's Pillar. [Online] 2018. [Cited: February 10, 2019.] http://www.pompeys-pillar.org/history/.

39. N.A. Visiting the Pillar. Friends of Pompey's Pillar. [Online] 2018. [Cited: February 10, 2019.] http://www.pompeyspillar.org/things-to-do/.

40. N.A. History of Advertising: No 182: Clara Peller's Hamburger. US Campaign. [Online] January 20, 2017. [Cited: February 12, 2019.] https://www.campaignlive.com/article/history-advertising-no-182-clara-pellers-hamburger/1421235.

41. N.A. O'Fallon Historical Museum. Visit Montana. [Online] 2018. [Cited: February 13, 2019.] https://www.visitmt.com/listings/general/museum/o-fallon-historical-museum.html.

42. N.A. The Stack, Great Falls, Montana Sep 18, 1982. Billings Gazette. [Online] August 22, 2017. [Cited: February 12, 2019.] https://billingsgazette.com/the-stack-great-falls-montana-sep/youtube_e99cda33-7eb6-5a4e-9fe2-102d670dd8ca.html.

43. N.A. Tenacity: The Miners of Great Falls. Visit Great Falls Montana. [Online] 2018. [Cited: February 11, 2019.] https://visitgreatfallsmontana.org/2017/07/20/tenacity-miners-great-falls/.

44. Devlin, Vince. G is for Great Falls: City Shakes Off Decades of Dust and Powers Forward. Missoulian. [Online] February 14, 2015. [Cited: February 12, 2019.] https://missoulian.com/news/local/g-is-for-great-falls-city-shakes-off-decades-of/article_3a202951-d76a-5387-9418-e2877dfb713b.html.

45. Company, Anaconda Copper Mining. Main Stack. Retrieved from https://en.wikipedia.org/wiki/File:Anaconda_Smelter_Stack_1920.png#filelinks

46. N.A. Climate Information. Montana Kids. [Online] 2018. [Cited: February 14, 2019.] http://montanakids.com/facts_and_figures/climate/Climate_Information.htm.

47. N.A. Montana. Ski Resort. [Online] 2018. [Cited: February 14, 2019.] https://www.skiresort.info/ski-resorts/montana/sorted/slope-length/.

48. N.A. The Big Sky. Rotten Tomatoes. [Online] 2000. [Cited: February 13, 2019.] https://www.rottentomatoes.com/m/big_sky.

49. N.A. Levee Tour. Fort Benton. [Online] 2013. [Cited: February 13, 2019.] http://www.fortbenton.com/leveetour.html.

50. N.A. Keelboats of the Missouri River. Travel Logs. [Online] 2018. [Cited: February 14, 2019.] http://travel-logs.us/boats-ships/Keel%20boats/Keel%20Boat.htm.

51. Cook, Rob. Cattle Inventory vs Human Population by State. Beef2Live. [Online] January 1, 2019. [Cited: February 5, 2019.] www.beef2live.com/story-cattle-inventory-vs-human-population-state-0-114255 .

52. Wick, Jessica. 14 Ways Montana Is America's Black Sheep... And We Love It That Way. Only In Your

State. [Online] December 30, 2016. [Cited: February 18, 2019.] https://www.onlyinyourstate.com/montana/americas-black-sheep-mt/.

53. N.A. The History of Montana's Cattle Industry. *Montana Kids.* [Online] 2018. [Cited: February 17, 2019.] http://montanakids.com/agriculture_and_business/farm_animals/History_of_Cattle.htm.

54. N.A. Grant Kohrs Ranch National Historic Site. *Visit MT.* [Online] 2018. [Cited: February 18, 2019.] https://www.visitmt.com/listings/general/national-historic-site/grant-kohrs-ranch-national-historic-site.html.

55. N.A. Grant-Kohrs Ranch. *National Park Service.* [Online] February 24, 2015. [Cited: February 19, 2019.] https://www.nps.gov/grko/learn/historyculture/conradkohrs.htm.

56. N.A. Grant-Kohrs Ranch. *National Park Service.* [Online] 2018. [Cited: February 19, 2019.] https://www.nps.gov/grko/index.htm.

57. N.A. Grant-Kohrs Ranch. *National Park Service History eLibrary.* [Online] [Cited: February 18, 2019.] http://npshistory.com/brochures/grko/ranchers.pdf.

58. Buckley, Jay H. Lewis and Clark Expedition. *Encyclopedia Britannica.* [Online] February 1, 2019. [Cited: February 19, 2019.] https://www.britannica.com/event/Lewis-and-Clark-Expedition.

59. N.A. Shep...Forever Faithful. *Fort Benton.* [Online] 2013. [Cited: February 19, 2019.] http://www.fortbenton.com/shep.html.

60. Inbody, Kristen. 75 Years of Honoring Shep's Story. *Great Falls Tribune.* [Online] March 16, 2017. [Cited: February 18, 2019.] https://www.greatfallstribune.com/story/life/my-montana/2017/03/16/years-honoring-shep-story/99278354/.

61. N.A. My 'Old Shep'. *Thyme Goes By.* [Online] November 15, 2009. [Cited: February 19, 2019.] https://thymegoesby.wordpress.com/tag/old-shep/.

62. Mason, Fergus. 10 Things Cowboys Carried With Them In The Wild West To Survive. *Ask a Prepper.* [Online] July 10, 2017. [Cited: February 19, 2019.] http://www.askaprepper.com/10-things-cowboys-carried-wild-west-survive/.

63. N.A. Louisiana Purchase. *Encyclopedia Britannica.* [Online] January 30, 2019. [Cited: February 19, 2019.] https://britannica.

64. N.A. Why Does My Border Collie Follow Me Everywhere. Wag. [Online] 2018. [Cited: February 20, 2019.] https://wagwalking.com/behavior/why-does-my-border-collie-follow-me-everywhere.

65. N.A. Virginia City Chinese. Montana Kids. [Online] 2018. [Cited: February 20, 2019.] http://montanakids.com/cool_stories/ghost_towns/chinese.htm.

66. N.A. Conrad Mansion Museum. Conrad Mansion. [Online] 2018. [Cited: February 21, 2019.] http://www.conradmansion.com/About-Family.html.

67. Ogren, Katlin. 5 Reasons to Eat Bison: The New Healthy Red Meat. Chicago Now. [Online] February 6, 2012. [Cited: February 21, 2019.] http://www.chicagonow.com/katalin-fitness-health-driven/2012/02/5-reasons-to-eat-bison-the-new-healthy-red-meat/#image/1.

68. Bison. National Park Service. [Online] 2018. [Cited: February 21, 2019.] https://www.nps.gov/yell/learn/nature/bison.htm.

69. N.A. Bison in Yellowstone National Park. My Yellowstone. [Online] 2018. [Cited: February 21, 2019.] https://www.yellowstonepark.com/things-to-do/wildlife/bison.

70. Weiser, Kathy. Ghost Town Ghosts in Bannack, Montana. Legends of America. [Online] March 2018. [Cited: February 24, 2019.] https://www.legendsofamerica.com/mt-bannackghost/.

71. Powell, Lisa. The perfect time (and place) to learn about the life of famous sharpshooter Annie Oakley. Dayton Daily News. [Online] July 20, 2018. [Cited: February 27, 2019.] https://www.daytondailynews.com/life-styles/darke-county-annie-oakley-center-tribute-little-miss-sure-shot/AVvcrM6vUVNYX5njsmojRO/.

72. N.A. Annie Oakley. Buffalo Bill Center of the West. [Online] 2018. [Cited: February 27, 2019.] https://centerofthewest.org/explore/buffalo-bill/research/annie-oakley/.

73. N.A. Annie Oakley in Europe. American Experience. [Online] 2018. [Cited: February 27, 2019.] https://www.pbs.org/wgbh/americanexperience/features/oakley-europe/.

74. N.A. Frequently Asked Questions About Annie Oakley. Annie Oakley Center Foundation, Inc. [Online] 2016. [Cited: February 27, 2019.] https://www.annieoakleycenterfoundation.com/faq2.html.

75. N.A. Annie Get Your Gun. Internet Broadway Database. [Online] 2017. [Cited: February 27, 2019.] https://www.ibdb.com/broadway-production/annie-get-your-gun-1440.

76. Barbee, Karen. [in person], 1980.

77. Chodosh, Sara. In a Montana town, a record-breaking 103-degree swing in 24 hours. Popular Science. [Online] June 22, 2017. [Cited: February 27, 2019.] https://www.popsci.com/one-wacky-month-in-montana.

78. Graetz, Rick and Graetz, Susie. A look back at some of Montana's coldest moments. Missoulian. [Online] February 24, 2019. [Cited: February 27, 2019.] https://missoulian.com/news/local/a-look-back-at-some-of-montana-s-coldest-moments/article_b5aabf0c-6f40-52c8-a038-33ffdb8667a9.html.

79. Traylor, Aaron. What Jeff Foxworthy Says About Montana. 100.7 Zoo FM. [Online] May 17, 2012. [Cited: February 27, 2019.] http://1075zoofm.com/what-jeff-foxworthy-says-about-montana/.

80. Broad, William. Snowflakes as Big as Frisbees? New York Times. [Online] March 20, 2007. [Cited: February 27, 2019.] https://www.nytimes.com/2007/03/20/science/20snow.html?pagewanted=all.

81. N.A. American Black Bear. Bear Biology. [Online] 2018. [Cited: February 27, 2019.] https://www.bearbiology.org/bear-species/american-black-bear/.

82. N.A. Black Bear Behavior. Florida Fish and Wildlife Conservation Commission. [Online] 2018. [Cited: February 27, 2019.] https://myfwc.com/wildlifehabitats/wildlife/bear/facts/behavior/.

83. N.A. American Black Bear. Washington Nature Mapping Foundation. [Online] 2018. [Cited: February 27, 2019.] http://naturemappingfoundation.org/natmap/facts/american_black_bear_712.html.

84. Reichard, Sean. Yellowstone History: Bear Feeding. Yellowstone Insider. [Online] July 11, 2016. [Cited: February 27, 2019.] https://yellowstoneinsider.com/2016/07/11/yellowstone-history-bear-feeding/.

85. Thomas, Andy. Charles M. Russell. Russell County. [Online] 2017. [Cited: February 27, 2019.] https://www.russellcountry.com/charles-m-russell.html.

86. Boggs, Johnny. Following Charlie Russell's Paintbrush. True West Magazine. [Online] September 12, 2009. [Cited: February 27, 2019.] https://truewestmagazine.com/following-charlie-russells-paintbrush/.

87. N.A. San Francisco Snowstorms. Mic Mac Publishing. [Online] 2005. [Cited: February 27, 2019.] https://thestormking.com/Sierra_Stories/San_Francisco_Snowstorms/san_francisco_snowstorms.html.

88. Thompson, Leslie. Nancy Russell: Wife & Business Manager. Sid Richardson Museum. [Online] March 8,

2017. [Cited: February 27, 2019.] https://www.sidrichardsonmuseum.org/blog/nancy-russell/.

89. N.A. Russell Funeral 'The biggest funeral we ever had". Great Falls Tribune. [Online] March 16, 2017. [Cited: February 27, 2019.] https://www.greatfallstribune.com/story/news/local/2017/03/16/rus_sell-funeral-big-gest-funeral-ever/99271264/.

90. N.A. Charles M. Russell. C.M. Russell Museum. [Online] 2019. [Cited: February 27, 2019.] https://cmrussell.org.

91. D'Ambrosio, Brian. Haunted by waters: 'A River Runs Through It' 25 years later. Missoulian. [Online] September 7, 2017. [Cited: February 27, 2019.] https://missoulian.com/entertainment/arts-and-theatre/haunted-by-waters-a-river-runs-through-it-years-later/article_b5e74c15-52cd-542d-b3dd-b2673059e262.html.

92. N.A. Head to beautiful Central Montana for the Montana Bale Trail! Montana Bale Trail. [Online] 2018. [Cited: February 27, 2019.] https://www.montanabaletrail.com/.

93. N.A. Battle of the Little Bighorn Reenactment. Visit MT. [Online] 2018. [Cited: March 3, 2019.] https://www.visitmt.com/things-to-do/events/2019-06/Battle-of-the-Little-Bighorn-Reenactment.html.

94. N.A. Indians Defeat Custer at Little Big Horn. History.com. [Online] November 16, 2009. [Cited: March 3, 2019.] https://www.history.com/this-day-in-history/indians-defeat-custer-at-little-big-horn.

95. N.A. The West Episode Six. Montana PBS. [Online] 2001. [Cited: March 3, 2019.] https://www.pbs.org/weta/thewest/program/episodes/six/yellowhair.htm.

96. N.A. Little Bighorn Battle Recreated. Billings Gazette. [Online] May 22, 2011. [Cited: March 3, 2019.] https://billingsgazette.com/special-section/travel-tourism/billings/all-around/little-bighorn-battle-re-created/article_9a978c28-6d1b-5215-8356-b2e4925adaa1.html.

97. Peglar, Tori. Grand Prismatic Spring at Yellowstone's Midway Geyser Basin. My Yellowstone. [Online] August 14, 2017. [Cited: March 3, 2019.] https://www.yellowstonepark.com/things-to-do/grand-prismatic-midway-geyser-basin.

98. Lundin, Caitlin. Who Was Chet Huntley: The Founding Father of Big Sky. Visit Big Sky. [Online] 2017. [Cited: March 3, 2019.] https://www.visitbigsky.com/blog/who-was-chet-huntley-the-founding-father-of-big-sky/.

99. N.A. The Big Sky Experience. Big Sky Resort. [Online] 2018. [Cited: March 3, 2019.] https://bigskyresort.com/the-big-sky-experience.

100. Thomson, Thomas. Chet Heads for the Hills. Life. July 17, 1970, Vol. 69, 3, p. 33.

101. N.A. Who is Chet Huntley? Visit Big Sky. [Online] 2016. [Cited: March 3, 2019.] https://www.visitbigsky.com/blog/who-is-chet-huntley/.

102. Rowley, Barbara. Big Sky Country. Snow Country. October 1990, Vol. 3, 8, p. 48.

103. Deane. Huckleberry, Blueberries Kissing Cousin. Eat The Weeds. [Online] 2012. [Cited: March 14, 2019.] http://www.eattheweeds.com/gaylussacia-huckleberry-history-2/.

104. N.A. Indian Dyes. Access Genealogy. [Online] October 18, 2018. [Cited: May 28, 2019.] https://www.access-genealogy.com/native/indian-dyes.htm.

105. N.A. History. The Round Barn. [Online] 2018. [Cited: March 14, 2019.] http://historicroundbarn.com/history/.

106. N.A. Montana. History. [Online] November 9, 2009. [Cited: March 14, 2019.] https://www.history.com/topics/us-states/montana.

107. Cook, Tom. Montana Horse Still Holds Record for Kentucky Derby. Independent Record. [Online] April 28, 2013. [Cited: March 14, 2019.] https://helenair.com/montana-horse-still-holds-record-for-kentucky-derby/article_dff034c8-b05c-11e2-b192-001a4bcf887a.html.

108. Hillenbrand, Laura. The Derby. American Heritage. May/June 1999, Vol. 50, 3.

109. Graetz, Rick. The Making of the Crown of the Continent. Missoulian. [Online] May 14, 2017. [Cited: March 15, 2019.] https://missoulian.com/lifestyles/territory/the-making-of-the-crown-of-the-continent/article_3d6be01c-c211-5ac2-983e-32744ec86969.html.

110. Franz, Justin. Rebuilding the Legend on the Lake. Flathead Beacon. [Online] May 28, 2017. [Cited: March 15, 2019.] https://flatheadbeacon.com/2017/05/28/rebuilding-legend-lake/.

111. N.A. Glacier. National Park Service. [Online] 2018. [Cited: March 15, 2019.] https://www.nps.gov/glac/learn/historyculture/places.htm.

112. N.A. Going to the Sun Road. Enjoy Your Parks. [Online] 2017. [Cited: March 15, 2019.] http://enjoyyourparks.com/GoingToTheSunRoad.html.

113. Wallenfeldt, Jeff. Missouri River. Encyclopedia Britannica. [Online] 2018. [Cited: March 15, 2019.] https://www.britannica.com/place/Missouri-River.

114. N.A. A Muddy River? Missouri River Water Trail. [Online] 2016. [Cited: March 15, 2019.] https://missouririverwatertrail.org/river-history/muddy-river.

115. Gonzalez, Mark. Continental Divides in North Dakota and North America. NDGS Newsletter. 2003, Vol. 30, 1.

116. Nixon, Chris. Owner. Bozeman Lehrkind Mansion Bed & Breakfast. March 15, 2019.

117. Kendall, Lewis. New brewery a descendant of Bozeman's beer history. Bozeman Daily Chronicle. [Online] April 14, 2018. [Cited: April 7, 2019.] https://www.bozemandailychronicle.com/news/business/new-brewery-a-descendant-of-bozeman-s-beer-history/article_2dfe0164-fc43-543a-8301-512a9696ca9e.html.

118. N.A. Daly Mansion History. Daly Mansion. [Online] 2019. [Cited: April 7, 2019.] http://dalymansion.org/DalyMansionHistory.html.

119. N.A. Marcus Daly. Encyclopedia Britannica. [Online] 2019. [Cited: April 7, 2019.] https://www.britannica.com/biography/Marcus-Daly.

120. N.A. Anaconda. Encyclopedia Britannica. [Online] 2019. [Cited: April 7, 2019.] https://www.britannica.com/place/Anaconda-Montana#ref255424.

121. Thornton, Tracy. Daly and Clark: Copper kings in contrast. Montana Standard. [Online] January 16, 2016. [Cited: April 7, 2019.] https://mtstandard.com/lifestyles/daly-and-clark-copper-kings-in-contrast/article_be0c2d94-e2b5-5007-9f2b-72456fee6621.html.

122. N.A. About. Conrad Mansion Museum. [Online] 2019. [Cited: April 7, 2019.] http://www.conradmansion.com/About-Family.html.

123. Conrad Mansion Family. Mountain Mouse Land. [Online] 2015. [Cited: Aril 7, 2019.] https://www.mtnmouse.com/montana/conrad_mansion_family.html.

124. Tabish, Dillon. The man and the mansion. Flathead Beacon. [Online] October 7, 2015. [Cited: April 7, 2019.] https://flatheadbeacon.com/2015/10/07/the-man-and-the-mansion/.

125. N.A. Copper King Mansion. Visit Montana. [Online] 2019. [Cited: April 7, 2019.] https://www.visitmt.com/listings/general/bed-and-breakfast/copper-king-mansion.html.

126. Hagenmeier, Jeffrey. The Copper King Mansion, W.A. Clark Mansion, In Butte Montana. Wandering Trader. [Online] January 10, 2019. [Cited: April 7, 2019.] http://wanderingtrader.com/travel-blog/united-states/copper-king-mansion-w-clark-mansion-butte-montana/.

127. The Mansion. The Copper King Mansion. [Online] 2019. [Cited: April 7, 2019.] http://thecopperking-mansion.com/the-mansion.

128. N.A. Butte: The Copper King Mansion. *Empty Mansion*. [Online] 2014. [Cited: April 7, 2019.] http://www.emptymansionsbook.com/butte-the-copper-king-mansion.

129. N.A. Bair Family Museum. *Visit Montana*. [Online] 2019. [Cited: April 7, 20019.] https://www.visitmt.com/listings/general/art-museum/bair-family-museum.html.

130. Anderson, Erin. Bair family collection of Western art. *Distinctly Montana*. [Online] September 9, 2005. [Cited: April 7, 2019.] https://www.distinctlymontana.com/montana-art/09/09/2005/bair-family-western-art.

131. Klassy, Todd. The story of Charles M. Bair. *Todd Klassy*. [Online] May 14, 2014. [Cited: April 7, 2019.] https://www.toddklassy.com/montana-blog/2014/5/11/the-story-of-charles-bair.

132. N.A. Moss Family. *Moss Mansion*. [Online] 2019. [Cited: April 7, 2019.] https://www.mossmansion.com/history/moss-family/.

133. N.A. Moss Mansion in Billings Montana. Total Transportation. [Online] 2018. [Cited: April 7, 2019.] https://mttotaltransportation.com/tours/moss-mansion-billings-montana.

134. N.A. Moss Mansion. Visit Montana. [Online] 2019. [Cited: April 7, 2019.] https://www.visitmt.com/listings/general/museum/moss-mansion.html.

135. N.A. 52 Interesting Facts About Montana, Montana State Symbols. The Fact File. [Online] February 28, 2019. [Cited: April 30, 2019.] https://thefactfile.org/montana-facts/.

136. N.A. Montana Memes. Meme. [Online] July 7, 2017. [Cited: April 30, 2019.] https://me.me/i/distance-from-se-montana-to-texas-587-miles-distance-from-17614563.

137. N.A. World's Shortest River. Montana Kids. [Online] 2018. [Cited: April 30, 2019.] http://montanakids.com/facts_and_figures/geography/Worlds_Shortest_River.htm.

138. N.A. Montana Facts and Trivia. 50 States. [Online] 2018. [Cited: April 30, 2019.] https://www.50states.com/facts/montana.htm.

139. Long, Tony. June 25, 1876: Was Custer Outgunned At Little Bighorn? Wired. [Online] June 25, 2009. [Cited: April 30, 2019.] https://www.wired.com/2009/06/dayintech-0625/.

140. Orcutt, Amanda. 50 Facts About Montana You Probably Didn't Know. Movoto Blog. [Online] 2016.

[Cited: April 30, 2019.] https://www.movoto.com/blog/opinions/montana-facts/.

141. N.A. Fishing Alone While In Montana May Be A Crime. Unaccomplished Angler. [Online] March 1, 2011. [Cited: April 30, 2019.] http://unaccomplishedangler.com/2011/03/fishing-alone-while-in-montana-may-be-a-crime/.

142. N.A. Montana Vortex and House of Vortex. Visit Montana. [Online] 2018. [Cited: April 30, 2019.] https://www.visitmt.com/listings/general/amusement/montana-vortex-and-house-of-mystery.html.

143. Traylor, Aaron. What Jeff Foxworthy Says About Montana. 107.5 Zoo FM. [Online] May 17, 2012. [Cited: April 17, 2019.] https://1075zoofm.com/what-jeff-foxworthy-says-about-montana/.

144. N.A. Jeff Foxworthy on Montana - You Might Live in Montana if... Montana Associated Technology Roundtables. [Online] May 6, 2010. [Cited: April 30, 2019.] https://matr.net/news/jeff-foxworthy-on-montana---you-might-live-in-montana-if/.

145. Morford, John. You Might Live in Montana if.... Billings Gazette. [Online] December 12, 2006. [Cited: April 30, 2019.] https://billingsgazette.com/entertainment/community/501blog/you-might-live-in-montana-if/article_d389d6d4-67ec-56db-a350-b89f04cac0d9.html.

146. Wick, Jessica. Most People Don't Know These 10 Movies Were Filmed In Montana. Only in Your State. [Online] January 31, 2016. [Cited: April 30, 2019.] https:www.onlyinyourstate.com/montana/movies-filmed-in-mt/.

147. N.A. Montana Filmography. Montana Film Office. [Online] 2017. [Cited: April 30, 2019.] https://www.montanafilm.com/film-community/montana-filmography-2/.

148. N.A. Legends of the Fall. Internet Movie Database. [Online] 2016. [Cited: April 30, 2019.] https://www.imdb.com/title/tt0110322/.

Add a ½ cup of Epsom salt, ½ cup of Borax and 10 drops of lavender essential oil to a hot bath. It helps tired feet and an exhausted body rejuvenate. The combination of ingredients reduces inflammation and swelling. This was a ritual after all the weddings and events that I executed. Give it a try!

INDEX